RAMAGE IN SOUTH ITALY

―――――

THE NOOKS AND BY-WAYS OF ITALY

*Wanderings in Search of its
Ancient Remains and Modern
Superstitions*

BY

CRAUFURD TAIT RAMAGE, LL.D.

―――――

ABRIDGED AND EDITED BY
EDITH CLAY

WITH AN INTRODUCTION BY
HAROLD ACTON

ACADEMY

CHICAGO

Published in 1987 by
Academy Chicago Publishers
425 North Michigan Avenue
Chicago, IL 60611
Copyright © 1965 and 1987 by Edith Clay

Library of Congress Cataloging-in-Publication Data

Ramage, Craufurd Tait, 1803-1878.
    Ramage in south Italy.

    Reprint. Originally published: London : Longmans,
Green, 1965.
    Bibliography: p.
    Includes index.
    1. Italy, Southern – Description and travel. 2. Italy –
Description and travel – 1801-1860. 3. Ramage, Craufurd
Tait, 1803-1878 – Journeys – Italy, Southern. I. Clay,
Edith. II. Title.
DG821.R34 1986 914.5'7048 86-22163
ISBN 0-89733-217-2
ISBN 0-89733-216-4 (pbk.)

CONTENTS

CONTENTS

CONTENTS

vii

CONTENTS

CHAPTER XXIII

CHAPTER XXIV

APPENDIX

ILLUSTRATIONS

ix

Note to the First American Edition

It may seem extraordinary that more than twenty years after the English publication of this book, I feel no need to amend my *Preface*.

In general, Southern Italy remains in much the same state as it was in 1964, except that practically the whole of the coastal region has been developed for tourists with innumerable hotels beside the once solitary beaches. An *Autostrada* has been constructed to Reggio Calabria, and to Apulia, which has greatly improved communications: on the whole these have not destroyed the magnificent scenery through which they pass. Alas, this cannot be said of the Government plans for further industrial and agrarian development which usually are carried out to the detriment of their surroundings. What is very striking has been the increase in archaeological activity throughout the whole of Southern Italy where many sites have been excavated which have yielded important discoveries, both for pre-history and the Greek colonisation in that area.

In fact, Ramage could easily find his way were he to start out again on his travels. I remember that W.H. Auden and Elizabeth Mayer remark in their Introduction to Goethe's *Italian Journey* (London, Collins, 1962, p.XIV) that they are amazed at the similarity between pre-French Revolution Italy, which Goethe saw, and post-World War II Italy.

Edith Clay
London, 1986

INTRODUCTION

ONE hears that Norman Douglas has but few readers among the younger generation: more's the pity. *Alone* is one of his perennially refreshing and most characteristic memorials, and among the vivid characters he evokes in its sparkling pages not the least memorable is that of the enterprising Scotsman, Craufurd Tait Ramage, author of *The Nooks and By-Ways of Italy*, with the explanatory sub-title *Wanderings in search of its ancient remains and modern superstitions*.

This minor classic has become a rarity since its lone publication in 1868, in an edition very trying to the eyesight. By reviving it Miss Edith Clay is conferring a favour on lovers of Italy and on those, who, like myself, cherish an amused affection for the author of *Nooks and By-Ways*, so superior to the voluminous, repetitious and prosaic travel literature of the period.

It is significant that the book should have been dedicated to the memory of General Carlo Filangieri, for Ramage's information on economic and social matters was evidently derived from those numerous friends to whom Filangieri had given him letters of introduction, and without whose assistance he might have succumbed to the fatigues of the journey.

Carlo Filangieri (1784–1867) was the eldest son of the famous reformer Gaetano Filangieri (1752–1788) whose monumental work *La scienza della legislazione* (1780) won him a European reputation. Goethe has left a charming description of him and his vivacious sister in his *Italian Travels*. He had married the Hungarian Countess Caroline Fremdel and his paternal family was of Norman origin. Educated in Paris at the military academy, Carlo became even more cosmopolitan than most Neapolitan aristocrats and he remained pro-French all his life. Having fought with gallantry under Napoleon and served with distinction under Murat's régime in Naples, he was in disgrace with the Bourbons when Ramage set out on his travels, but he was reinstated by Ferdinand II and he played an important role in subsequent events, above all in the recovery of Sicily after its secession in 1848. On this account he has not been treated fairly by historians. His son Gaetano (1824–1892) was also a public figure, an archaeologist and compiler of six erudite volumes of *Documents for the History, Arts and Industries of the Neapolitan Provinces*, and the founder of the Filangieri Museum, of which Baron Francesco Acton, its present director, has recently produced a handsome catalogue.

Ramage's dedication is therefore a curious link with Neapolitan history. One seems to hear Filangieri's voice when he writes: 'The French certainly conferred a great benefit on the country by reforming the legal code, which, before their time, exhibited a strange incongruous mass . . . The Code Napoleon . . . supersedes these multifarious enactments, modified, indeed, by the immemorial customs of the country, though it was not without a struggle that it maintained its ground on the return of the Bourbons.' It was General Filangieri who eventually got rid of the Swiss mercenaries whose presence was far more galling to him than to the Neapolitan masses.

Norman Douglas has written so perceptively about the merits of this book that it would be gilding the lily to expatiate on his remarks. The author of *Old Calabria* was temperamentally attuned to his fellow Scottish humanist who 'did not collect bric-a-brac like other travellers; he collected knowledge of humanity and its institutions, such knowledge as inscriptions reveal'. One can only add that *The Nooks and By-Ways* has gained considerably in interest owing to the general improvement in communications and accommodation, which have drawn and will continue to draw more travellers to this supremely picturesque and romantic part of Italy, still almost insulated from the twentieth century. Even the cleverest photography can scarcely render justice to such scenery. Perhaps when both painters and public grow tired of abstractionism, mute inglorious Turners and Constables will wander in Ramage's footsteps, for the variety of landscape to be enjoyed in South Italy should prove a perpetual stimulus and inspiration. If the modern traveller is blessed with a classical education he will enjoy it all the more, with Ramage as a valuable *vade-mecum*.

Ramage chose to ramble through South Italy in 1828 when the expensive Austrian army of occupation had been reluctantly withdrawn from Naples and the well-meaning but inept and gouty Francis I attempted to restore law and order in a kingdom infested with secret societies plotting to revive the Constitution of 1820. These sects had cropped up like mushrooms after the Austrian retreat. Much of their hocus-pocus I am inclined to attribute to ennui. Provincial boredom is still endemic, in spite of the introduction of the cinema, radio and television, which may even aggravate it by contrast and comparison with the illusionary *dolce vita* of large modern cities, so that there is a swelling tide of emigration to the North, whither the mirage, or Fata Morgana described by Ramage, seems to have shifted from the Straits of Messina. Too late the Piedmontese deplore the effects of their conquest of the Two Sicilies. Though politicians may deny it there is still melancholy truth in Ramage's remarks on 'the bitterness with which the inhabitants speak of their countrymen in other parts of Italy, even of those of another province. Imagine a Lancashire man looking upon a man of Yorkshire as scarcely belonging to the same country, and you will have some idea of the feelings that prevail here.'

Metternich was standing in the background with folded arms and an 'I told you so' expression. British diplomats like William Noel Hill and the consul, Sir Henry Lushington, who employed Ramage as tutor to his sons, tended to patronize the constitutional movement. Fortunately for King Francis, his bugbear Lord William Bentinck, who had sponsored the ill-fated Sicilian Constitution, was now Governor-General of distant Bengal. As Ramage observed, opponents of the government considered all Englishmen their friends. 'But it would be absurd in me,' he added sagaciously, 'to inter-meddle with the internal affairs of a country of which I know so little, and I have as yet seen nothing to incline me to believe that the body of the people is fitted for a representative form of government.'

Everything went wrong in the Two Sicilies under Francis's feeble reign. Desperadoes and brigands like the three swashbuckling Capozzoli brothers terrorized the hilly Cilento region between the gulfs of Salerno and Policastro; conspiracies were rampant everywhere. To cope with the situation the languid government enlisted the police, who began to gain that ascendancy which they never wholly lost. As Ramage records, the population was disarmed, and this put them at the mercy of the brigands, 'who used to enter villages at midday and carry off respectable inhabitants to their fastnesses, from which they were not released till their friends had paid a ransom'. No doubt the government often acted inconsistently, but we should bear in mind that in the Cilento region the secret sect of *Filadelfi* were hatching an insurrection at the very time Ramage was writing: 'In the population of Policastro, which consists of seven thousand, only sixty were found worthy of being entrusted with arms.'

Obviously the season was not propitious to a solitary tour of the kingdom of Naples, yet young Ramage was determined to brave every danger, equipped with his stalwart umbrella and an insatiable curiosity. His reckless resolve to visit remote and primitive villages regardless of scorching heat and every physical discomfort astounded the local authorities when it did not kindle their suspicions. 'I can perceive,' he wrote, 'by the political turn they give to the conversation, that they suspect I have other objects in view than those I profess. I have no doubt that I increase their suspicions by the perfect candour with which I express my opinions on any subject they choose to start.' But his transparent innocence must have been a talisman: was he not a classical crusader?

Henry Swinburne and Keppel-Craven, as he reminds us, 'had gone pretty nearly over the same ground; but they travelled with all the attendance of high rank, and protected by a constant guard of soldiers. I went alone, often on foot, without a guard, always unarmed, and only once with a guard of armed men across a dangerous pass of the Southern Apennines.' His outlook was pleasantly tolerant and democratic, but we should not forget that an Englishman in those times was, as Norman Douglas pointed out, 'a far more self-assertive and self-confident creature than nowadays'. He paid not the slightest attention to friendly warnings. 'Onward I was resolved to go, till I knocked my head against an impenetrable wall, and you will be amused to see how gradually one difficulty after another disappeared.' Sometimes, as on the road to Taranto, he was forced to admit that his friends had been right. No water was to be found, and he had never experienced the pangs of thirst so strongly before. 'My umbrella was scarcely any protection, and my clothes would scarcely fit an Irish beggar. Perched on the back of my mule, which had an uneasy movement, holding my umbrella over my head as best I could, I looked forward anxiously for the first Pisgah view of Taranto.' One cannot help admiring such stubborn self-confidence. It is a welcome change from the modern *Angst*.

Miss Edith Clay deserves our hearty thanks.

HAROLD ACTON

Florence, July 1963

EDITOR'S PREFACE

My attention was first drawn to Craufurd Tait Ramage when his grand-daughter, Miss Mary Hill, showed me the *Letters* (Appendix, 197) which he had written to his mother, Mrs Black, who had been twice widowed and left practically penniless with two small sons to educate. At this time she was housekeeper to the fifth Duke of Buccleuch at Drumlanrig Castle in Dumfriesshire. Later I became acquainted with *The Nooks and By-Ways of Italy: Wanderings in Search of its Ancient Remains and Modern Superstitions.* Ramage as a young man, with his amazing capacity for assimilating knowledge, seemed to me such a versatile, eccentric, and endearing character; and his book of such interest and entertainment that I resolved to attempt a new edition. This resolve was given impetus and encouragement by Mr Edward Hutton and Mr Harold Acton to both of whom I am deeply indebted. Mr Hutton, in fact, told me that he and the late Mr Norman Douglas had had the same feelings about Ramage and had intended to republish his book forty years ago. Now that increasing interest is being shown in Italy's 'deep south', it seems an appropriate moment to show through the eyes and words of Ramage what his experience of that part of Italy was one hundred and thirty years ago.

I have spent some months in Italy following Ramage's route, and was astonished to find, in the majority of instances, how accurate a recorder he was – apart, of course, from the improvement of roadways and hostelries and the disappearance of brigands and mosquitoes; and apart from the great alteration that has unfortunately, from an aesthetic point of view, changed the face of the countryside due to subsequent agrarian policy. This is especially noticeable along the Ionian coast of the Gulf of Taranto.

Craufurd Tait Ramage was born on the 10th of September 1803 at Annefield, near Newhaven in Midlothian. His father was John Ramage of Leith and his mother was Elizabeth Lumsdaine. He was educated at Edinburgh High School and at the University, where he graduated on M.A. in 1825. While at the University he took private pupils, including Archibald Campbell Tait (Archbishop of Canterbury 1869–1882) with whom he maintained a lifelong friendship. After leaving the University he became tutor to the younger sons of Sir Henry Lushington, Bart., H.B.M. Consul at Naples, and lived with them there from 1825 to 1828. Between April and the end of June 1828 he undertook his solitary tour of the Kingdom of the Two Sicilies which is the subject of this book. He returned to Naples for a short time and then proceeded homewards via Rome, Florence, Vienna, and Munich. For thirteen years after his return to England he was tutor to the family of Thomas Spring-Rice, later Baron Monteagle. When he was thirty-six he married Mary Paterson, daughter of Robert Paterson of Ninfield, Dumfriesshire in Cheshire, who was eighteen years his junior: they had two sons and three daughters. In 1841 Ramage was appointed vice-master of Wallace Hall Academy at Closeburn in Dumfriesshire, and succeeded to the rectorship in 1842. He was nominated Justice of the Peace for Dumfriesshire in 1848 and in 1852 the degree of LL.D. was conferred upon him by the University of Glasgow.

Ramage devoted his leisure to literary pursuits and his publications were: *Beautiful Thoughts from Greek Authors*, with translations by the Author, Liverpool, 1864, with a second edition in 1873; *Beautiful Thoughts from Latin Authors* etc., Liverpool, 1864,[1] with a second and third edition; *Beautiful Thoughts from French and Italian Authors* etc., Liverpool, 1865, with a second edition in 1875; *Beautiful Thoughts from German and Spanish Authors*, etc., Liverpool, 1868; also *Defence of the Parochial Schools of Scotland*, Edinburgh, 1854; *The Nooks and By-Ways of Italy*, Liverpool, 1868; *Drumlanrig Castle and the Douglases*, John Anderson, Dumfriess, 1876; and *Bible Echoes in Ancient Classics*, Edinburgh, 1878. He died at Wallace Hall on the 4th of December 1878.

Although the *Nooks and By-Ways of Italy* was published forty years after Ramage returned from Italy, it must be remembered that he was only twenty-four years old when the diaries and letters from which it was compiled were written. Ramage was undoubtedly one of the world's eccentrics, if only because of his mode of dress – 'I have a white merino frock-coat, well-furnished with capacious pockets, into which I have stuffed my maps and note-books; nankeen trousers, a large-brimmed straw hat, white shoes, and an umbrella, a most invaluable article to protect me from the fierceness of the sun's rays' – and his learning and command of languages, both ancient and modern, is remarkable. Almost every page is self-revealing and shows him to be perceptive, logical, modest, accurate, full of commonsense, very practical, and blessed with a strong sense of humour, be it dry or sardonic at times – 'I find they have a custom here of allowing the beard to grow for a month after the death of a relative, and that they show their grief also by wearing their linen unwashed and unchanged till it is worn away with filth. This custom, however, I suspect, is observed by many who are not mourning for the death of a friend'. It is incredible that the hardships which he

---

1. On 5th November 1864, when sending a presentation copy to a friend, Ramage wrote he was 'glad to find by the sale of the Latin work that a large number of our countrymen can enjoy the strong meals of the ancients and cannot have bowed the knee to the frivolous literature of the passing day'.

endured and the squalor which he encountered seldom made him complain. In his mad haste to accomplish all he had set out to do, it is the intense heat which seems to have been his greatest trial.

His appreciation of, and delight in the beauties of nature are obviously deeply felt and often poetically expressed – 'I was so charmed, however, with the appearance of the mountains and the coolness of the air, that I resolved to face the brigands. Accordingly, I proceeded to ascend the mountain-range, which was covered with magnificent oaks, beeches, and gloomy pines, that had borne the blast of many a winter. Every step presented new beauties, and opened to the eye fresh objects of admiration. There was a wildness in the scenery, and a gloom in the darkly-wooded mountains, that overpowered the mind. All was silent save the sound of some distant water-fall, or the low moaning of the breeze through the aged forest. At times the piercing scream of the eagle startled the air, or some wild goat would dart away to its secret recess.' And again – 'I am not so bitten with the anti-quarian mania but that I believe a varied landscape, such as that which I was now admiring [the summit of Monte Stella] speaks far more powerfully to the heart, and has a greater moral effect, than any work of man, however magnificent, even though it may be a memorial of one of the brightest pages of human history.'

Ramage's writing is enlivened by most vivid and penetrating similes. For example, when speaking of the Neapolitans – 'They are like their own Vesuvius, which, after appearing to have slumbered for many years, bursts forth suddenly, more terrible than ever, and causes the whole land to tremble.' Or, when describing the professors of Naples University – 'Like to those phosphorescent fireflies which appeared the other evening at Velia, their teaching is brilliant, and reflects light, but there is no heat.'

His attitude to politics and religion is irreproachable. On one occasion at Capo di Leuca he 'found it was approaching the hour when Mass was to be performed, and it was, of course, expected that I should attend. I told them that I was an Englishman, and that my principles did not admit of my join-ing in their form of worship. I would stop, however, till my muleteer per-formed his religious duties, and would, meanwhile, descend to the shore to admire the works of the great God, whom we both worshipped, though under different external forms. This pleased the old man (the priest), who could not but see that I had some tincture of religion, and he said he would pray that I might see the error of my ways; to which I replied, that I had been taught in our heretical country that the prayers of a righteous man availeth much.'

As regards the customs of the country, he is careful not to give offence and is condemnatory of those who behave otherwise – 'I have seen some of our

B

countrymen place themselves in a conspicuous position, that they might in this way show more clearly their opinion of the folly of whatever ceremony they might be witnessing. This does not accord with what I consider right. In passing through a foreign country merely to gratify our curiosity, we are bound to respect the prejudices of the people; and if we cannot look upon their superstitious observances without lifting up our testimony, we had better stay at home.'

One is constantly left breathless by the amount of sightseeing Ramage did in a day. For example, he says he went from Catanzaro to Crotone, and from Taranto to Brindisi via Manduria. On another amazing hustle, he left Rossano for Cassano via Sybaris, and later the same day went from Cassano to Civita and back again to Sybaris, returning to Cassano while there was still light enough to visit the monastery. Since the distance covered must have been about fifty-two miles, this expedition seems almost impossible. We must remember, however, that Ramage hired a mule at Rossano (although he had to dismount as it refused to go at more than 'a snail's pace') and took 'active ponies' when he got to Cassano; also that he was travelling from daybreak until dusk.[1] During the course of his wanderings he hired a carriage on at least three occasions, and went by sea from Policastro to Paola; from Taranto to Gallipoli, from Brindisi to Trani, and when he visited Manfredonia and Viesti. At other times he travelled on foot or on mule- or ponyback. Also, since he repeatedly set out at daybreak and seldom stopped for the night before dusk, he would have had seventeen or eighteen hours 'at his command', although he usually spent two to three hours in the middle of the day at rest.

It is unfortunate that no dates are given in *The Nooks and By-Ways*, and I have been quite unable to trace any of the original manuscripts for this book, with the exception of the letters mentioned earlier.

For the more human side of his character, we may reflect on his attitude to wine and women. As regards the former, we find him enjoying *moscato* 'with great zest', and at Cutro he indulges 'in a very fair modicum of wine', while at Trebisacce he 'furnished' the coastguard 'with somewhat more wine than was exactly consistent with propriety': indeed, to such an extent that the poor man became 'quite obstreperous in his mirth' – all this because (for once) Ramage had 'nothing better to do'. Obviously he was not unmoved by women. At Strongoli 'the sparkling eyes of the younger sister' proved a great distraction, and on another occasion, 'the youngest daughter was one of the most entertaining girls I had ever met with'; in fact, he goes

1. Dr Gisela Richter informs me that when she was at the British School of Archaeology at Athens many years ago, it was quite usual for her fellow-students to *walk* from Athens to Marathon and back in a day, a distance of about forty miles.

on to say, 'I verily believe that I should have committed all kinds of follies' if his time had not been limited.

In my opinion, Norman Douglas in *Alone* gives such a delightful and penetrating account of Ramage's character and activities that it cannot be bettered – 'One grows attached to these *Nooks and By-Ways*. An honest book richly thoughtful, and abounding in kindly twinkles ... A shrewd book, indeed ... I wish I had encountered it earlier. It would have been useful to me when writing my own pages on the country it describes. I am always finding myself in accord with the author's opinions, even in trivial matters such as the hopeless inadequacy of an Italian breakfast. He was personally acquainted with several men I have mentioned – Capialbi, Zicari, Masci; he saw the Purple Codex; in fact, there are numberless points on which I could have quoted him with profit.'

With the exception of Lenormant, the well-known French traveller, I have confined my bibliography to English travellers, but few of them went further south than Naples or Paestum. Reflecting on their writings it seems to me that only Norman Douglas and George Gissing made my pulse beat faster by their poetical descriptions of the wild and rugged beauty of Southern Italy and their real understanding of its inhabitants: with Ramage, of course, I quite simply fell in love. Of the other travellers, Henry Swinburne is, I think, the best value, and I suspect that Ramage had a copy of his book in one of his 'capacious pockets'; as indeed, Augustus Hare had of *The Nooks and By-Ways*. Lady Blessington is a brilliant and thought-provoking writer and gives a vivid account of the circle in which she moved in Naples: some of her writings show a more serious and deeply interesting side of her character. Colt Hoare, Keppel-Craven, Eustace and the rest are often very 'meaty', but to me they lack inspiration and are often prosaic, although Strutt can provide a little light entertainment at times. Lear, who can be immensely amusing, used, I suspect, artistic licence with his pen as well as his brush.

I have had most reluctantly to abridge *The Nooks and By-Ways* and much that I should have liked to include has had to be omitted. Ramage's expeditions in and around Naples; the Sorrentine peninsula, and his final tour from Naples to Rome must await future publication should this present book be favourably received. I have confined this edition therefore to the tour Ramage made through the Kingdom of the Two Sicilies in 1828, although his *Letters* give a brief account of some of his further travels. Those whose interest is aroused by this work may seek out the original 'Ramage'.

The four illustrations by Giacinto Gigante (1806–1876) and Achille Vianelli (1803–1894) are reproductions of the charming watercolours purchased by Ramage from the artists. They are now in the possession of his grand-daughter, Miss Mary Hill, to whom I am indebted for allowing them to be reproduced here. The other twelve illustrations are of sepia drawings by Antonio Senape, which have recently come into my possession and are reproduced here for the first time. Senape was born in Rome; he worked in the Kingdom of the Two Sicilies between 1818–1847, and also in Malta and Provence.

I have given much thought to the question of the footnotes and bibliography relating to the archaeological sites. If any readers of this book are specialists in this field, they will already have far more knowledge than I am competent to convey or they will know where they should look for it. On the other hand, the non-specialist reader may wish to be better informed, and I have therefore drawn attention to reports on these matters in the footnotes if I have thought that information might not be included in the works cited in the bibliography. Where the footnote simply says *Bibliography*, it is suggested that the works of Bérard and Dunbabin should be consulted first.

The first new edition of *The Nooks and By-Ways of Italy* will appear in Italian published by Istituto Grafico Tiberino di Stefano De Luca of Rome. This contains the major part of Ramage's text relevant to his tour. In addition, there are the following appendices: (a) *Extracts from the writings of other English travellers in South Italy*. (b) *Inscriptions:* Mr P. M. Fraser, Fellow of All Souls College, Oxford has contributed a learned article on these and here usually the single word indicates where Ramage recorded inscriptions in his text. (c) *Classical Texts:* Ramage liberally sprinkled his book with quotations accompanied by his own translations; here Ramage's references only are usually given, although the quotations are always apt and often amusing. (d) *A list of Greek words recorded by Ramage as being in use in South Italy in his day:* omitted from this edition.

This book does not contain Ramage's *Preface* which is chiefly concerned with acknowledging his 'many obligations' to General Carlo Filangieri, Duke of Taormina and Prince of Satriano, to whom he inscribed the Dedication. Also, long historical accounts of places visited by Ramage have often been omitted since these facts can easily be found elsewhere.

Ramage's book was compiled from letters, based on diaries, written to his cousin, Mr Morris Charles Jones of Gungrog. He says in an introductory note that he was prevented from publishing an account of his tour earlier from fear that he might inadvertently draw the attention of a suspicious government to those from whom he had received hospitality, and who had poured out their grievances to him. Finally, due to the abridgements made in this edition, it has been thought better to divide the book into Chapters instead of Letters, as in the original edition.

EDITH CLAY

London, May 1964

ACKNOWLEDGEMENTS

IN addition to the persons mentioned previously, I owe a debt of gratitude to many friends who have helped me in various ways, and I would especially like to offer my warmest thanks to Signora Paola Zancani Montuoro who, from the inception of this book, has given me much encouragement and advice and to whom I am continually indebted for her generous hospitality. I wish also to express my particular gratitude to the following: Miss Yvonne ffrench, Mr and Mrs Marc Fitch, Mr John Fleming, Mr Anthony Forster, Mr Peter Fraser, Mr Richard Garnett, Mr John Greenwood (of the Italian State Tourist Office in London), Mr and Mrs Denys Haynes, Miss Lorna MacEchern (Private secretary to the Duke of Buccleuch), Dr J. Millar (Rector of Wallace Hall Academy, Closeburn), Dr Gisela Richter, Mr J. R. Seaton (of the National Library, Edinburgh), Professor Arnold Toynbee, Mr Raleigh Trevelyan, and to officials of the Austrian Institute in London and of the Central Bureau voor Genealogie at The Hague.

I am most grateful to the Trustees of The Marc Fitch Fund who generously made a grant of £250 towards my travelling expenses in connection with this book, and to the Shell International Petroleum Company, whose Italian branch made available to me a set of their excellent maps of Italy.

Finally, I must thank Mrs Emily Villiers-Stuart who, with patience and good humour, drove my car several thousand miles during the summer of 1962 when I was following in Ramage's footsteps.

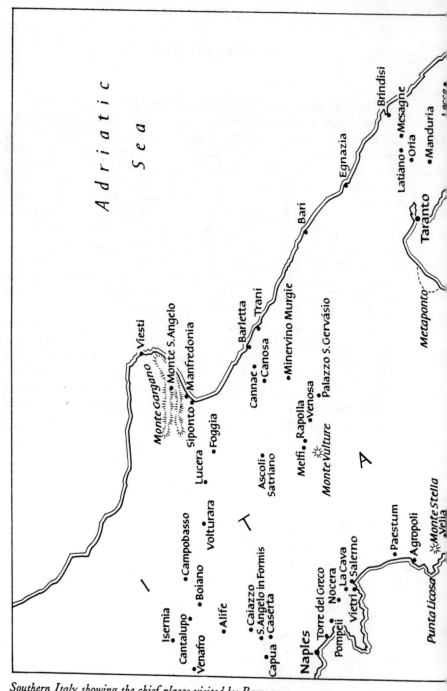

Southern Italy showing the chief places visited by Ramage

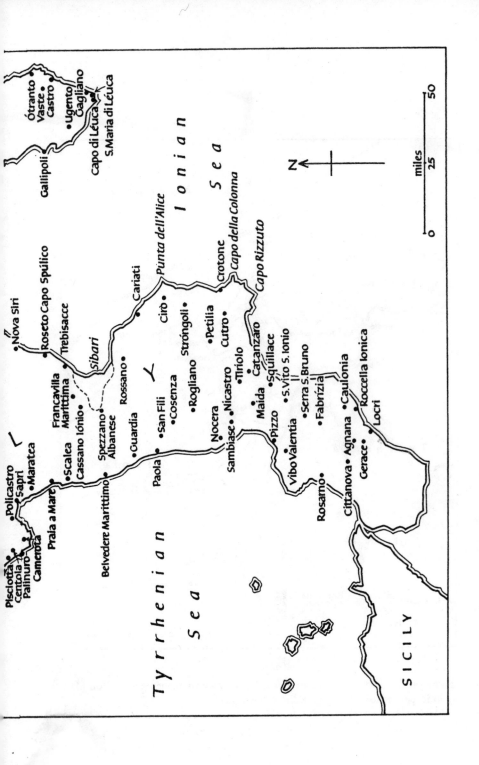

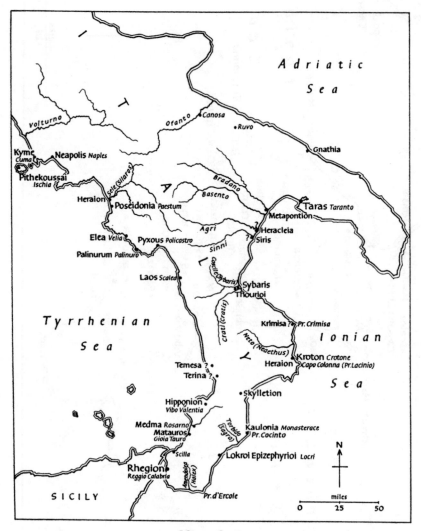

Magna Grecia

(Based on the map in *La Magna Grecia* by U. Zanotti-Bianco and L. Von Matt, by kind permission of Stringa Editore, Genova)

Pæstum, April 29, 1828.

I HAVE got safely to the end of my first day's journey, and, when I tell you all the fatigues I have undergone, I dare say you will allow that I am pretty well seasoned for the tour I have undertaken. Last night Sir Henry Lushington[1] gave a ball to the fashionables of Naples, and it was three before everything was quiet. As I had resolved to start at four, I had many little arrangements to make which I had not been able to overtake. About four I got into an open cabriolet, much of the same description as the old cabs you may have seen in London, but of a more picturesque form. The gaudy trappings and the gayness of the colours seem to harmonise with the beauty with which Nature has clothed herself here. You know that Naples stands at one corner of an extensive bay, and that at the opposite side rises a ridge of mountains of considerable height, which gradually sink down to a point opposite to a small island called Capri, celebrated as the spot where the Emperor Tiberius spent many of his last years. It was towards this ridge that my journey was first directed, and nothing could exceed the beauty of the scene, when the streaks of early light shot from behind the distant Apennines. Long ere the sun's rays could reach me, they had tinged with a purple hue the lofty peaks of these mountains, and gradually the picturesque island of Capri became illuminated. The bay lay unruffled before me, thickly studded with tiny boats, whose lateen sails were unfurled, ready to receive the morning breeze. Vesuvius rose by my side, still exhibiting proofs of its late commotions in the smoke that issued ever and anon from its crater. Nature smiled in all her loveliness, and seemed to invite man to partake of her joy. The coast along which we were passing was crowded with signs of human existence. The peasants were hastening to the market with fruit and vegetables, and many a fair dame bade us God speed as we hurried along. The houses exhibited an appearance of decay, which was but too emblematic of the people to whom they belonged; yet we were passing through the summer residences of the proud aristocracy of Naples. The architecture showed few traces of that purity of taste which might naturally be expected in a country abounding with the classic models of antiquity, and the grotesque

1. See *Letters*, p. 197.

figures that adorned the exterior of many buildings might well have issued from the brain of the national favourite – Pulchinello.

You must know that I had a companion with me, a young priest, who was going about thirty miles in my direction, and whom the cabman entreated should be allowed to occupy part of my vehicle. I yielded to his wishes, though I afterwards repented, as I found myself forced into a discussion of doctrinal points of religion at a time when I would much rather have enjoyed the glorious displays of God's goodness before me.

We first reached Herculaneum[1] ... The ruins lie in some places about one hundred feet below the surface; in other parts they are less deep. A considerable part has been excavated, and many valuable vases and statues have been discovered.

We next passed through the village of Torre del Greco, which has been often destroyed by the lava of Vesuvius ... In a short time we reached the gate of Pompeii[1], and here, though I was strongly tempted to take a farewell glance of its ruins, I considered it better to hurry forward on my journey. We were now close on the ridge of mountains to which I have alluded. The gloom of their darkly-wooded sides, the massive buildings of a monastery that were seen on the declivity, and a ruined castle, formed a strange contrast to the smiling and lovely aspect that Nature had assumed around. We entered the struggling village of Nocera, and, as we passed through its busy streets, I thought that I could distinguish a difference in the countenances of the people. They are descended from a colony of Saracens, and they are said still to retain many peculiar customs, indicating a race distinct from that which peopled the rest of Italy. The Church of Santa Maria Maggiore stands on the site of a Roman temple, resembling in miniature the Pantheon of Rome, and containing some very fine columns of variegated marble.

As we drove along, we passed through patches of lupins, which my charioteer said they made use of in three different ways. They feed their cattle with them when they are green; in the low warm country they find it difficult to procure green food for their cattle and horses, and are obliged to strip even the trees of their leaves for this purpose. Besides, they use the lupin to manure the land, by ploughing it in before it is ripe, and some they allow to ripen for seed. This is the *tristis lupinus* of Virgil (*Georg.* i. 75), and the epithet is really deserved, as it is remarkably bitter, and causes you to put on a rueful countenance when you

1. For reports on recent excavations *see* bibliography.

chew it. Before it can be eaten, which it is by the common people, it requires to be steeped and macerated in water for some time. The flower is white, and, like the sunflower, turns with the sun, and is so sensitive to its rays, according to Pliny (xviii. 36, i.), that the husband-man may know the hour of the day by its position, even when the weather is cloudy . . .

The country on which we were now entering has long been the resort of all who wish to study an Italian landscape in its perfection. The mountains rise to a considerable height, and are covered with wood to the summit. The fields around exhale the perfume of the orange and citron flowers, while the vine is trained in graceful festoons from tree to tree. Here, too, the monks had erected a monastery – La Cava – which is one of the most celebrated in Italy. It was at one time very rich, but the French in their visit to Italy confiscated the greater part of its property, and when the Bourbons recovered their throne, they did not think it necessary to restore it. I had visited it some years ago, and had spent a few hours very pleasantly in wandering through its grounds. Its library still contains many interesting manuscripts illustrative of the Lombard princes of Salerno.[1]

They pay, or rather used to pay, great attention to their garden, and had fruits of the most luscious kinds at all seasons. They contrived to cause their fig-trees to produce fruit twice a year, which, indeed, is not unusual in the neighbourhood of Naples. The fig-tree bears fruit at the usual time, at the latter end of August or September, and again in May, and is thence called *Fichi di Pasqua*. The manner in which this is brought about in the gardens at Naples is by covering the trees with mats all the winter; and in this way the small figs, which remained green on the tree in the autumn, are preserved, and ripen in the spring, as soon as the tree begins to shoot, and produce these early figs . . . [Ramage parted with his companion] at Salerno, a city of considerable size, situated on a bay somewhat resembling, though much larger than that of Naples. On consideration, I thought it my best plan to hire a boat here to carry me across the bay, about twenty miles broad, to a small village, Agropoli, which I saw on the opposite side. I had passed, about three miles before we reached Salerno, a few fishermen's huts,

1. The Abbey of La Trinità della Cava, founded in the eleventh century, was noted for its magnificent collection of manuscripts which was fortunately preserved intact during the Second World War.

and it occurred to me that I might get a boat at a reasonable rate there. This spot was called Vietri, and thither I trudged with my knapsack on my back, and my umbrella over my head to ward off the intense heat of the sun. Here I found a boat, but lost two precious hours before I could get the boatmen under way. As we advanced into the bay, we had a beautiful view of the romantic coast of Amalfi and the fabled islands of the Sirens, which I intend to visit when I return from my southern tour. The City of Salerno, too, added to the beauty of the scene. Above it rose a ruined castle, overgrown with ivy, and its dark masses carried the mind back to the gloomy period when it was first erected. Yet it ought not to be called gloomy, as Salerno then flourished under the paternal sway of a race of Lombard princes, and enjoyed a degree of prosperity which has long since passed away. We know from history that literature was encouraged, and that its school of medicine was one of the most celebrated in Europe . . . [Ramage quotes from a Latin poem] '*Regimen Sanitatis Salernitanum*', addressed by the school of Salerno to Robert of Normandy, the eldest son of William the Conqueror . . . Moderation in toddy, light suppers, an easy mind, 'not to be passion's slave,' and moderate exercise, formed the recipe which the doctors of Salerno prescribed to their patients, if they wished to enjoy good health and a long life . . .

By degrees we left the coast behind us, but I found that we had still a great distance before we should be able to reach Agropoli, and, to my annoyance, a strong southerly breeze set in, which would effectually prevent us from reaching it before midnight. The boatmen, too, assured me of its continuance, and, though it was evident that they wished to induce me to put back, the appearance of the sky confirmed their statement. Agropoli was therefore quite beyond my reach, unless I was willing to remain at sea all night, and this idea I did not quite relish, as I might be tossed overboard, and no one would be the wiser. In this dilemma I took the following determination. I had consulted my map, and I saw that the ruins of Pæstum, where there was an eating-house (for I had already visited it), might be reached by walking along the coast, if the boat could get beyond the mouth of a river called Sele, the ancient Silarus,[1] which I saw fell into the bay. I gave directions,

1. Excavation of the important archaic sanctuary, dedicated to Hera, and discovered by P. Zancani Montuoro and the late U. Zanotti-Bianco at the mouth of this river, has continued since 1934, *see* bibliography.

therefore, that they should pull the boat on shore as soon as they got beyond the river, and though they attempted to dissuade me by representing all sorts of dangers and difficulties, I kept to my resolution, and at last was landed on a sandy beach. The sun was set, and I had still about five miles of unknown ground before me.

My map showed me that there might be a near cut across the country to Pæstum; but when I attempted to leave the shore, I found myself in a marsh, which I concluded to be occasioned by my proximity to the mouth of the river. This, in fact, was the *stagnum Lucanum*, salt marshes, alluded to by Plutarch (*Crassus*, 2.), where Crassus defeated a large body of insurgents under Spartacus. Two years ago I had crossed the Silarus nearer the hills, and I was much struck with the grove of holm-oaks, the ilex of Virgil (*Georg.* iii. 146), which were growing plentifully around . . . I saw there was no possibility of penetrating in the direction I had begun, and must therefore keep along the sandy shore. Luckily the moon rose, else I should have been in an awkward predicament. I began to doubt whether I should be able to find any mode of reaching Pæstum that night. If the marsh continued, it would be impossible; but I might get on to Agropoli by creeping along the shore . . . Amidst these not very pleasing cogitations, I came suddenly upon a party of fishermen, who had drawn up their boat on the shore, and were cooking some fish for supper. They were not a little surprised to see me at such an hour, and I did not know whether I ought to be pleased or alarmed at the rencontre. In this vicinity an Englishman and his wife, Mr and Mrs Hunt,[1] had been shot and robbed a few years before, and this did not fail to be recalled to my recollection. However, I went boldly up and inquired if they could point out any path across the marsh to Pæstum, where I wished to rest for the night. They were very civil, and told me that about two miles farther on I should come to a ruined tower, and there I should find a path leading on to Pæstum.[2] They at the same time offered me part of their supper, and even wished me to spend the night with them under their boat, which served them for shelter. The night, indeed, was beautiful, and if there had been necessity for the step, I might have run the risk, but, on the whole, I thought it needless to throw temptation in their way. Thanking them for their

1. See *Letters*, p. 203.
2. For reports on the extensive excavations undertaken at Pæstum (Poseidonia) in recent years *see* bibliography.

courtesy, I continued my course, and ... as I came upon the tower, turned into the country; I kept along the path for some distance, when I reached the ruins of the Temples of Pæstum. I now recollected sufficient of the locality to have no further fears of reaching the *locanda*, the Italian word for an eating-house, for it cannot be dignified with the title of an inn. No one would ever think of sleeping in it unless they were in my predicament. The daylight had now for some time left me, but the moon shone bright. Everything around was silent as the grave. The wind had died away, and I heard no longer even the ripple of the waves. I had no occasion to hurry to the *locanda* to secure a bed, as it was not likely that any other wearied traveller would be there. I turned therefore, into the ruins of the temples – into that one dignified with the title of the Temple of Neptune[1] – and seated myself on what is supposed to have been its ancient altar. The massive pillars threw a deep shade across the ruins, and formed a beautiful contrast with the parts illuminated by the pale light of the moon. There was perfect silence, yet I was in the centre of what had once been a populous town. Its inhabitants must have been rich and highly civilised, else they could never have raised to their gods such a magnificent edifice. It still remained a monument of their power, while their names and deeds of glory had long passed into oblivion. It is curious that these temples should not be alluded to by ancient writers, and were even unknown to travellers till the middle of the last century. The columns only remain, but they are sufficient to show the ancient magnificence of the temples.

All this was very pleasant, but the air of this place is said to be particularly fatal at night. I was still unprovided with shelter, and it was possible that I might be refused admission at such an hour. It was past ten, and I was quite certain that they had been long shut up. I had little difficulty in finding the *locanda*, as there are only four houses in the vicinity. On knocking, a voice called out, *Chi è?* – i.e. who is there? *Un inglese* – an Englishman, said I. They were unwilling to open the door till I entered into an explanation of the accident that had brought me to Pæstum at such an hour, and after some parleying I was admitted to the house. When the man saw that I was really what I had represented myself, he became civil, and told me that I might have a bed upstairs. He seemed, as far as I could judge from his face, to be an honest man – at all events I was in his power, and must abide the consequences. He

1. Now thought to be dedicated to Hera.

6

lighted a fire and broiled a sausage, and with some coarse black bread and miserable wine, I contrived to make a supper. My bedroom was up a flight of steps; the room contained a few boards that served as my bed, a stool, and a box which contained I know not what. There was no glass in the window; the shutters merely closed, and that not very perfectly . . .

II

AT daybreak I was roused by a scarecrow of a boy suffering from dropsy, and I found that this was a very prevalent disease in the vicinity, arising from the stagnant water which they are obliged to drink. All the peasants whom I met on my former visit had a pale, unhealthy appearance, which is caused by the *miasmata*, or marsh. On descending from my room I found a blazing log of wood, by no means an unpleasant sight at this hour, and all I could get for breakfast was the everlasting sausage and their coarse bread. Some peasants came in, and by them I was told that Stella[1] was distant about twenty miles. I talked of brigands, and inquired whether I should be in danger of falling in with them, but they assured me that nothing of the sort existed in their neighbourhood. Having paid my bill, which amounted to little more than a shilling, I hoisted my knapsack, and commenced the toils of the day.

I think that I have not told you the manner I am equipped. I have a white merino frock-coat, well furnished with capacious pockets, into which I have stuffed my maps and note-books; nankeen trousers, a large-brimmed straw hat, white shoes, and an umbrella, a most invaluable article to protect me from the fierceness of the sun's rays, which will increase as I advance to the south.

Thus equipped, I began my second day's journey without the slightest idea where I should find shelter for the night, quite certain that it was impossible to have worse accommodation than I had had, if I could find any at all. Still I was quite fresh, and the novelty of my position gave a zest to all my fatigues. The morning was delightful; the sun was now above the horizon, and illuminated the gloomy scene I had traversed the previous evening. The glare of the sun, however,

1. Monte Stella.

was not in keeping with the surrounding objects. The obscure light of the moon was better suited to the desolate appearance of the place ... The walls of the ancient town are still visible in many parts, and are to be traced for about two miles, but as I had already walked along them on my former visit, and they had often been examined by antiquaries, I did not think it necessary to make a longer stay.

After I had passed the walls and a small stream that runs on the outside, possessing the property of petrifying or rather encrusting wood and twigs if they are kept long enough in it, I found myself in a plain covered with thick brushwood, which completely obstructed my view, and I can scarcely imagine how I should have been so lucky last night as to have made my way so easily, particularly as I find it traversed in every direction by paths, along which cattle have evidently passed. The slightest deviation would, I can now see, have landed me in a quagmire. I had glimpses of the hills towards which it was my purpose to advance. I heard the tinkling of the goat's tiny bell, and I knew the herdsman must be somewhere near, but I could see nothing of him, and I trusted to my good fortune to be able to extricate myself from the labyrinth in which I was involved. We are told by some of the Roman poets that Pæstum was famed for its roses; nothing of the kind, however, met my eye ...

After I had proceeded thus for about a mile, I came suddenly upon a deep part of the marsh, which induced me to thread my way to the shore, where I was sure to be able to get on, though with some additional fatigue. I was startled every now and then by large black snakes darting across my path, that seemed quite as anxious to get out of my sight as I was to avoid them ... The little streams coming down from the hills around are allowed to find their way as best they can to the sea, and as there are no banks, they spread over this low land, and have made the whole more or less of a stagnant marsh. Another enemy began to annoy me in a serious way. Large droves of buzzing flies gathered round me, and I had no mode of defence except to tie my handkerchief round my face, yet still they contrived to insinuate themselves, and their sting gave me great pain. Virgil (*Georg*. iii. 147) alludes to these flies in speaking of a hill in this quarter, and here they are in full vigour after an interval of eighteen hundred years ... After a variety of doublings to avoid bogs, and stepping into several, I managed to reach the beach somewhat beyond the spot where I had left it yesterday evening. The bay looked quite calm, except here and there where the morning breeze created a slight ripple. It was untenanted in its wide extent . . . I cannot imagine where the harbour of Pæstum could have been, and yet in former times there must have been some port, as it was evidently a large city, and, besides, was sacred to Neptune. The shore seems quite unsuited for any safe anchorage, being unprotected from the north and west. I could perceive no remains of any pier, or mole, that might have been thrown out for the purpose of protection.[1]

I sauntered along the beach in the direction of Agropoli, which is placed at the end of the plain where the shore begins to be somewhat precipitous. I was approaching the hills seen on the south side of the Bay of Salerno. They rise to no great height, nor are they remarkable for their picturesque appearance, except in one direction, where they bend round and form a kind of amphitheatre. At last I reached a small stream falling into the sea, and while I was cooling myself before I attempted to wade, I observed two men approaching from the opposite side, and waited to see how they would manage to cross. One of them was a fat, jolly priest, who had evidently not stinted himself of the good things of this life, and the other was probably his servant. At all events, the priest mounted on his back, with his dress drawn up over his ears, and was thus ferried across. I entered into conversation, and inquired what he called those flies from which I had been suffering so much, and he said *tafani*, which seems to be a corruption of the *tabanus* of the Latins. He said that they were *diavoli*, 'devils', and in that I agreed with him, though I was glad to learn that I should get rid of them as soon as I left this marshy ground. I then put in my petition that the same kindness should be bestowed on me by his servant as he had received, and I was at once carried over, to the great amusement of the priest. I offered him some trifle, but he refused to accept it. I now began to leave the plain and to ascend the hills, which are of a white, chalky character, and even at this early hour of the morning the reflexion of the sun's rays became very disagreeable. They are the ancient Montes Petilini, to which the band of rebellious slaves, headed by Spartacus, retreated when defeated by the consul Crassus, 71 BC. I saw in the distance some peasants working in the fields, and I met a band of

1. No evidence has yet been found for a port or docks at Pæstum, but it has been suggested that the Poseidonion might be at Agropoli, *see* P. Zancani Montuoro, *Arch. Stor. Cal. Luc.*, XXIII 1954, p. 165 sqq.

women, who took fright at my appearance, and scampered off in the utmost confusion. What they could have imagined me to be I cannot conceive, for they gave me no opportunity of questioning them. I did not think it necessary to enter the village of Agropoli, which lay a little to the right, though the inhabitants maintain that St Paul, on his way to Rome, honoured them with his presence, and they point out the exact spot where he first placed his foot. During the Middle Ages, AD 879, it was occupied by a band of Saracens, who maintained a garrison at this point to overawe the country, and there is still a spot called Campo Saraceno. When they retired, it is said that they destroyed what little remained of the city of Pæstum. Some Saracenic inscriptions attest their presence in former times. It was sacked in 1535 and 1542 by the Turks, when three hundred of its inhabitants were carried off as slaves to Constantinople.

I saw in the distance some of the young damsels of Agropoli, employed in the same way as our Scotch lassies may be often observed by the traveller. They were busily engaged in washing their linen in a burn, apparently kilted high above the knees, but I did not approach to disturb them in their occupation. It is said, I know not how truly, that these girls are considered marriageable at the early age of twelve, and this arises from the peculiar mildness of their climate.

Leaving Agropoli to the right, I began to proceed up a small glen, and I was surprised to observe how far advanced the vegetation was, compared with what I had left yesterday in the vicinity of Naples. I was only about sixty miles farther south, and yet the foliage was completely expanded and the fruit was beginning to form. The soil seemed to be particularly well suited to the olive-tree, which in some cases had attained a magnitude I had never before observed. The vine was trained in the same manner that I had been accustomed to, from tree to tree, and the graceful festoons added much to the beauty of the scenery. It was not without great delight that I came to some lofty plane-trees, forming a kind of irregular avenue to a miserable house, and under the shade of these trees I took shelter from the heat of the sun, which was now beginning to be oppressive. The edifice had the appearance of what might be supposed to be a farm-house, but had all the gloom of desolation around it. It was a pretty spot, however, and might have been made a delightful residence. I saw no signs of human existence, and I felt no inclination to disturb the repose of the inhabitants, though I began to feel the effects of my sausage breakfast. I determined to stop at the first repectable house that I met, and try how far the hospitality of the country was likely to go.

It was not long before I was able to put this intention into effect, for I reached a house which was in a tolerable state of repair, and to which the proprietor was making some further additions. This augured well, and I walked up to the door, where a good-looking girl appeared, yet before I could reach her she had vanished, and immediately afterwards a man came forward, to whom I addressed a petition for wine, for which I was prepared to pay, and if they had none, water would be a very valuable commodity in my eyes. I told him that I had come from a distant land to admire the beauties of his country. He required, however, no incitement to give me all and more than I required. He called for chairs, and we sat down under the shade of a tree, while he directed the servant to bring out some refreshment. It was indeed scanty, and of very coarse quality, but it was evidently given with good will, and that would far more than have compensated for even less luxurious fare. The bread was coarse and old, the cheese I could scarcely make any impression upon, and if this may be taken as a sample of their mode of diet, I would back Scotland against Italy, even with her oat-cakes and porridge. In the wine, however, he beat us, for he produced some of a very excellent quality, and if it had been iced, it would have been nectar itself. In entering into conversation with my host, I found him express himself in a manner far superior to what I could have expected in this remote spot, and I could not help expressing my surprise that I should have fallen in with a gentleman of so accomplished a mind, when he laughed, and holding up his hand, which had lost two fingers and was otherwise mutilated, added that he had not always led so quiet and peaceful a life as he now did. He had served several campaigns under Napoleon, had witnessed the burning of Moscow, and in the fatal retreat had escaped with the loss of several of his fingers and toes. He was now living on a small property which he had inherited, and said that he only regretted having no outlet for his surplus produce . . . I inquired what were the principal articles of commerce, and he said that he dealt chiefly in oil and Indian corn, but many of his neighbours fed pigs in great numbers, and the bacon was exported through Naples to various parts of the world. The olive-tree begins to bear in its fifth year, and sometimes even in its fourth. The cattle are not only numerous but of a very large size, and in the vicinity of Potenza and Avigliano are of a milk-white colour, such as Theocritus (*Idyll*. 32) describes those consecrated to the sun. He spoke of the exquisite flavour of the hams from the pigs feeding in the woods. Nature seldom changes in these matters, and in this case we find she has remained steady. Cassiodorus, who lived in the fifth century, refers to this article of commerce abounding in Lucania, and the sausage, which is the only food I have yet been able to procure, is nothing else than the *lucanicæ*, of which Cicero (*Ad Fam.* ix. 16) speaks when he says: 'I used formerly to be delighted with your olives and pork sausages.' ... Here is the mode in which the epicure Apicius (2, 4) tells us they were made: 'An intenstine stuffed with minced pork, mixed with ground pepper, cummin, savory, rue, rock parsley, berries of laurel, and suet. The intenstine is drawn out thinly and hung up in smoke.' You must know that Lucania was the ancient name of the part of Italy in which I am now travelling ... The Italians now call it *salsiccia*, and we may trace the origin of this work to Varro and Macrobius ... From Macrobius (*Sat.* vii. 8) we find that it was more frequently called *isicium*, hence *salis isicia*, i.e. sausage of salted pork, and from this we get the present Italian word *salsiccia*, which has passed into our word sausage through the French *saucisse*.

He spoke also in enthusiastic terms of dried figs, which are found more particularly at Cilento, in this province, and which are what the Romans called *caricæ*, so highly prized by the ancients that they were accounted food for the gods ...

Being now refreshed, I tore myself away from my intelligent host, as I saw that I must advance a few miles farther before the sun was in its mid-day fury, if I meant to reach Stella before sunset. My host told me that there were ruins on its summit, and this made me the more anxious to put my plan in execution. He pressed me to remain, but the hot season is fast advancing, and I am aware that I shall find it to increase every day as I proceed southward. I do not mean to omit the examination of any interesting spot full of historical recollections, but I shall not tarry longer than is absolutely necessary for the object I have in view. I parted from my host with considerable regret, but I at last began to ascend the hill in the direction of a village, Torchiara, which was about four miles farther on. As I advanced, the country became more bare, and the rock protruded with an unpleasant glare. No attempt had been made to level the path along which I was proceeding, and, from its appearance, I should imagine that in the winter season the water flowed along with considerable force. On reaching Torchiara, a large church was the first object that attracted my attention, and, as it seemed a handsome building I expected to find the inhabitants comfortable, and the village of a higher grade than I had anticipated. In this, however, I was mistaken, as, though the houses were built with stone, they were uncemented by mortar, and had a wretched unfinished look. What I could see of their interior as I passed along quite corresponded with the discomfort of the exterior. Of course there was no attempt at regularity in the erection of the houses; but what was most surprising, and showed the apathetic disposition of the people, was, that they had left the road, I cannot call it street, between the row of houses in the same state as it had come out of the hands of nature. The rocks in many parts protruded considerably, and it was not without an effort that I climbed up. A very little labour would have made it level, but they say, I suppose, as we used to do too often in Scotland, it just does *weel eneugh*. It was now necessary to make some inquiries respecting the road I ought to pursue, and I thought that the best place to obtain this information would be the *locanda*. The people stared at me as I passed along, making, however, no observation, and I did not enter into conversation with any of them till I reached the *locanda*, which I easily recognised by the various objects hung up at the door. There was only one apartment, and it was crowded with peasants. It was not plastered; was low-roofed, dark and dingy, though it perhaps looked more so from the bright sunshine which I had just left. I glanced hurriedly over the contents of the little shop while I called for a flask of wine. As the apartment was small, they had everything suspended from the roof, except the wine; hams, which seemed to be well dried and smoked; long strings of sausages; small round cheeses made from goats' milk; and a variety of dried fruits, such as raisins and figs, which were hung up in nets. Two tolerably sized casks of wine completed the contents of the shop. There were three small tables and several benches of the rudest construction, on which were lolling several Salvator Rosa looking men, their countenances exhibiting the same angular form and the same dark piercing eye. Some had evidently drunk a sufficient quantity of my host's wine, and were very boisterous in their mirth; but, as I was aware of the excitable temperaments of the southern Italian, I did not know how soon their knives might be at each other's throats. A party of them were playing at a game of cards, which I found to be usually kept by the landlord, no doubt as a means of inducing people to frequent his shop. The game was of the nature of what they call *scopa*, but I found it to be somewhat different from the game of that name played by the Neapolitans. My appearance among them of course attracted attention and excited their curiosity. With some difficulty I made my host comprehend that I was on my way to Stella. I was sadly annoyed to find my Italian, on which I piqued myself, and on which I was complimented by the better educated, was with difficulty understood by the peasants, and, what was more distressing, I found great difficulty in understanding their language. However, we managed to get on pretty well, and I had rather an interesting conversation with the party, which was now increased by a large proportion of the inhabitants of Torchiara ... The door was crowded, and they were climbing on each other's backs to look in at the windows. I was, no doubt, regarded as a great curiosity, as no Englishman had ever probably passed through their village before. I may tell you, that to declare yourself an *inglese* secures respect wherever you go, and I am sorry to think that a *scozzese* would not sound so important in their ears. Our conversation turned on the constitution of England, of which some of them seemed to have a pretty correct idea. They inquired whether we did not often behead our kings, and they had an imperfect notion of our parliaments. Our conversation was suddenly put an end to by the appearance of an officer of gendarmes, who strutted into the apartment with a consequential air, and demanded to know who I was. There is no advantage to be got in resisting these Jacks in office, and I therefore told him that I was an Englishman travelling through the country by permission of his government, as my passport would show. He had done nothing more than his duty in questioning me, as the government find it necessary to be on their guard against insurrectionary movements, and I had, no doubt, in his eyes, a suspicious look. I stated my desire to visit Stella, when one of the party said that a friend of his was in the village who was going to its vicinity, and that he would be my guide if I delayed a short time.

Accordingly, ere long, we were on our way. The path lay along the ridge of a hill, a small portion of which was covered with vines, and our view extended across the valley of the Alento to a forest, which my guide called Monteforte. To the west he pointed to a wood of pines, from which, in former times, they get resin, but the manufacture had long since ceased. The village of Copersito lay below us, about which there is rather an amusing legend. You must know that Salerno, which I have already mentioned, possesses the sacred body of the venerated St Matthew, and that it was conveyed thither by land from I know not what place. At all events, the monks, who were toiling under the weight of the body, reached Copersito with difficulty, fainting from heat. Water could not be found till they prayed to the apostle, when it burst suddenly from the rock, and the water is now considered to be a cure for every kind of disease. This is no doubt very silly, and we may laugh at it, but I could match it with many equally superstitious notions in Ireland. Barregoween well, in the county of Limerick, is visited by crowds of people every week, with the idea that they can be cured of their diseases by the water blessed by St Patrick.

After passing through several small villages, I reached Il Mercato, situated at the foot of the hill where the ruins of which I was in search were said to be found. It consisted only of half a dozen houses, but I was now so completely knocked up, that, without rest, I could proceed no further. Luckily one of the houses was a *locanda*, being part of an old monastery, the inmates of which had been turned adrift by the French when Murat occupied the throne, and which still continued to form part of the royal domain. It is in a sadly dilapidated state,[1] and a few years will level it with the ground. It is amazing how numerous the monasteries were in this beautiful corner of Italy: St Franciscans, near Agropoli; Austin Friars, at Copersito; Reformed Fathers and Benedictines, at Lauriano; Capuchins, at Perdifumo; and many others, who it is needless to enumerate. The French may have acted from interested motives in much they have done in Italy, but in reducing the number of monasteries I have no doubt that the country has been benefited.

I did not quite like the appearance of my host, and the ruined monastery seemed a fit place for a deed of darkness, but my exhaustion precluded the possibility of my advancing a step farther without rest. I inquired if he had any room where I could lie down for a couple of hours, when he showed me into a cell once occupied by the monks, about eight feet square, and containing a few boards, on which I could stretch myself. I smiled at the idea of resting on such a bed, but, at all events, I should enjoy quiet and coolness for a short time, and I told

1. The Capuchin Monastery of San Martino, now (1962) restored and inhabited by this Order.

him to call me in two hours if I did not make my appearance. I inquired what dinner he could procure me, and was highly delighted to find that he had some excellent fish. I placed a bench against the door, that the noise might awake me if any attempt were made to break in upon my privacy. I slept soundly, and at the hour I fixed my landlord awoke me, when, on looking up to the mountain, I was sadly disappointed to find it covered with a thick mist. I called for my dinner, and had it brought out into the open air, as the heat was no longer so oppressive. I looked out with longing eyes to see the fish I had been promised, when, to my consternation, a dish made its appearance containing cold salted fish, swimming in vapid vinegar, and spiced with every herb, I am quite sure, that the Mountain Stella could produce. It was the most abominable compound that I had ever tasted, but mine-host looked so wistfully in my face to hear its praises, that I could not find it in my heart to tell him so. Sausage was again my dinner, with the coarse black bread of the country. The wine, too, was miserable, but I had made up my mind to rough it. While I was thus employed, I was surprised to see a manufactory busily at work on the opposite side of the road. It was not a large one, nor very important; it was a potter merrily employed at his trade, turning out the common earthenware used by the peasants. I inquired where he found a market for his merchandise, and he told me that this village had fairs at certain periods of the year, when he disposed of large quantities of his goods. There was no appearance of wealth about himself or his house, which consisted only of one apartment, but, notwithstanding this apparent poverty, I had heard him loudly carolling some merry lay of his country while he was turning his wheel. The peasantry of Italy are a gay, merry race, who have few wants, and, knowing nothing of those luxuries which have become necessaries for all classes among us, live perfectly satisfied with the little they possess.

This fair, to which the potter refers, may possibly be that mentioned by Cassiodorus as taking place in the fifth century near Leucothea, now Licosa, which is at no great distance from the spot where I was sitting . . .

I had engaged my friend who had accompanied me in the morning to remain till I was ready to proceed on my journey, as I saw that I should probably be benighted, and unable to find the ruins of Petilia. We started about five in the afternoon, but, though the sun's rays were no longer so powerful, it required considerable resolution to persevere in the ascent. As we mounted, however, the air became fresher, and there was some appearance of change in the vegetation. My eye has been little accustomed for some years to the sight of grass, and it was not, therefore, without delight that my foot once more trod the green sward ... In the lofty region above us, ever and anon, as the mist cleared away, we had a glimpse of a ruined castle perched on the top of a rock, but my time would not permit of my ascent to it ... Tradition has handed down that it was destroyed by a piratical band of Saracens ... I climbed up for about a mile farther, when I reached the summit of Stella, on which there was a small piece of level ground, where a chapel had been erected to the Madonna della Stella. There were no ruins that had the slightest appearance of bearing any very ancient date, but there were a good many foundations of ruined buildings a little below the chapel; and if Petilia was of small size, it may have been placed on this spot, though it must have been of difficult access. There were two towns called Petilia,[1] one in this part of Lucania, and another at Strongoli, among the Bruttii, which will be mentioned hereafter. At least, this is what Antonini and Romanelli[2] maintain, but having been on the spot, and seeing the small space of ground which it could occupy, I confess that I entertain grave doubts whether the true position has yet been discovered. At such a height water would fail, and even the difficulty of procuring provisions would be great.

You must not suppose, because I was disappointed in the object of my search, that I was not amply rewarded for the fatigue I had undergone. I would willingly have endured a thousandfold as much more to have enjoyed the magnificent scene that lay before me. I am not so bitten with the antiquarian mania but that I believe a varied landscape, such as that which I was now admiring, speaks far more powerfully to the heart, and has a greater moral effect, than any work of man, however magnificent, even though it may be a memorial of one of the brightest pages of human history. It was truly a noble landscape that opened to my view as the mist cleared away. The sun was approaching the horizon, and its rays tinged with a golden hue the sea, which was smooth as glass. All the rocks were touched with the same bright light.

1. It is generally supposed that there was only one town of Petilia at Strongoli (p. 133), but for a second town in Lucania *see* V. Panebianco, 'A proposito della capitale delle confederazione lucana' (*Rassegna Storica Salernitana*, VI, 1945).
2. Baron of San Biagio and D. M. Romanelli, topographers and historians.

I must have been about fifteen hundred feet above the level of the sea, but so nearly perpendicular was the mountain in some parts that it looked as if I could have thrown a stone into the water, and everything around was so silent that I imagined I could have heard its plunge to the bottom. In other parts the mountain slanted away gently, and the vegetation seemed to continue to the very edge of the water, for you must recollect that we have no perceptible tides here. The shore wended away to the north with numerous indentations, and immediately off the promontory there was a small island, which, on referring to my map, I found to be Licosa, the ancient Leucosia or Leucothea, the residence of a siren, a fabulous lady, who is said to have charmed men to their destruction. It seems a mere rock, and likely enough was always so, but the fable was an allegory to show that, whatever might be the outward appearance of the lady, if the imagination clothed her with beauty, it was sufficient to lead the individual to his ruin. From this bright and lovely scene I turned round and looked into the interior. My eye rested on the lofty Apennines, and below them stretched the gloomy forest of Monteforte, which my guide told me was the abode of a band of brigands. I have heard so much respecting them, and some of the statements have been of so alarming a character, that I thought it wise to hear what my guide, who lives in their vicinity, thought of them. I expressed a desire to visit them, which I secretly thought was putting my head into the lion's mouth, and inquired whether he imagined I should be plundered of my property. He told me that a solitary traveller ran no risk; but they levied heavy contributions on rich proprietors. From the statements he made, I see that they have established a species of *black mail (sic)*, and, if I fall in with such parties, I have some right to claim kin with them, in consequence of the same practices that once prevailed in my own country ...

The gloom of evening had now settled on the valleys below, and I saw that the sun was almost touching the horizon; and however unwilling I was to depart, I had no alternative, as the twilight in this part of the world is of short duration ... I saw a village at the foot of the hill, towards which there was a pretty easy descent, and I thought it better to take my chance of finding lodgings there. I parted from my guide, and made a hurried descent, knowing, that before I could reach it, evening would already have set in. The appearance of the houses augured ill for my night's rest, though I had no doubt that I should find some shelter. I lost no time in putting an end to my doubts, entering the first open door that I reached, and causing great consternation to two old women, who were the only occupants. I had some difficulty in making my wishes understood, when an objection was started, which had never occurred to me. It appears that there is a law which forbids anyone, under a severe penalty, from receiving a stranger in his house for the night without the permission of the magistrate, and it happened that this village was in union with another two miles distant, and there the magistrate resided. It was vain to argue that I was exhausted by fatigue, and that I could go no farther . . . I saw I must yield to necessity, and walk off a couple of miles to the village, which I found to be called Porcile.[1] It was now quite dark, and I should have had some difficulty in finding my way, if I had not fallen in with a man who was going to the same place. I entered into conversation with him, and his head was evidently full of Carbonari, to whom he seemed determined to believe that I belonged. It is a society united by sacred bonds to overturn their present form of government, and to introduce the constitutional principle. I wish them every success, but I am not here with the view of taking any part in their proceedings. At last we reached Porcile, and I requested my companion to point out the house of the syndic, or chief magistrate of the village. I made my wants known to him, produced my passport, and stated that I wished to pass the night in the village if I could procure a bed. He told me that, if my passport was approved of by the head of the police, he would give me a bed, and he was civil enough to accompany me to that officer, who we found seated at a large table, with a quantity of papers before him. The room was but dimly lighted by two lamps; but while he was examining my passport I threw my eyes over the apartment, and observing a picture, evidently executed by a young artist, I remarked that it was a creditable performance. It was a casual observation, but it touched on a secret spring, and cleared away any difficulties that he might have been inclined to throw in my way. It turned out to be a painting executed by his only son, and of whose talents as an artist his father was evidently proud. My passport was at once declared *en règle*, and the syndic very kindly offered to furnish me with a bed in his own house. The character of the Lucanians for hospitality has in no way degenerated from early times. Ælian (*Var. Hist.*, iv. 1) tells us that there was a law that if a

1. Unidentified.

stranger arrived at sunset, with a desire to spend the night, and was refused, the party should be fined for his inhospitality ... My arrival soon became known to the whole village of Porcile, and the syndic's house – *palazzo* as they call it, for every respectable edifice is here dignified with the title of palace – was soon crowded by the principal inhabitants of the village. It was amusing to find myself become a person of such importance, but I would have willingly foregone all my new-born dignity for the quietness of my bed-chamber. The apartment into which I was introduced was of considerable size, and had evidently been in former times rather elegantly furnished, though the dust of age had now given it a dingy hue. The chairs were of that old-fashioned form which leads us back to the time of Elizabeth, and had been richly gilded. Their covers were of faded satin. The walls of the room were hung round with paintings of the ancestors of my host, but the light was not sufficient to enable me to decide whether they possessed any value as works of art. I find that it is by no means uncommon to have a bed even in their reception-rooms, and it was so here.

I carried my politeness as far as my strength would allow. At last, however, I could bear my chair no longer, and I requested permission to recline on the couch. While I was resting they brought for my examination a variety of coins and cameos, of which some seemed to be of considerable value. They talked very highly of a marble statue which was in their church, and they prevailed on me to accompany them to look at it. It had no pretensions, however, to antiquity ...

After a delay, which appeared to me endless, supper was announced and we proceeded into another apartment, where I found the lady of the house, rather advanced in years, ready to receive me. I scanned with curious eye the appearance of the supper-table, which was groaning under a load of provisions. It showed that they were behind us in two articles – table-linen and earthenware. Their manufactory of table-cloths has not advanced beyond the very coarsest material, and the plates were of a rude, ungainly appearance. Silver forks and old silver-handled knives in great quantities proved the wealth of the family. The centre of the table was furnished with a dish of excellent salad – a great luxury in this climate. Then we had a roasted kid, rabbits, and what they called *gelatine di porco*, and *insalata di capretto*, swimming in oil. Celery and beans closed the repast. The wine was of excellent vintage, and there was a simplicity and homeliness which showed that they were truly happy to receive a stranger from a distant land at their hospitable board.

At last, however, we parted, and I was not sorry to stretch my wearied limbs on my couch.

III

I BEGIN to be alarmed respecting the result of my journey, as I have three times met one of those omens which the Italians consider of dire import. You will laugh when I tell you that this is the third morning that I have had a priest in his canonicals crossing my path, but I assure you that the people of this country look upon such an event as 'no canny'. Why they should regard the priest in this light, to whom they are so subservient, I know not, yet such is the case.

I had a clean and comfortable bed, a luxury of no common occurrence unless you are received by a private family ... The breakfast of the Italians is light – a cup of coffee generally, with a glass of a kind of liqueur, called *rosolio*, made from the fig; this was served up to-day, and shortly after sunrise I bade my host adieu, with a thousand thanks for the hospitality with which I had been received. Nothing could exceed the kindness of the whole family; and when my host learned that I intended to examine the ruins of the ancient city of Velia, he gave me a letter to a friend, Don Ervasio Passaro, who resided in its vicinity. The younger part of the family accompanied me about a mile out of the village, and we parted with great regret. Before leaving the village I paid a visit to the priest Pietro Zammarella, who has collected a small museum of antiquities, coins, cameos, and seals. There was a seal more particularly which had been found at Baiæ, and which was the nearest approach to printing that I had seen. The letters were raised as in our type, and when covered with ink gave the name as distinctly as it is now seen on this paper SEX POMPO VALENTIS ... [Here follows the description.]

The small valley through which I now continued my journey was beautifully wooded; the common oak, the *quercus* of the ancients, the dark evergreen ilex, plane-trees interspersed with the elm, were everywhere around. The vine was trained up the elm in graceful festoons, but, with the exception of a few patches here and there, man had left the country in a state of nature. The first village to which I came was Acquavella, which had the appearance of being entirely deserted. The inhabitants were nowhere to be seen, while it swarmed with dogs, who commenced a fierce attack, and whom I kept at bay as well as I could with my umbrella, roaring lustily for assistance. This brought out several of the peasants, and I was saved from the fate of Actæon. On reaching a small square in front of their church, I found a large party seated, and as I wished to visit Torricelle, where I was told last night I should find some ancient remains, I proposed that one of them should accompany me as guide; but they all refused with the exception of a poor boy, who volunteered his services, and with him I started. Our way lay up a hill, and when I had nearly reached the summit, I was sadly startled to observe a party of men rushing after me at a very hurried pace. It was quite vain to attempt to elude them in a country of the topography of which I knew nothing, and I thought it best to show no symptoms of alarm. I kept advancing at my usual pace, and in a few minutes two of them came abreast of me, with whom I entered into conversation, though feeling not much at my ease. I told them the object I had in view, and I was soon satisfied that they had followed from mere curiosity. They seemed, however, to imagine that I had some other object than that which I professed, and they continued to pester me with their impertinent inquiries. They gave me some further information respecting the brigands of Monteforte, which did not encourage me to place myself in their power. Two days ago they seized two of the rural police, and as yet no tidings have been heard of them. They are a *comitiva*, as they called them – that is, a band of five brothers, who have continued for fourteen years the torment of this part of the country. The Baron of St Magno was carried off some time ago, and had to pay two thousand ducats – about 400 *l.* – before he was released. It seems that they now wish to leave the kingdom with their plunder, but the government refuses to enter into any terms with them. At last we reached the edge of the ridge and looked down upon a level plain, about a mile in breadth, through which I observed a river to flow in a sluggish stream; and this I knew to be called Alento, the ancient Heles, called by Cicero, 'a noble river'. The descent from this ridge was in one part somewhat precipitous, and there a baronial castle had once stood, now in ruins. There were some very aged chestnut-trees growing in its courtyard and in one of its towers, which proved that some centuries had elapsed since it had been inhabited. The plain below was of a marshy character from the overflowing of the river, and this is believed to be the origin of the ancient name of the river Heles, from the Greek Eλη, 'marshes'. Its exhalations render all the villages within several miles particularly unhealthy. I saw not a patch of cultivation so far as the eye could reach, though I was told that many years ago an attempt had been made to introduce the cultivation of rice, which produced such disease among the inhabitants that four thousand of them were cut off. At present this plain, which I have no doubt might be brought under cultivation, is entirely barren.

I had at first intended to return to Acquavella ... as, however, it would add several miles to my journey, I determined to descend into the valley of the Alento, and thread my way as best I could towards its mouth, in the vicinity of which were the ruins of the ancient city of Velia. I found my descent far less easy than I had expected, though I at last succeeded in getting rid of the brushwood; and on attempting to cross the channel of the river, I came upon a small footpath, along which I proceeded. Sauntering thus carelessly along, I found myself suddenly in the midst of a party of men who were reclining on the ground. They were fully armed, and I imagined that I had fallen into the lions' den. They were equally astonished at my appearance, and all started to their feet without an instant's delay. They were sad cut-throat-looking fellows; I should not, however, have felt so much alarmed if I had not come so suddenly upon them. There were large patches of brushwood in different parts of the plain, and it was on turning a corner that I lighted in the midst of them. I did not pause a moment; merely saluting them, I continued to walk forward, though I fully expected to hear a halt called, though not a syllable was uttered by any of the party, even my salute being unacknowledged. As soon as I was hid by a clump of brushwood, I confess that I hurried on somewhat more rapidly than was quite consistent with the bold front I had assumed in their presence. It was very much in the *sauve qui peut* style, and I did not stop, except to throw a hurried glance behind me, till I had put a considerable space between me and the cause of my terror. At last I reached a road, which was, no doubt, that along which I should have passed if I had returned to Acquavella, and here I met a small party of women who were returning from labouring in the fields. If they formed a good specimen of the fair ladies of the valley of Alento, they have

23

little to boast of in respect to beauty. Several of them were evidently young, but exposure to the sun's rays and constant labour had wrinkled their foreheads, and given them an appearance of age, to which their years did not entitle them. The climate of Italy brings them naturally to early maturity, and at twenty the bloom of youth is nearly gone. Of course in the higher classes their personal charms last somewhat longer; yet, as they take little exercise, they are apt in a few years to become stout, and lose the elasticity and joyousness of youth. Behind these women followed two oxen, one of which carried the inverted plough, reminding me of the allusion in Virgil (*Eclog.* ii. 66) . . . This plough was of very slight form, and used in some light sandy soil on the declivities of the hills. In ancient times, the plough turned upside down used to be dragged home with its tail and handle over the surface of the ground, to which Horace (*Epod.* ii. 63) alludes . . .

Inquiring of the ploughman what he called the share, he said *gomere*, which is evidently the *vomer* of the Romans. It is made with two ears jutting out, rising in the middle, with a back which he called schiena. The wood of the plough, from the handle to the share, he called *ventale*, a corruption of *dentale*. The whole was light and easily moved, as some of the ground where he was employed was of an open texture. It was made of elm, which is very abundant in this quarter, and was so made in former days Virg. (*Georg.* i. 170) . . . As I was talking to him, I saw some hurdles at the side of the road, and inquired what was the use of them. I found that they were used as we do harrows, for levelling the ground. The ground on the side of the river is in parts hard, and requires to be broken with mallets before it can be smoothed for the grain . . .

I do not know that the river Alento is entitled to the epithet *noble*, applied to it by Cicero, though it may in the winter season be swollen to a considerable stream; but at present it had not much water. There was no bridge nor boat; but as it did not seem to be deep, I plunged at once into the channel, and had no difficulty in reaching the opposite side. The road again began to ascend the valley, but as this was leading me away from a ruined tower, which I believed to be that of Castellamare della Bruca, and which I wished to examine, I struck out of the path into the fields. Here I fell in with a peasant at dinner with his wife, child, and donkey, and I could not help thinking, on looking at their miserable food, that the donkey fared the best of the party. Their dinner consisted of coarse bread and a flask of wine, which they were quite prepared to share with me. I did wrong, perhaps, in refusing to accept their offer, as the pleasure of conferring a favour makes all the world akin. From them I found that the gentleman for whom I had a letter of introduction resided about a couple of miles beyond the tower that I saw before me. The heat of the sun was now quite intolerable; and though I should have wished to have taken a glance at the ruins of Velia, which were close to the castle, it was impossible, as there was not even a tree under which I could rest. Besides, it was of no consequence, as I intended to return. I had now reached a sandy beach, of the same character as that near Pæstum, and I had much difficulty in bearing up against the direct and reflected rays of the sun. I cannot express the delight I felt when I threw myself down under some antique olive-trees, which completely sheltered me. These olive-trees must be many centuries old; their trunks were completely hollowed out, and they seemed to be chiefly nourished by their bark, which was immensely thick. At last, I mustered strength to proceed forward, and reached the house of the gentleman whose hospitality I must put to the proof. Its exterior was in no way inviting, and its desolate appearance made me suppose that it was uninhabited. I ascended by a rude stair to the door, and after knocking some time I roused a boy, who had been asleep, and found that his master had gone to a neighbouring village, and would not return until evening. There was no *locanda* within several miles of Velia, and I was therefore obliged to take it for granted that he would be willing to receive me. I directed the boy to find some one by whom he could forward my letter, and I entered the house, which I found to consist only of two small apartments, almost destitute of furniture. My host usually resides in Naples, and only occasionally comes down here for a few days to look after a small property which he possesses. In the lower part of the house he has a machine for extracting the juice from the olive-berries, as well as a wine-press.

After a few hours' rest, towards evening I sallied forth to visit the ruins of Velia, and proceeded again along the beach which I had passed in the morning. The evening breeze was cool and refreshing, being just sufficient to make the waves break on the shore with a quiet and peaceful murmur. After leaving a few fishermen's huts I saw no one, though in former times it must have been a joyous scene of human happiness. Velia[1] was a Greek colony, which, we are told, was founded about 540 BC by some Phocæans of Asia Minor, who preferred exile with liberty to an enslaved country. In such matters, history is constantly repeating herself. The Puritans acted the same scene many thousand years afterwards, and fled their country to enjoy freedom of religious worship, which, however, they were equally unwilling to grant to others. These Phocæans found themselves unable to resist the power of Cyrus the Elder, and took refuge at this spot, which was at that time unoccupied, as it is now. The enterprise and industry of its inhabitants soon raised the city to importance, and one of the Greek schools of philosophy derived its name from Velia. In Roman times, the balminess of the air made it the residence of invalids, and Horace (*Epist.* i. 15, 1.) ... seems to have visited it in consequence of some weakness of his eyes. The last effort it made to attract the attention of the world was by producing the poet Statius about AD 61, and from that time its name is scarcely mentioned in history. I was curious, therefore, to see what time and the more destructive hand of man had left of this once-famous city. I reached the ruined castle, now called Castellamare della Bruca, evidently a fortress of the middle ages, of considerable strength before the invention of gunpowder. It must, at all times, have been the site of whatever work of defence the city possessed, as it stands on the highest ground where the hill terminates towards the sea. The city was placed behind it, partly along the top of the ridge and partly in the plain below. The walls may be traced imperfectly for a circumference of about two miles, constructed of large squared blocks of stone, placed over each other without cement, though not in the style of what is called Cyclopian architecture. That style of architecture was a rude and gigantic form of building, where large polygonal masses of stone, unshaped by the hand of man, were fitted to each other without cement by their own superincumbent weight. In Scotland, we are in the habit of ascribing every wonderful building to the Peghts, believed by the ignorant to be some supernatural beings; so in Greece and Italy they considered the Cyclopes to be the authors of every edifice more than usually gigantic, and of whose erection they had no tradition. I looked anxiously for the re-

1. Excavations have been undertaken here intermittently since 1926 and are now (1962) being conducted on a large scale by the Italian archaeological authorities, *see* bibliography.

mains of a temple to Ceres or Proserpine, which is mentioned by ancient writers. I saw nothing, however, to fix its position. There was, indeed, a small vaulted chamber, which I find that the peasantry called *catacomba*, and which had something of the appearance of an inscription on its roof. I could trace one or two Greek letters, or what had some resemblance to them. Of the city itself nothing remains, except here and there foundations of edifices, respecting which there is no tradition. Many of the sepulchres have escaped, and the inscriptions upon them show that they are the receptacles of generations far apart. Some are inscribed with the earliest Greek characters, leading us back to the times of its foundation, while the *hic jacet* of another brings us down to the period of Roman dominion. I was much struck by the simplicity of a small monument raised by an affectionate parent to his beloved daughter. It was merely a white marble slab, with two full-blown roses engraved on it, and the inscription, 'To Nike, daughter of Zoilus'. This little monument had survived to bear witness to far-distant generations of love and affection, while sepulchres of far loftier pretensions had long ago mingled with the dust of those who had erected them.

In the vicinity of the castle[1] there were several buildings of a later date, and among them one which had been used as a chapel. One tower of the castle still remains, which I entered, and was proceeding to ascend a ruined staircase, when I found myself attacked in a way that makes me now laugh, though I do assure you that it was very distressing at the time. I was covered from head to foot by a host of stinging insects, and when I gave a glance at them I found them to be nothing else than fleas. You may suppose that I made a hurried retreat; but they were not to be got rid of in this way, and I found myself in a state of the utmost torture. Luckily I was within a few hundred yards of the sea, and I had no way of relieving myself except by stripping and dashing into the water. In this way I got myself put to rights, and, on inquiry, I found that the tower was made use of as a pig-fold, and that these insects are the result of the unclean state of such animals. I shall never be able to think of Velia without a shudder at the recollection of the torture I endured. This adventure put an end to my meditations, and I returned to the house, where I found my host waiting my arrival, and was received with great kindness . . . We spent the evening pleasantly in the open air, and

1. A Greek temple has since been excavated on the hill-top beside this tower.

were joined by several of his friends, one of them being an antiquarian, well versed in the literature and ancient state of his country. He told me that there was a small village, about two miles distant in the interior, called Catona, where the ruins of ancient buildings are found, and it is supposed to be the site of the villa of Cato, which is mentioned by Plutarch (*Cat.* 20). He spoke also of a hill, called Li Candidati, on the declivities of which many ancient sepulchres had been found, so much so that he was inclined to believe that the inhabitants of Velia must have buried many of their dead here. I asked him where the Portus Veliensis, or harbour, could have been, as I saw no spot where vessels could have been anchored with safety; and yet Cicero, when he was flying from Rome after the assassination of Cæsar, landed here, and tells us that he found Brutus with his ships at the river Heles. According to this gentleman, there were two ports: one close to the foot of the mountain, Lago di Castello, about a quarter of a mile from the sea; the other is called Porticello, at the mouth of the river. Close to it you see a column, in which there was an iron ring till very lately, to which the vessels had been moored. Virgil says (*Æn.* vi. 366) . . . 'Seek the harbours of Velia', as if there had been several.

While we were seated, I was astonished to observe the field before us sparkle with fire from a number of small flies which were flitting about. I was unable to lay hold of any, as they appeared to lose their phosphoric light as soon as they rested on any object. They called these flies *lucciole* . . .

The white hellebore, which Pliny (xx. 21, 2) speaks of as excellent, and as growing among the vines at Velia, is no longer found here, but grows abundantly on Monte Stella, which I visited yesterday.

IV

IT is, perhaps, as well that these letters will not be able to reach you till you know that I am in comparative safety, as I have no doubt my friends would conjure up all sorts of dangers, that would exist nowhere except in their own imagination. All that I have seen of the people pleases me; nothing can exceed the kindness and hospitality of every one with whom I come in contact, and if I had only seen the sun set from Mount Stella I should have considered myself amply repaid for whatever fatigue I have undergone. I perceive that mental energy can sometimes supply the place of physical exhaustion, and as I am anxious to visit the remains of the cities of Magna Græcia, which were placed along the south-eastern coast of Italy, I am determined to allow nothing, except positive illness or capture by the brigands, to prevent me from putting my plan in execution. Till I actually see these much talked-of brigands, I shall believe them to be only men of buckram, and shall act as if they did not exist.

The Italians are obliged to keep very early hours at this period of the year, as the heat is so oppressive from eleven till three that they never think of venturing out. For the first two days I paid no attention to the heat, but I see that I must make arrangements to rest several hours at mid-day. My host and myself were on foot before daybreak, and proceeded to the beach on a sporting expedition. I had observed yesterday several nets stretched from a number of poles, and had imagined that it was for the purpose of drying, though it seemed to me an unnecessary trouble. I find now, however, that it is with the view of catching quails, which come over from Africa at this period of the year in large numbers; and as they are short-sighted creatures, and tired with their long flight, they fly up against these nets, and are either shot or so entangled in the meshes that they can be caught by the hand. They make an excellent dish, as I have often found at Naples, and from the conversation of my friends I perceived that they were considered a great delicacy. You will laugh to hear that I was furnished with a gun, who had never fired a more deadly weapon than a popgun; but I thought that I should sink in the eyes of my friends if I confessed ignorance in such matters, and I resolved to be very cautious as to the direction in which I pointed my weapon, and to be in no hurry to use it. When we reached the beach we found the servants already watching, and we were all stationed at different parts, to include as large a space as possible. You may be sure that I chose as distant a point as I could well do, that if my slugs did not kill a bird (a very unlikely feat) they might run no risk of doing mischief. Here we stood, immovable as statues, for upwards of an hour, but no quails made their appearance. They say that they are always preceded by a large quail, who is their leader, and whom they seem to obey. This is the *ortygometra* of Pliny (x. 33, 2); and they observe that they are more plentiful when the south wind blows. I have nothing of the sportsman in my nature, and soon got tired of watching.

I was delighted when the overseer announced to us that we must give up all hopes this morning of having any sport, and I delivered up my gun to one of the servants with great pleasure. Pliny (x. 33, 4) assures us that quails live on poisonous herbs, probably hellebore, and that they are the only animal, besides man, who is afflicted with epilepsy . . .

Some fishermen had landed, and I proceeded with my friends to view the result of their night's labour. They had not been very successful; and as this was Friday . . . fish had a higher value than on any other day of the week. There was the same squabbling as to price that may be seen with the dealers in that article in every other country. At last a satisfactory arrangement was made between them, and I am sure that the poor fishermen had the worst bargain. The fish consisted chiefly of anchovy and sardine, called by them *alici* and *sarde*. From October to the end of April these fish abound here. I was surprised to find a man, who had been watching their proceedings, step forward and claim an item of the small sum they had received, as the tax imposed by government. I find that there is a regular guard of these tax-gatherers along the whole coast of Italy for collecting this paltry sum, and for preventing the people from carrying off the smallest quantity of salt water from the sea. Salt is a monopoly in the hands of government, and produces a considerable revenue each year, which would be annihilated if the people were allowed to take salt water, and by mere exposure to the sun produce crystallised salt. It is necessary, therefore, for the security of the revenue, that this restriction should be maintained; and when any infraction of the law is discovered, it is punished by imprisonment and fine. I wished to take another glance at the ruins of Velia, as my antiquarian friend of last night offered to accompany me and give me the benefit of his local knowledge. We were joined at the ruins by a gentleman on horseback, whom I found to be the proprietor of the ground, called Don Teodosio de Domenicis. He told me that several of the tombs had been opened, and that they had contained coins, bracelets, small images, and urns, though I could not find that he possesses any of them. The government claims whatever is found in such excavations, and it makes everyone cautious of confessing that they have such treasures. As there is always a great demand at Naples for antiques – so much so that there is actually a manufactory of such articles – it is likely, if he made any such discovery, he would dispose of them there.

We first examined the south-east corner, where a number of sepulchral inscriptions are found. The first is a monument half covered with earth, with the figure of a naked man on horseback, having a sword or spear in his hand. Below is a Latin inscription, the first words of which only are legible: HIC IACET CALIMORPHVS. The remainder is still covered. It is said to be upwards of twelve feet in length, having been at one time uncovered. The next object in this quarter was an ancient tomb, built of rubble-work. The proprietor said that this tomb had never been examined. In this neighbourhood they find quantities of vases full of ashes; and, indeed, this seems to have been where the inhabitants of Velia were buried. . . . [Here follow 5 Inscriptions and descriptions of them.]

My antiquarian friend pointed out what he thought might have been the Temple of Proserpine, and showed the holes through which oracles were delivered; it appears to me, however, to be a building of the Middle Ages. Along the brow of the hill is the appearance of a paved road; and there is an ancient cistern, which has been modernised.

The castle derives its epithet, Bruca, from a wood, which at one time extended nearly to the sea, but which is now seen at some distance up the valley of the Alento. The proprietor of the ground kindly invited me to dinner, and as he promised to show me some ancient inscriptions which he had discovered in excavating at Velia, I was not unwilling to accept his hospitality, particularly as I must allow the heat of the day to pass before I could proceed on my journey. I returned to my host to thank him for his kindness, and though he was anxious that I should remain the rest of the day, my time was too precious to allow of any sacrifice to mere pleasure. Accordingly I bade him adieu, and, shouldering my knapsack, ascended the hill to the village Ascea, where I had agreed to dine. The declivity was covered with vines, olive-trees, fig-trees, and oaks. This village was miserable enough, and contained only one tolerable residence – that of the gentleman from whom I had received the invitation. I believe that he has accumulated his property chiefly by his own industry; and his manners were of a far higher tone than any I had yet met in my travels. Above his door he had inscribed, in legible characters, the two following sentences: 'Pride is the character of the scoundrel' and 'Misery is the result of idleness and vice'. This gave me some insight into his character, and our conversation tended to confirm me in my previous good opinion. He received me with great cordiality; and though his house was deficient in many particulars which we think necessary for our comfort, still it was the best I had yet seen. In the entrance-hall of his house my attention was drawn to the skin of a large wolf, which Don Teodosio had shot after it had killed fifty sheep. He says that they are still more numerous than sheep-owners like. The room into which I was ushered was the dining-room, and here I found three very beautiful girls busily employed in laying out the table for dinner. They turned out to be my host's daughters; and I was not sorry to have accepted his invitation, as it enabled me to see a fine specimen of Italian beauty. I had as yet been unfortunate in that respect, and was beginning to have a poor idea of the ladies of this part of Italy; but the youngest of these girls was one of the most enchanting I had ever met with. Her figure was slight and well proportioned, her features oval, with arched eyebrows, and her smile most bewitching. In fact, it was well that my time was limited, else I verily believe that I should have committed all kinds of follies. At last dinner was announced, and we sat down to a plentiful display of food; but I was amused to find that every dish consisted of fish, which was dressed in a variety of ways. It was Friday, and my host is a rigid observer of the rules of his Church, though, if he had known in sufficient time that he should have had the honour of my company, he would have taken care that some meat should have been prepared for me, as he was aware that we differed from him in that respect. I could not help smiling at the idea of their fasting on such food as was before me, and told him that I should have no objection to fast once a week on these conditions. I assured him that I could forgive the want of variety in the food, as his wine was first-rate, being a strong white wine, which he called *vernaccie*, from the name of the grape from which it was made. In his garden I saw many pear and apple trees, with apricots, from which he said that he had always an abundant crop. Being an epicure in our common straw-berries, I inquired if he grew *fragole*;[1] he said that they are found in the mountains of the interior, but it was too hot near the coast. It was the custom of the house for the daughters to wait at table, at which I was not a little pleased, as, being a stranger, I received most marked attention. The eldest son was also a fine intelligent boy. I was strongly urged to remain till next day, and had difficulty in prevailing on my-self to give a negative to their pressing invitations; but I kept to my

1. Strawberries.

resolution of moving forward as soon as the heat of the day was passed.

[Here follow 3 Inscriptions seen in the house.]

At last I bade adieu to my kind friends, regretting that we should never meet again, and proceeded on my solitary journey towards a small village called Pisciotta, about eight miles distant. On inquiry, I found that there were two roads by which I might approach it, one along the face of a perpendicular rock, and the other by the beach. The first would have been the most picturesque, and I was much tempted to choose it; but I was not sure that I might not be overtaken by the dusk of evening, and I understood that the path was in some places so narrow that a false step would precipitate me many hundred feet below. It is only used in stormy weather, when the beach cannot be approached, as, though there are no tides, the wind sometimes drives the sea to the foot of the rocks . . . By degrees the hills approached the shore, and I then saw that it would be necessary to descend to the beach. I was not sorry that I had adopted this plan, as the rock was not continuous, but a succession of depressions and heights, up and down which I must have clambered with great fatigue. I crept along the bottom of this rocky coast for several miles, and as I saw no sign of human habitation, I began to fear that I might have missed the path leading to Pisciotta, which I knew to be situated a short distance from the shore. At last, towards sunset, I saw a tower which was to be my guide, and in a short time I met a police-officer, or *gendarme*, who of course demanded to know who I was, and whence I came. It is difficult at first to submit to these demands, as at home we come and go without any one making us afraid. Here, however, government keeps a sharp look-out on all travellers, and no one can leave his parish without a permit, which he is bound to show when he is called upon. I accordingly produced my passport for the two officers (for he had now been joined by another), and they could not deny that it was perfectly *en règle*. They began to question me as to the object of my journey, but I declined to give them satisfaction, and demanded that they should conduct me to their superior officer. They were so little accustomed to such cavalier treatment, as the whole country is at their feet, that they debated whether they should not arrest me. I showed, however, no symptoms of fear, and threatened them with all kinds of punishments from their government if they dared to disregard my passport. At last they allowed me to proceed, and I ascended a steep rock, partly by stairs and partly by a winding path, to the village Pisciotta. It was the largest which I had yet seen. The people stared and scarcely treated me with common civility when I inquired for the house of the judge, who is always the superior officer of the district. I did not like my reception, and was afraid that I had fallen into a nest of hornets. After making many mistakes, which I began to suspect arose from the intentional mis-direction of the inhabitants, I at last found the house of the judge, to whom I presented my passport, and stated that I meant to remain in the village, if it were possible to find a bed. He consulted with his clerk, and they agreed that Donna Laura would be able to accommodate me. Laura was a very ominous name. Think of the famed Laura, for whom Petrarch sung and sighed! I longed to have my doubts resolved, and, pleading fatigue from my journey, I requested the servant to conduct me to the house of my hostess. I might have saved myself all anxiety on the subject, as you can scarcely conceive a more uninteresting figure, fat, round, and dumpy; but she had a good-humoured face, and promised to give me a clean bed, as well as the best supper she could provide. Altogether, I believe I ought to be pleased with my good fortune.

While I was waiting for supper, and feeling anxious to retire to rest, I was annoyed by three of the inhabitants making their appearance to pay their respects to me. I could well have dispensed with this honour. I could not, however, get rid of them without actual rudeness, as they were ushered into my presence without notice. One of them was a Frenchman, who had resided here for twenty years, and was now pre-paring to leave it, from the annoyance he received from government on account of his political sentiments. It appears that the government is afraid of an insurrection at this moment, and they are placing all suspicious persons under strict surveillance of the police. At one time there was a Masonic lodge at Pisciotta, in which the greater part of the inhabitants were enrolled; and as this is connected with the system of Carbonarism,[1] it causes Pisciotta to be regarded with great suspicion by government. This may account for the insolent conduct of the *gend-armes* whom I had met. He apologised for the incivility with which I

---

1. The *Carbonari* (charcoal-burners) were members of secret societies which flourished especially in the *Regno* against the Bourbons and were Revolutionaries, very much on the left, working for the unity of Italy.

had been received by the inhabitants when I was inquiring my way to the house of the judge; they had imagined that I was the bearer of government despatches, and few of them feel good will to the underlings of office. This explained satisfactorily what had struck me so forcibly, and I find that I run no danger from brigands in this part of the country. I can hear of no ancient remains at Pisciotta . . .

This morning my French friend was with me at sunrise, and we proceeded to visit the natural grotto that he had spoken of the night before. I begin to suspect, however, that this was a mere pretext to detain me, in order that he might try to discover if I was not an English agent on a political mission, as he pushed me very strongly on such subjects. After walking about a couple of miles along the hills, and through an uninteresting country, we reached a place where the grotto was said to be; but he could not find the entrance, and he asserted that it must have been blocked up. This was very teasing, as I have no wish to add unnecessarily to my fatigues, and, besides, the freshness of the morning was spent in this fruitless search. Neither did his conversation compensate for the delay, as he was a shallow, vain coxcomb, prating of constitutions and constitutional government with a volubility truly distressing, and with increased fluency from his entire ignorance of the subject. I may be doing him injustice, but I could not help suspecting that he was a spy, to find out if I had any ulterior object different from that which I professed. It is so unusual for a foreigner to visit this part of the country, that I can perceive that I am an object of curiosity to both the government officers and their opponents. The latter consider all Englishmen their friends; but it would be absurd in me to intermeddle with the internal affairs of a country of which I know so little, and I have as yet seen nothing to incline me to believe that the body of the people is fitted for a representative form of government. They are, indeed, dissatisfied, and I have no doubt that many of them would willingly see a change. On our return, we met the judge, who behaved with great incivility, possibly from my intercourse with this Frenchman. I lost no more time, starting at once with a boy to conduct me to a spot said to be the tomb of Palinurus[1] . . . The country through which I passed was partially cultivated; there was the same lonely and desolate appearance from the few inhabitants I met. The tomb is

1. Tombs dating from the sixth century B C, have been excavated at Palinuro in recent years; also houses, *see* bibliography.

situated at a place called Torrione,[1] near to the village Torracce, a few hundred yards from the shore, and three miles from what is called the promontory of Palinurus. It had very much the appearance of a ruined watch-tower, and however I might be inclined to believe it to be the spot so beautifully alluded to by Virgil, I confess that my belief was of a very doubtful character. It is, however, much resembling the tombs at Velia, though very much larger, being filled up with stones and lime. At one time it was larger than it is at present, as the hill is covered with its remains; and the peasants say that coins have been found, though they could show none. There is a chamber below, so filled with stones that it cannot be entered. On one side you see the remains of plaster, composed of small pieces of stone and lime. I think it is an ancient building, but of what epoch it is impossible to say. It is a curious circumstance that there should be a fair held at this uninhabited spot on the 4th of August, for three days; and one cannot help imagining that this may be a continuation of those meetings mentioned by ancient writers, at which games were celebrated in honour of Palinurus. The spot where the fair is held is marked by a small chapel and a clump of very aged trees, under whose branches the peasants assemble at a stated period to exchange their various commodities.

I dismissed my guide, and lay down under the shade. It was a quiet and peaceful scene, but sad and melancholy. I regretted when I felt myself obliged to move forward. I was in a mood little inclined for exertion, and could have passed hours under this shady retreat. I had still about six miles before I reached Centola, where I intended to remain for the day, as I meant to examine the promontory Palinurus to-morrow. My friend at Ascea furnished me with a letter of introduction to a gentleman at Centola, so that I had no fear of being able to find accommodation.

The country still continued to be uncultivated, and the bare white limestone rocks are disagreeable to the eye. The few peasants I met looked strangely upon me, and were anxious to know on what errand I was bent ... I reached at last a small river called Molpa, the ancient Melphes, which I had some difficulty in crossing. Here was situated the parish mill, to which all the grain must be sent to be ground. In every parish there is a mill under the control of government, and it is in this way able to tax the people at its discretion.

1. Torre di Caprioli.

It was now past mid-day, and the heat was most exhausting, yet I had still a steep ascent to mount before I could reach Centola. Half way up the hill I came to a monastery, and I resolved to take shelter, if the good monks would admit a heretic. I rang the bell, and after some delay a young monk made his appearance, when I stated to him that I was a foreigner, and should be obliged to him if he would allow me to remain a short time, till I had recovered from my exhaustion. He conducted me at once to the superior, who received me with great cordiality and politeness. He gave directions that dinner should be got ready, and regretted that it was not such as he could have wished, since the rules of his order compelled them to live in the most temperate manner. I was conducted to the refectory, a large gloomy hall, with two long tables and some rudely constructed wooden benches; and here the inmates of the monastery crowded round me. They had no appearance of living on spare diet, being as jolly a set of fellows as could anywhere be met. They eat twice a day – at eleven o'clock in the morning, and at seven in the evening. Three dishes were all they were allowed – soup, maccaroni, and an omelette, with fruit in its proper season. Their garden showed that, whatever else they neglected, they paid due attention to horticulture. Any one might enter their society who could muster a sum of thirty ducats, about five pounds of our money; but there are only fifteen monks at present, who are supported principally by the voluntary contributions of the people.

This monastery had, like many others, been suppressed by the French, and it has never recovered the blow it then received. They have a small library, chiefly of old theological works, in a confused and dirty state, showing that study formed no part of their duty; and I was amused when the superior apologised for its appearance by remarking that they had not found time to arrange it since they were visited by the French. They had been restored to their monastery for fifteen years. They inquired if I were not a heretic; and when I acknowledged that I was what they so denominated, they expressed their regret that I should be doomed to eternal damnation. I asked if they did not think it sinful to receive me in their house; when they remarked that I was *un uomo*, a fellow-creature, and that as God made the sun to shine on the just and the unjust, they had no right to refuse me the slight assistance they could afford me. When I stated that I intended to remain the rest of the day at Centola, the superior pressed me kindly to accept of a bed, which, however, I thought it better to refuse, and to press on to Centola.

Accordingly, I made my way to the syndic's house, and found him to be a young man of pleasing manners. Having seen that my passport was regular, he invited me to accompany him to his brother's house, and here they proposed that I should take up my residence for the night. They offered to prepare dinner, and when I refused on the plea of having already enjoyed the hospitality of the Capuchin friars, they brought out *rosolio* and prepared coffee for me. Nothing, in fact, could exceed the genuine, unaffected kindness of these simple people. I declined, however, their proposal to remain the night, and proceeded to deliver my letter; but the maidservant who answered my summons had evidently been roused from her slumbers, and was in bad humour. She told me that her master was enjoying his siesta, and could not be disturbed, nor would she admit me within the house before her master gave permission. There was no use disputing the point with her, nor did she indeed give me an opportunity, as she slammed the door in my face, and I imagine retired to finish her disturbed slumbers. Thus within an hour I had called up a variety of human passions and feelings. What a contrast between the kindness of the monks and the unmannerly rudeness of this girl! . . .

I found a tree, under whose shade I sat down. I made a pillow of my knapsack, and was soon soundly asleep. How long I may have reposed I know not, but several hours must have passed, as the sun was far advanced in its course when I awoke. I started up in some alarm to examine if all my goods were safe; everything was right, and I felt quite refreshed by my slumbers. I returned to the house of the gentleman, and, having presented my letter, was received with the utmost kindness by the whole family. The lady of the house was particularly pleasing, and the house was soon crowded by all the respectable inhabitants of the village. We had a very interesting conversation on a variety of subjects, and, in return for the information I communicated to them respecting England and its customs, I gleaned all I could respecting their municipal system . . . [Here follows a discourse on the office of syndic (mayor), local administration, etc.]

V

THOUGH I am not one of those who think we are bound to observe this day (Sunday) with the same strictness that characterised the Jewish Sabbath, still I am of opinion that it is right, as far as it is possible, to abstain from all secular pursuits. It is necessary for the tone of the mind as well as for the strength of the body that a day of rest should intervene, and it is only reasonable that this small portion of our time should be devoted to the performance of our religious duties. It is with regret, therefore, that I am unable to delay my journey, but as my mode of travelling renders me nearly independent, I am not likely to lead others astray.

At daybreak I took an affectionate farewell of my host and his family. They have a custom in Italy particularly disagreeable to us. At parting you are expected to kiss all the males of the family, and as some indemnification for this horrid nuisance, I took care that the ladies should not pass unnoticed; but I can assure you that, even with this set-off, I cannot reconcile myself to the form. I started with a little boy to guide me to Palinurus, which I found to be about four miles distant. The weather had changed; the sun was not, indeed, entirely obscured, but there was a thick haze all around, and a feeling of oppression, which I knew to be the precursor of the *scirocco*. This wind is found generally to last for three days, reaching on the second its height, and on the third gradually dying away, when the sun again shines forth with un-diminished splendour. Those whose constitutions have been long exposed to the climate feel its effects acutely in excessive languor both of mind and body; on me it has not yet any effect, though I perceive sensibly enough the difference between the stifling closeness of this day and the free, unembarrassed circulation of yesterday's atmosphere. We again crossed the river Molpa, and descended by a narrow footpath to the port of Palinurus, where I found a village of fishermen.

Along the coast of the Neapolitan dominions to the southern extremity of Italy, nature has not furnished a single tolerable harbour for even moderately-sized vessels. This port of Palinurus, formed by the projection of the promontory, is the best, but it is unprotected from the north and north-west, and its entrance is only of sufficient depth for small merchantmen. I found on my arrival that my friend had given orders that one of his boats should be at my command, and an intelligent fisherman offered to accompany me to two grottos, which I knew previously were well worthy of examination. The one is called La Grotta degli Stucchi, and the other La Grotta delle Ossa, that is, the grotto of bones. We rowed a few hundred yards under the promontory till we reached a cave, which was partly natural, and partly hollowed out by the inhabitants to procure *stucco*. It was twenty feet by thirty broad, and the waves, as they dashed ceaselessly against the sides of the cave, produced innumerable echoes, seeming to run along under the promontory and conveyed from one to the other to a great distance. The fisherman told me that there were a variety of branches to the cave, running upwards of a mile inwards, and this no doubt caused the countless sounds which met my ears; but as there was no remarkable object to be seen, I did not make any further examination. It was not unpleasant again to breathe the open air. We then rowed round the weather-beaten headland of Palinurus, and as the breeze now began to blow fresh from the south, the waves were dashed with some violence against the whitened rocks, which rose for several hundred feet perpendicular from the sea, and on their summit was a small fortress, which had been erected by the French, now nearly in ruins . . .

As we cleared the promontory, I found Palinurus to present three distinct headlands, called by the inhabitants Punta delle Quaglie, where quails are caught in great numbers, Frontone, which is the principal point, and Punta di Molpa, from the river close to it. It was the scene of several shipwrecks mentioned in ancient writers, and was particularly fatal to a fleet of Augustus, who himself narrowly escaped a watery grave at this spot. The bones of his sailors were, according to a tradition of the inhabitants, collected and placed in a grotto, which I was on my way to visit, called from that circumstance La Grotta delle Ossa. It is asserted that these bones became petrified, and have been preserved for nearly two thousand years. I had great doubts of the possibility of any such process being able to be carried on in a cave open to the external air, as the bones must have been completely decomposed before any process of nature could change them into stone. There is no doubt that this singular phenomenon has occasionally occurred in respect of animals, as you see in any museum of natural curiosities examples of this kind, but it must have been produced under different

1 Lake Avernus, *top*
Amalfi

2 The Temples of Paestum, *top*
Castellammare

circumstances from those in which the bones of these mariners were placed. I was not, therefore, disappointed when I found it a cave containing a fine collection of stalactites, which you know assume at times strange appearances. Some of the stalactites were no doubt like the bones of men; but the grotto of Adelsberg, in Styria, contains many still more wonderful, the stalactites assuming in one instance the appearance of drapery of most delicate texture. It hangs so elegantly and gracefully that no art of man could equal it. I mention this drapery because there can be no doubt that it is entirely the work of nature, though you are shown at the same time the head of a man with features well formed, and this is also said to be the unaided production of nature. Of this, however, we may have some doubts, as a few touches may have been furtively added to make it look what it now appears. I left this grotto of Palinurus satisfied that it had no pretensions to be considered the extraordinary natural curiosity which native writers would have the world to imagine. In the course of conversation with the fishermen, I was not a little surprised to hear that the *jactus reti*, the throw of a net, is not unknown among them; they buy what the Neapolitans call *vuolo*, which is nothing else than a corruption of the Greek word βόλος, and take their chance of the quantity of fish the throw may produce. This custom is alluded to . . . in Suetonius (*Clar. Rhet.* c. 1) . . .

I left the boat at the mouth of the river Molpa, a lonely spot with nothing but a ruined watch-tower, and engaged one of the fishermen to attend me till I thought it proper to dismiss him. There were said to be some ruins on the hill immediately above, and as some geographers have asserted that there was an ancient town called Melphes,[1] of the same name as the river, I thought it not improbable that this might be the site. I contrived to scramble up at some risk, and found on the top a considerable piece of level ground, which was partially cultivated. The ruins, however, were of the Middle Ages, and could not be confounded with any Greek or Roman structure. It could never have been of great size, but tradition hands it down that the Saracens landed here in 1464, and, plundering the village, carried off the greater number of its inhabitants as slaves to Africa.

Why it should have been selected by Maximianus, the colleague of Diocletian, as the place of his retreat when these two emperors,

1. Post-holes for buildings, probably of the town of Molpa, have been found on the hill-top overlooking the sea.

AD 305, abdicated, is not told us; but here he was residing in AD 306, when he was induced by his son Maxentius to quit his retreat in Lucania, and again resume the purple. It is, indeed, prettily situated on a hill looking down to the north on the river Molpa, and having the river Mingardo to the south, with the sea at its foot stretching far as the eye can reach . . . From this eminence I descended to a small plain which 'ed to the river Mingardo, and was not a little surprised to hear approaching the sounds of the spirit-stirring bagpipes. For an instant I thought myself in some remote glen of my native country, and expec-ted to see a Highlander in full costume appear; but a very different sight met my eye. It was a shepherd clad in the rudest habiliments, made out of the untanned skins of the animals which he tended. The soles of his feet were protected by a piece of leather, which were fastened by cords of goat's hair. The longest of the pipes was upwards of four feet, and the bag was proportionally large, but the sounds grated harshly on the ear. The music of this instrument is heard to greatest advantage at a distance, and I fear I am unpatriotic enough to give the preference to the Irish over the Scotch pipe; at least, I have never heard any sound from the latter able to compete with those produced by the celebrated Gansey, so well known to all those who have visited the south of Ireland. This instrument is very common in the mountainous parts of Italy, and the peasantry at a certain period of the year crowd into Naples, where you see them serenading the images of their Madonna at the corner of every street with the hopes of collecting a few pence from the more religious part of the community. The airs which he played were wild, and, as he receded in the distance, had a pleasing effect. These pipes are made by the shepherds themselves, and, when they visit the towns, I have found that two of them generally travel together and play in concert . . .

After crossing the Mingardo, a small muddy stream, I dismissed my guide, and proceeded on my solitary way towards Camerota, a village which I understood to be about six miles distant. I had soon cause to regret this proceeding, as I got entangled on the face of a hill covered by a kind of stunted oak, and was fairly bewildered. To add to my diffi-culties, I reached a spot where several footpaths diverged, for there was not the slightest appearance of a road, and I had no idea what direction I ought to take. It was needless to halt in hopes of meeting any one, as the place was evidently little frequented. I determined to keep towards the shore, as I might, perhaps, be able to get clear of the brush-wood, which confined my view to a few yards around. I turned my steps, therefore, in that direction, and reached the summit of a hill, where I fell in with two shepherd-boys reclining under a green arbour, which they had formed with the branches of trees . . .

I got myself set right, and entered into conversation, inquiring whether they attended mass, which they assured me they did, men-tioning a small chapel in the vicinity, and the name of the padre. Not much could be expected of them; their knowledge of religion was con-fined to some slight acquaintance with the Ten Commandments and a prayer to the Virgin Mary. I was glad to know that some attempts had been made to instil the principles of religion into their minds.

I had no longer any difficulty in making my way to Camerota, which I found prettily situated on the face of a hill. The first building I reached was a monastery, and, recollecting the kindness of my friends at Centola, I determined again to make trial of monkish hospitality. How different, however, was my reception to-day! Some time elapsed before my knock was attended to, and when I made my request to be allowed to rest a short time under their roof, I saw it was received with great reluctance by the doorkeeper. I was inclined to walk off, had I not been prevented by my desire of seeing how the matter would end. The young monk reported my arrival to his superiors and, ere long, several monks made their appearance with very flushed faces, attended by a young man well dressed, and evidently possessed of some authority. This gentleman demanded, in a loud and authoritative tone, who I was, and what I wanted; to which I naturally answered, 'That I had not the honour to be acquainted with the individual who addressed me, and that I was not inclined to satisfy any stranger who addressed me in the uncivil tone which he had assumed.' The monks, I saw, stood aghast, at what, no doubt, appeared to them my fool-hardiness. I was much more inclined to laugh than to be angry at the adventure; my opponent was unprepared for my answer, and expected that I would be overwhelmed by the information he now conveyed to me. He exclaimed, in a highly indignant tone, *Io sono il Judice Reale del Distretto!* – 'I am the Royal Judge of the District', muttering at the same time *Corpo di Bacco* – an oath which the Italians are much in the habit of using when they are in a passion. It has been handed down to them from their pagan ancestors, and means, 'by the body of Bacchus'.

It is less offensive to my ears than *Corpo di Cristo*, which you constantly hear used in a very blasphemous way . . . To cut short any further altercation, I begged that he would examine my passport, and he would then see that he was called upon by his government to protect and assist me, as far as was in his power. He was obliged to confess that there was nothing irregular in my passport; but I had lowered his dignity before his clerical friends, so that he could not recover his temper; and as his discourteous tone continued, I refused to have any further communication with him. To try how far the hospitality of the monks would stretch, I requested a glass of water, when the superior pointed to a pump in the court-yard, and told me I could find it there. I smiled, though a little nettled at this additional rudeness, and left the monastery, saying that I perceived that the Judge of Camerota was equally distinguished for his courtesy as the monks for their hospitality. I was amused at this adventure, and laughed heartily, as soon as I got beyond the walls of the monastery . . .

I expected to hear more of this adventure, and you will find that I was not mistaken. The village was at no great distance from the monastery, and on my way I joined a peasant, to whom I told how I had been treated by the judge, of whose name he feigned ignorance. The *locanda* was kept by the collector of the land-tax, and, while I was seated there, a person of respectable appearance came in, and entered into conversation with me in reference to my interview with the judge. I inquired if he knew of any ancient remains in the vicinity, and he offered to point out to me the ruins of a Greek church. I found it to be a small chapel, and that little of it remained. His object, however, was to draw me aside and make me a communication, which, I saw, was intended to frighten me. He told me that the judge had positive orders from his government to stop all persons travelling through the country, though they were furnished with a regular passport, and that, if I remained at Camerota, he would be under the disagreeable necessity of putting me under arrest. I was highly indignant at this attempt to alarm me, and told him at once that I did not believe a single word of the statement, as I had left Naples only a few days before, and I could not imagine that a government would act so unjustly as to give me a passport to travel through its provinces when it knew the orders it had previously issued. Besides, I had waited, by request, on the Minister of the Interior to explain to him fully the objects I had in view, and the route I intended to follow. He had been kind enough to point out objects of interest, which might be worthy of examination, and to give me advice as to the dangers which I ought to avoid. He had even granted me a passport of a peculiar kind, to free me from the annoyances of such men as this judge; and it was too much to ask me to believe that a gentleman of his high character – Minister of the Interior for the King of the Two Sicilies – would act so treacherously, as he must have done, if the statement he now made was true . . . I offered to accompany him at once to the presence of the judge, who might act as he thought proper; but he might rest assured that I would not allow the rights of my country to be trampled on in my person with impunity. This offer embarrassed him, and he muttered something as to his friend not wishing to place me in any difficulty. I told him that I would not allow my plans to be deranged in the slightest degree by any threats that might be held out; nor would I give any information as to the course I intended to pursue. If he had no further communication to make, I begged that our conference might end. I was much tempted to remain at Camerota for the night, and see whether the judge would dare to put his threats in execution; but a considerable portion of the day was still at my command, and I thought it folly to waste it on such a purpose. I rested at the *locanda* for several hours, and heard nothing more from the judge. Towards evening I determined to walk forward to San Giovanni a Piro, and I requested the landlord to inform the judge that, if he wished to have any further communication with me, he would find me at that village.

The country through which I now passed was rather better cultivated than that which I had seen in the early part of the day, and though the *scirocco* still blew, it was less oppressive than it had been in the morning. I fell in with a muleteer who was proceeding to San Giovanni, and I mounted one of his animals; there was no saddle, however, and I soon discovered that the fatigue of walking was nothing compared to the disagreeable jog of the mule. He complained bitterly of the badness of the times, and was no friend of the present government. I had often remarked a small bag suspended round the necks of the peasants, and I had imagined, knowing how superstitious the Italians were, that it was some amulet or holy relique to guard them against the evil eye; but I find from the muleteer that it is what they call *carta di sicurezza*, a paper giving a description of their personal appearance, their height, the colour of their hair, and any peculiarity that may serve to distinguish one man from another. This must be worn by every person in the kingdom, and of course a certain sum of money must be paid for it. This is nothing else than a poll-tax, the most unjust of all, severely felt by the poor and not at all by the rich. It must be renewed every year, and if any one be found without this paper he is liable to be thrown into prison.

At the entrance to the village I parted from my companion, and proceeded to present myself before the chief magistrate. I had some misgivings as to my night's rest when I observed the wretched appearance of the houses. The people crowded to their doors as I passed, and seemed amused, if I may judge from the peals of laughter I heard behind me. I made my way to the syndic's house, which was in a sadly dilapidated state, and with scarcely a vestige of furniture within. What must I expect to find at the public *locanda* if the chief magistrate resided in such a hovel? He was not at home, and I was obliged to wait, hungry and tired, till he made his appearance, as no one would dare to receive me till my passport was found to be good. When he returned, I found him to be quite civil, and he immediately despatched his servant to search for a bed, which was furnished me by the old lady who kept the shop of the village. The sun had been set for some time, and it was quite dark when I issued forth to proceed to my lodgings. A boy carried a small lamp before me, the glimmering of which was just sufficient to prevent me stumbling over the uneven street of San Giovanni. The shop was crowded with peasants, whose noise and turmoil augured ill for my repose, and I inquired with eagerness where I was to sleep. Luckily, my bed-chamber was separated from the shop, on the opposite side of the narrow lane up a ruinous stair. I ordered supper, which was to consist of broiled sausage and cheese, with the best wine she could furnish. My table was a large box, and I sat down on a hard bench. The bed looked so filthy that it was impossible to think of undressing, but I had no doubt that I should sleep sound enough on the coverlet. My landlady came in to say that her son must sleep in the same room with me, and I inquired where she would find a second bed. She pointed to the bench on which I was seated, and said he would stretch himself on the top. I remonstrated strongly against this intrusion, and examined the bolt of the door with a view of securing myself. Alas! it was boltless, and I was entirely at their mercy. I placed my money and whatever articles of value I had with me under my head, and I did not feel quite at my ease, as you may suppose.

VI

THANK God, I was neither robbed nor murdered last night, though I had some doubts whether I should again see the light of day. With such misgivings, you will readily believe that I had no inclination to sleep till I surveyed my companion for the night, and could judge by his appearance whether he was likely to close my career. I tried to nourish my lamp, till I might be able to see him; but not all my ingenuity could succeed to keep in its flickering light. I dare say that the very methods I took to make it burn caused it to go out; at all events, I was now in total darkness, stretched on the top of my bed, watching anxiously to hear a footstep, when at last some one stealthily approached, and I was somewhat relieved by the appearance of a glimmering light. The door opened, and a tall man entered, with a peasant's large cloak wrapped round him; and, as the light of the lamp fell on his countenance, my fears made me suppose that I had never seen any one more strongly marked with all the evil passions of our nature. I remained immovable on the bed, apparently asleep, watching anxiously all his proceedings. He blew out his lamp and lay down at full length on the box, where I soon found, by the regularity of his breathing, that he was fast asleep. I was now satisfied that I had nothing to fear, and, as my day's labour had thoroughly worn me out, I soon forgot all my anxieties and dangers.

This morning I was afoot by daybreak . . . I had some doubts what course I ought to pursue, whether I should remain a few hours at San Giovanni, or proceed on to Policastro. I felt some curiosity to witness a procession, which I understood was to take place this morning, to the Madonna della Pietra Santa with the view to obtaining her intercession to procure rain. The *scirocco* generally brings with it showers of rain, and the priests, therefore, have wisely chosen this day to offer up their prayers. The morning was lowering, and I saw clearly that some rain must fall. This is a common method with the priests of working on the superstitious feelings of the people, and in these remote parts is not, perhaps, much to be wondered at; but you will be surprised to hear that I have seen, even in Florence, the same farce acted with all the solemnity which the archbishop of that city and his attendant priests could communicate to it. I left San Giovanni without waiting for the procession, since, if it were to prove eminently successful, I must be detained in this miserable place, or else I must submit to be thoroughly drenched, as I am sorry to say that my umbrella is already in a sad state of dilapidation. The peasants were beginning to leave the village to proceed to their labours in the field, and I joined a party who undertook to point out the way to Policastro, which I could see on the coast, about ten miles distant across a plain, through which flowed the river Bussento. The country was partially cultivated, the vetch and the Indian corn were beginning to appear; but they were suffering from the long drought. I had not passed over many miles before a drenching shower began to fall, when I took refuge in a hut which happened to be near, and I requested permission to remain till the rain had ceased. The interior was the very picture of misery, and contained an old man on the verge of the grave; but not a word of dissatisfaction with his lot fell from his lips. I found that the river Bussento was of considerable size, and could only be passed by boat, *scafo* as they call it. It was well that I became acquainted with this fact, as I should have landed myself in marshes at the mouth of the river, towards which I was wending my way, as the direct road to Policastro.[1] The old man gave me directions where I should find the boat; but, between my stupidity and the difficulty of making out what he exactly meant, I derived little benefit from his information. The river Bussento rises in the mountains of Sanza, and, after receiving several small tributaries, disappears in a deep abyss at a spot called Tironi, and having run about three miles underground, issues forth at a place called Li Zirzi, six miles from Policastro. The mountainous nature of the country, and perhaps the earthquakes which rend the ground, may be the cause of these streams sinking and again starting suddenly from the surface . . .

On leaving the hut I met a peasant, whom I hired to be my guide to Policastro. As I was walking along, I happened to sneeze, when my companion immediately exclaimed, *Criste Santo*! 'The saint save you! ' which is the compliment paid in this part of Italy to those who are thus affected . . . The boat was, as might be expected, of rude construc-

1. Policastro, the Greek Pyxus and Roman Buxentum, *see* bibliography.

tion, though easily enough paddled across. Soon afterwards we met a pretty girl, the wife of my guide, who had been selling vegetables at Policastro; and I allowed him to return with her, as I saw that I should have no further difficulty in finding my way. On reaching the public square of Policastro, which is a considerable town, by far the largest I have seen since I left Naples, I met one of the armed police; and being by this time pretty well acquainted with the impertinence of these subordinates, I requested that he would conduct me to the house of the syndic. We found the worthy magistrate industriously employed in reducing oak bark to a state fit for tanning leather. He directed me to proceed to his chancellor, whom I found sick in bed, and rather testy at my intrusion. He insisted that I should proceed to Bonati, a village five miles distant, for the purpose of showing my passport to the judge of the district, which I positively refused to do, unless he sent me under arrest. He told me that, wherever I passed the night, the magistrate of the village would require the signature of the judge. I told him, however, that I should go on in the route I had already determined, till I was actually stopped, and that all I wished from him was permission to examine the antiquities of Policastro . . .

I proceeded to the house of the curate, whom I thought not unlikely to be acquainted with the ancient remains of his own city, and from whom I might derive some information, if he were inclined to be civil. I found him engaged in the performance of his religious duties in the cathedral. I waited till he had concluded, and met him at the door, when I explained to him the objects I had in view; but he was a sad barbarian, ignorant and rude. Several of his congregation, however, who overheard our conversation, came forward and offered at once to point out the small remains of the ancient town, which we know to have been called Buxentum. The name of the river which I had crossed is only a slight corruption of this word. In front of the cathedral lie several fine marble pillars, half buried in the earth, and which must have belonged to a temple, probably on the site of the cathedral . . . [2 Inscriptions are now described.]

. . . I was told that I should find some ruins on the hill above the city, and accordingly I proceeded to examine them. I was joined by a considerable body of the police, who are here always armed with a carbine; and as we passed through the narrow lanes of the city, the people crowded after me, calling out, *'Che c'è?'* – 'What is the matter?'

49

evidently imagining that I was some important captive. In passing through the town, I was astonished to see on several doors a St Andrew's cross marked distinctly in red, and on inquiring of my guide what it meant, he coolly said, 'An enemy hath done this,' or, at all events, words to that effect. Political feelings run very high here, and they show thus their secret feelings to each other, condemning their enemies by the *sanbenito* cross, used in former times by the Inquisition to indicate the flames in which the impenitent were to be immersed. The Neapolitans call a door thus marked *macreata*, and at one period it became so serious a nuisance, and created such bad blood, that a law had to be passed against the practice, inflicting the severest penalties on all who should be guilty of damning their neighbours in this way. On ascending the hill I found the ruins of a castle, which had once been of considerable strength, having the date 1393 above one of its gates, but it is said to be of a much earlier period. Several of the police left me here to proceed, as they told me, in search of some unfortunate *Carbonari*, who are hunted at present like wild beasts. You must know that a few years ago the country was in a state of insurrection, which was suppressed by a small Austrian force. The inhabitants are not devoid of personal courage, if you take them individually; but they have no confidence in each other, and cannot, therefore, fight as a body. In consequence of this insurrection the whole country was, of course, disarmed and put at the mercy of the brigands, who used to enter villages at midday and carry off the respectable inhabitants to their fastnesses, from which they were not released till their friends had paid a ransom. Some progress has been made towards organising an armed force throughout the country; the government, however, is naturally afraid of trusting arms to the landed proprietors, who have generally evinced a desire to have some influence in the management of their affairs ... In the population of Policastro, which consists of seven thousand, only sixty were found worthy of being entrusted with arms.

I could find no more ancient remains. .... The marsh at the mouth of the river renders the city unhealthy, and the archbishop, with the principal inhabitants, are said to leave it from May till December. After resting a short time at Policastro, I proceeded on my way along the coast. As the mountains seemed to approach the shore, I suspected my onward course would be tedious and fatiguing; and as I wished to reach Maratea, a village fifteen miles distant, I determined to hire a boat, if such a thing could be procured. I soon fell in with a few fishermen's huts, and had no difficulty in making a bargain with them to carry me to Maratea, stopping on my way at Sapri, which is supposed to be the site of the ancient Scidrus.[1] The boat had not the luxurious and easy movement of a Venetian gondola, yet I have never enjoyed one of them so much as that in which I was now embarked. The rain which had fallen a few hours before had communicated freshness to the air, and as I stretched myself at full length on the hard bench, with my umbrella above me, I congratulated myself on my wisdom in choosing this mode of proceeding. We soon entered a small and beautiful harbour, near which was situated the village of Sapri.

There was more appearance of comfort in this village than in any I had yet seen. The houses were interspered with gardens and vineyards, and the late shower made everything look fresh and cool. I was struck by the luxuriance of their fruit-trees. The orange and citron-trees were flourishing in all their beauty. The *albicocco*, our apricot, seemed to thrive – the Neapolitan *crisciommolo*, of which they are so justly proud.

The Italians are as fond of all kinds of green herbs as their ancestors were in Roman times, and the salad forms always a principal part of their frugal meals in the country. I could with difficulty get over the flavour of the strong-smelling garlic, of which they seem particularly enamoured. I met several respectable inhabitants, with whom I entered into conversation, and they pointed out to me an ancient inscription built into the pedestal of a holy cross in the middle of the public piazza. It was much worn away, but I was able to decipher it [2] . . . [Here follow 4 Inscriptions.]

I have been deeply affected, as all must be, with some of the sepulchral inscriptions that are found in the museums of Italy . . . [2 Inscriptions.] Peace is the predominating idea in their epitaphs; hope in ours.

The stairs of one of the houses showed a specimen of coarse mosaic; the site of the ancient town, (Scridros) however, had been nearly half a mile from the present village, on the north side of the little bay, at a spot

1. Scidros has not yet been identified, but is thought to be near Sapri; *see* bibliography.
2. Now (1962) practically unreadable.

now called Camerelle. Here many coins and cameos have been found, and the foundations of houses are still to be seen. More particularly there are considerable remains of a theatre, with eight niches and some of the steps still existing, two small aqueducts, city walls of a reticulated structure, a portico of considerable length; but I saw no inscriptions, though such have been found both in the Greek and Latin languages. It was a Greek city, mentioned by Herodotus (vi. 21), from whom we learn that it was a colony of Sybaris, and was one of the places to which the surviving inhabitants of that city retired after its destruction in 510 BC. Though it appears from its remains to have been a city of considerable size, and possessed the only tolerable harbour between Naples and Sicily, it is never mentioned connected with any historical event, and drops altogether out of view at a very early period.

I met the boat at a point of land forming one side of the harbour. The two points of the harbour are guarded by two towers, the one to the west called Buondormire, and the other to the east, Lubertino. I was not sorry to get on board, as the rays of the sun reflected from the sand rendered all exertion unpleasant. As we advanced, the mountains approached close to the shore and overhung the sea. There was a winding path along the face of the hills, but at this period of the day it would have been madness to have attempted to proceed on foot. There was not a breath of air, and the heat was greater than I had ever experienced; yet the boatmen seemed to suffer little inconvenience, though their bodies were exposed, uncovered, to the direct rays of the sun. I am now cautious, as I suffered last year by imprudently exposing myself a very short time on my way to the palace of Tiberius, on Capri, when I received a sunstroke, and suffered for several months considerable inconvenience.

As we were on our way to Maratea, the boatmen told me of a strange phenomenon, of which I am sorry that I did not hear before I left Sapri. They maintained that close to Sapri, near a rock called Scialandro, a stream of fresh water bubbles up in the midst of the sea in such quantities, that when the weather is calm you can drink it unmixed with salt water, but when the wind blows it gets mixed, and you can only see the bubbling in the sea.

After proceeding for ten miles through this heated furnace ... the mountains were seen to recede somewhat from the shore, and a deep valley ran far into the country. Here Maratea was situated, and here

I intended to take up my abode for the night. My boatmen had no regular papers, and suggested a difficulty which had not occurred to me, that if they made their appearance at the usual landing-place, they would be asked for the register of their boat, and that the consequence of their not having it would be that we should be all arrested. Of course this did not suit my purposes, and what I had experienced already of the police of this country made me quite satisfied that they were stating what would certainly take place. I did not choose to run any such risk, and insisted that they should land me at once on the shore, and I should make my way to the village, exciting as little attention as possible, and keeping my own counsel as to the mode by which I had approached. I crept slowly along the shore, and as soon as I saw a chance of mounting the rocks with any degree of safety, I left the coast that I might avoid encountering any of the police. The inhabitants had with great industry cultivated every little spot in this narrow valley, yet the bare limestone rock constantly protruding had an unpleasant effect to the eye. Before I left Naples, I had been furnished by the Prince of Satriano, one of the ablest and most illustrious of the Neapolitan nobility, with a number of letters of introduction to his friends in different parts of the country, and among them was one addressed to the Baron di San Biagio, of Maratea. As soon as I thought that his household was likely to be awake (you see that I benefit by experience), I waited on the baron, who insisted that I should do him the honour of remaining with him for the night – an honour which I assure you, after my last night's troubles, I was not slow to grant. Nothing could exceed the kindness which I received, and indeed the only danger seems to be lest it should degenerate into the opposite by its excess. I have never felt so strongly as I have done within the last few days the difference between filth and cleanliness. The warmth of the climate generates insects of all kinds in a very prolific way, and I no sooner think that I have got rid of my tormentors than I receive a fresh supply from some other quarter. I can verily believe these to be one of the plagues of Egypt.

Maratea is situated on the declivity of a high hill, and is so surrounded by mountains, that from November till the end of January the rays of the sun do not reach it. The olive, however, was growing luxuriantly; and I was surprised to see quantities of myrtles, the bark of which, when reduced to powder, I was told, was used for tanning leather. They are famed for cheese, and in Naples most of the cheese-mongers and pork-sellers are from this little village.

In the evening I paid a visit to the syndic, whom I found superior to any I had yet met in this office, and from whom I received much civility. He proposed that I should accompany him through his village, and that we should visit the monastery of San Biagio, situated on a high hill above Maratea ... The evening is the period of the day that all the inhabitants assemble in the open air, and generally in the public square. It was crowded as we passed through it, and all rose to salute us with much ceremony. Before we could get half way up the hill, the sun was approaching the horizon, and I was obliged to be satisfied with a glimpse of the lofty mountains of Calabria, which rose in the distance, and whose tops were gilded by the rays of the setting sun.

You are aware that the Romish Church asserts that the power of working miracles has descended to her from the time of the Apostles; and you will not be surprised, therefore, to hear that the monks of San Biagio animate the devotion of true believers, and fill their own pockets, by the exhibition of a miracle regularly every year. They contrive by some means, I dare say not remarkable for ingenuity, to cause a statue of our Saviour to perspire manna; and if I had felt much anxiety to witness it, I might have gratified my curiosity by the sacrifice of a few days, as it takes place this week. I have already, however, seen enough of these mummeries at Naples and its immediate vicinity. The manna, is of course, a cure for all sorts of diseases, and brings a considerable sum into the treasury of the monastery. If any one happens to recover, after he has employed this manna, the monks take care that it should be announced in all parts of the country; and, in cases of failure, they have it always in their power to say that it arises from a doubt in the mind of the patient as to the efficacy of the remedy.

I have inquired respecting ancient remains, as geographers are inclined to place the city Blanda[1] on this site; but I can hear of nothing, except, indeed, a tower on the shore, which they call Torre di Venere. No coins or cameos seem ever to have been found here. The evening had now closed in before I again reached the house of my host, and I was not sorry to observe, on my return, symptoms of supper at an earlier hour than is usual among the Italians. Their hours of eating do not correspond with ours. They rise at daybreak ...

1. This site is still unidentified, but *see* bibliography.

About mid-day they dine, and, of course, the food depends on the wealth of the individual; it is, however, rather in quantity than quality that they differ. They then retire to bed, and the house is shut up till four in the afternoon, when they take a cup of coffee, and about ten at night they have a substantial supper. At least, I observed that their supper exhibited, according to the custom of their progenitors, a greater variety of dishes than any other of their meals. The sausage generally appears in some form at every meal, and this evening we had it served up surrounded by the snow-white maccaroni ...

Before we sat down to supper, the baron showed me a very beautiful brass image of Cupid, which had been found at a small village, Rivello, a few miles from Maratea; the god was blinded with a fascia, and held a heart in his left hand, in which there had once been some precious stones. It is prettily designed, and of superior workmanship. The baron said that Rivello[1] seems to have been the site of some ancient town, from the ruins of the buildings of a reticulated structure and the form of a circus, which can be distinctly traced.

While we were conversing, a man came in to say that a friend had been severely stung during the afternoon by hornets, and wished some juice of the fig to rub over the place, as it is considered a sedative to the pain on such occasions. The juice must be taken before the fruit is ripe, as it possesses a peculiar acidity at that stage They use it, also, to remove warts, the *verruca* of the Romans. Pliny (xxiii. 63, 1) refers to ... 'the milky juice of the fig' being made use of for this very purpose ... The hornet is a great annoyance in the summer months in Italy. Last summer, while I was residing at Sorrento, there was a lane which it was impossible to pass with any safety from the vicious attacks of these insects.

VII

You must not be alarmed at the account of this day's proceedings, though I confess a speedy and melancholy conclusion had nearly been brought to my projected tour. Luckily, no serious injury had befallen me, though I feel somewhat stiff and bruised.

1. *See* P. Zancani Montuoro: 'Siri-Sirino-Pixunte' (*Arch. Stor. per la Cal. Luc.*, Anno XVIII, 1949, fasc. I–II).

You will observe that my face is still turned towards the south, and I hope that I shall be able to continue in that direction for another two hundred miles; but what has happened to-day will be a warning not to be too sanguine, as I am exposed to a variety of disasters, any one of which may close my career. I had some hesitation this morning how I should proceed, whether by boat or on foot: I found, however, from my friends, that the coast continued for the next ten miles of the same rocky, precipitous character, and therefore I thought it the wisest plan to hire a boat to convey me to a celebrated grotto, about ten miles along the coast.

In descending to the shore, I passed upwards of fifty women carrying large bundles of wood, which I find are sent to Malta for the consumption of that island. It must be a laborious employment, and I was sorry to hear always performed by women. On stepping on board my boat, the custom-house officer insisted on satisfying his curiosity as to the contents of my knapsack. What contraband articles were likely to be conveyed from Maratea it is difficult to imagine; probably a bribe was all he wanted from me to leave it untouched. I laughed at the absurdity of his proposal, and made no objection to as minute an examination as he chose.

The mountainous character of the coast continued for about ten miles, and we found several small islands, probably those mentioned by Pliny as *Ithacesiæ*. The village of the Madonna della Grotta[1] is situated at the spot where the mountains begin to recede from the shore, and consisted of only a few houses, which had all of them a small piece of cultivated ground in front. I had some difficulty in finding the grotto, of which I was in search, as the few people I met seemed to look with suspicion upon me, and gave me very indistinct directions. At last, however, I reached the stair, which, from its worn appearance, had evidently been passed by many a religious devotee, but it was now covered with moss, and had long ceased to be frequented, except by a few in its immediate vicinity. It was a magnificent natural grotto, about fifty yards in length, and about sixty feet in height. In the centre was a large baptistery plentifully supplied with water by drops from the roof. At one side a small chapel[2] was rudely constructed, where the statue of the Madonna was placed. While I was examining the grotto, a poor man made his appearance, to whom the care of the chapel was entrusted,

1. Praia a Mare. 2. This is still a place of pilgrimage.

3 Santa Lucia, Naples, *top*
Lacco Ameno, Ischia

4 Capri, *top*
Tasso's Villa, Sorrento

and he spoke in glowing terms of the peculiar sanctity of her statue, and assured me that the Virgin was so enamoured of this spot, that she had refused to leave it. In proof of this he told me the following legend. It would appear that three centuries ago this statue used to be visited by crowds, who believed that it possessed a power of curing disease. The priests of a neighbouring village, Ajeta, wished to turn this to their own advantage, and, under pretence that the Virgin would be more comfortable in their church than in this dark, damp grotto, transferred the statute with great ceremony to Ajeta. The morning after her arrival the people crowded to the church to pay their adorations, when they were amazed to find the statue had disappeared. Messengers were immediately despatched to the grotto, and there the Madonna was found to be placed in her long-accustomed haunt. Thrice an attempt was made to remove her, and as often she is said to have returned to her residence in the grotto. There could no longer be any doubt respecting her decision, and the priests of Ajeta were forced to give up their golden dream of riches and influence. The festival takes place on the 15th of August.

While I was meditating on the follies and superstitions of mankind, I forgot the slippery state of the stair, and, before I could save myself, I was brought with great violence to the floor, rolling in a very undignified way to the bottom of the stairs. Luckily my knapsack saved my head, or I verily believe my skull would have been fractured, and my career closed at once. I found, however, that I had sustained no serious injury, except that my clothes were covered with green moss, and that I had more the appearance of a merman than of the human being. My ankle feels a little stiff, but I ought to be thankful that I escaped so easily.

I intended to have had some refreshment at this village, but there was no house of public entertainment, and I was obliged to go on for six miles to Casaletto.[1] Nothing could exceed the dreariness and barrenness of the coast, and as the heat soon began to be excessive, I regretted that I had dismissed the boat. I was now leaving the ancient Lucania, the modern province of Principato Citeriore, and passing into the country of the Bruttii, the modern Calabria, said to be the native country of brigands. Of course, I cannot altogether divest myself of this idea, which was so impressed upon me before I left Naples, and I feel not altogether at my ease. On reaching a height, which enabled me to look

1. Unidentified.

down into a glen, into which the footpath led, I got a glimpse of some one concealed in the brushwood. It was a lonely spot; I had left all houses far behind me, and I had met no one since I left the village. I regretted that I had no weapon of defence, as it was disagreeable thus to be at the mercy of a single man. However, I had no alternative except to advance, and on approaching nearer, my anxiety was relieved as I saw that he was a man far advanced in years, with whom I could have no difficulty in coping, even if he were armed. I entered into conversation with him, and found that he was on his way to Casaletto; his language, however, was a dialect which I had difficulty in understanding, and we would carry on little conversation. The ground was very uneven, now a deep ravine and then a high hill, so that, on my arrival at Casaletto, I was thoroughly knocked up; and, if I am not able to arrange my hours of travelling better, I fear that I shall soon be stopped by illness. The *locanda* of Casaletto was equally miserable with all of the kind I had yet seen, and after resting about an hour, I proceeded in the direction of Scalea. From time to time I took refuge under the umbrageous shelter of an elm, and at last determined to remain until the heat of the day abated. I was on the point of dropping asleep, when a person of respectable appearance rode up, and entered into conversation, inquiring in an earnest tone, whether I had heard of the *portentoso miracolo* ('wonderful prodigy') which had lately taken place at the village of Ajeta, the very village which the old sexton had spoken of a few hours ago. It immediately occurred to me that it might be some curious natural phenomenon well worthy of examination, and I was prepared to sacrifice a few days, if it turned out to be so. I requested that he would be kind enough to explain to what he particularly referred.

I never witnessed a more solemn or awe-struck countenance than he displayed while he told me his story. My own feelings were a mixture of disappointment and amusement. It was a new version of the old farce of the monks of San Biagio, which I mentioned in my last letter. It would appear that a statue of our Saviour had suddenly begun to emit from its pores some liquid of a sweetish taste in a miraculous way, and my informant had been waiting on the judge of the district at Scalea to report the continuation of the miracle. He told me, if I wished to have a detailed account of their proceedings at Ajeta, I ought to pay my respects to Signor Pelerino, the judge, and I would have my curiosity satisfied. Accordingly, as soon as I reached Scalea, I proceeded to present my passport, and to receive permission from him to remain in his village. The subject of the miracle was evidently deeply impressed on his mind, and I had no difficulty in obtaining from him the following account, which will amuse you:

In the beginning of last February, the inhabitants of Ajeta, a village twelve miles distant from Scalea, had their attention first drawn to the following miraculous occurrence. Don Francesco Lo Monaco, a gentleman of considerable landed property, and of reputed sanctity, announced to his friends, that a statue of our Saviour, in his private oratorio, had suddenly begun to exude manna, and that he had found the floor and the statue bathed in the precious liquid, when he entered in the morning. His intimate friends were first admitted to witness the miracle; the prodigy was soon noised abroad, and a vast concourse of peasants assembled from all directions. The syndic of the village immediately communicated the proceedings to the judge, and the judge thought it right to examine more minutely into the matter. He proceeded with his chancellor – clerk, I suppose – to the village, but found on his arrival, that the miracle only took place at stated periods. He had only got comfortably settled in bed, when a servant came in breathless haste to announce that the statue had begun its operations. The judge did not choose to be thus disturbed, and sent for answer that he hoped to be able to witness it in the morning. This was intended to show that he suspected some trick, and was not going to be easily imposed upon. Next morning he proceeded to the chapel, and found the floor covered with moisture, the statue still dripping, and several pails full of the liquor, which had exuded in the night. This was a sufficient confirmation, it would appear, to the judge, and he confessed, with a countenance full of unaffected feelings, that he was so overcome with his own unworthiness to witness such a manifestation of God's presence, that he lay prostrate before the statue for an hour, repeating prayers and thanksgivings. Of his thorough belief I could not have the slightest doubt, and that he was a really pious man everything seemed to prove. It was his duty to report the whole proceeding to the *sotto-intendente*, who is the second in authority in the province. He resided at Paola, a distance of fifty miles, but he came accompanied by the criminal judge to Ajeta, and the two returned fully satisfied that they had witnessed a most wonderful miracle. The priests now came forward, and asserted that the proper place for the statue was their church, and though the proprietor demurred to their demands, he at last yielded, and it was agreed that it should be transferred with all due ceremony to a niche set apart for it. The inhabitants attended in crowds from the neighbouring villages, and the letter of the parish priest to the judge, which I saw, stated that the people walked *con molta decenza*, showing evident signs of penitence for their sins. Most of them were in tears, and many of them beat their breasts. The letter concluded by assuring the judge that it was a most pleasing and edifying sight. No sooner, however, had the statue been placed in the church, than all appearance of moisture vanished; and though prayers, petitions, and incense were offered without ceasing, they were all without avail, and the statue remained dry as a piece of stick. Two days it was kept in the church, but on the third the people demanded that the statue should be restored to its old haunt. This accordingly took place, and the following morning it of course began its operations once more. The priests, however, again interfered. The same ceremonies with the same result took place, and that statue now remains in the private chapel of Lo Monaco. It still continues to give forth a liquid, and at this moment all the villages within a distance of fifty miles can furnish specimens of it. The judge produced a small flask, and as a particular favour allowed me to taste it. It was sweetish, and had exactly the taste of sugar and water.

I listened to this story with great patience, and without any appearance of incredulity, till I heard the whole; I then stated, in a way least likely to hurt his feelings, that, as I was what he would regard as a heretic, I was very sceptical in all such matters, and could not doubt that he must have been in some way deceived, and that if he would only take proper measures to discover it, I had no doubt he would find it so. I pointed out various ways in which it might be accomplished, and proved by his own statement to me, that he had allowed his feelings to get the better of his judgment, for he had yielded to the mere appearance of moisture, and had proceeded no farther in his examination. When he found that I was not to be convinced, he begged that I would accompany him to Ajeta; and he promised that I should have the whole weight of his official authority to enable me to discover the imposture. This, however, was quite out of the question. I told him that I knew too well the superstitious character of his countrymen, and their excitable temperament, to venture on any such Quixotic enterprise. I was satisfied that he would protect me as far as was in his power, but an unreasoning mob was the last danger I should wish to face, and I did not believe that the few police he could muster would be any protection in case of a commotion. I recommended to him to examine the matter a little more minutely, and I had no doubt that he would find he had been imposed upon. He was a delightful old gentleman, and it seemed, when I thought of it, presumptuous in a young man as I was to give advice to one who must be highly honoured by his government, to occupy the responsible position that he did in the province. I spent several pleasant hours with him, and on his hearing that I was on my way to Paola, he was kind enough to offer me permission to proceed in a boat, which he was sending there on public business, and as there are no ancient remains between Scalea and Paola, I have accepted this offer. The distance is about fifty miles, and then I intend to strike into the centre of Calabria, said to be, so far as I can understand, rather a dangerous enterprise.

VIII

You will be surprised to hear that I have remained another day at Scalea, owing to a slight breeze blowing from the south, which prevents the boat from starting.

I am lodged in the house of a policeman, dirty and uncomfortable, yet I contrived to sleep soundly for many hours, till I was awoke at daybreak by a fearful uproar that took place in my room. I had entered the house after sunset, and the dimness of a small lamp was scarcely sufficient to enable me to examine into what sort of bed-chamber I was ushered. On awakening, I found it was the sleeping apartment of a very heterogeneous collection of animals. Above me had roosted a number of chickens, while ducks and pigs had spent the night amicably together on the floor. It was the pugnacious or playful propensities of two young pigs that had created all the tumult, as they had upset the pole upon which the chickens sat, and they naturally took refuge on my bed. The insects within my bed, however, I found now to be a much greater nuisance, and I had no other alternative but to withdraw myself from their presence, only too well satisfied if they did not pursue me in overwhelming numbers.

I proceeded to the shore to see if they were making any preparations for our departure. The wind continued unfavourable, and they gave no hope of our starting before evening. In a short time the beach exhibited an animated scene, from the inhabitants crowding to make their bargains with the fishermen, who had returned with a considerable load of fish. They were of several kinds, of which two were familiar enough to me, the *palamaji* and the *sarde*; of these I bought for twopence as much as I thought would make a tolerable breakfast.

The *sarde* (sardines) are the *Alausa pilchardus*, the pilchard so plentifully caught in its season on the Devonshire coast, and consumed by the inhabitants of that county in pies. The *palamaji* are no doubt the *pelamides* of Pliny (ix. 18, 1.), which he maintains to be the tunny of one year old. I am not ichthyologist enough to contradict his statement; at all events, it is an excellent fish in this season of the year.

Scalea is situated on the brow of a hill, the summit of which is crowned by the ruins of an ancient castle, which must at one time have been of considerable strength. The range, along which I have been passing for several days, ends here, and a plain of some twenty or thirty miles in breadth lies before me, through which passes a small river called Lao, falling into the sea about three miles from Scalea. It rises near Viggianello, like many of the rivers in this part of the country, from springs gushing from a hill. The marshes formed at its mouth cause the autumnal months to be particularly unhealthy at Scalea, and the inhabitants even now have a sallow, pale look. There seems every reason to believe that the ancient city, Laus,[1] was situated in the plain about a mile from Scalea, where there is a pillar of cipollino marble, a piece of marble pavement, and some appearance of the remains of an aqueduct. I cannot hear, however, of any inscriptions having ever been found at this spot ... My guide was the gaoler of Scalea, whose office at present is very much of a sinecure, as he has only four prisoners confined on a charge of petty larceny. His prison, indeed, is not of very ample dimensions, being only a couple of apartments in what is called La porta di Cimalonga, a small tower which

1. Laos has not yet been identified, but is thought to be near Scalea, *see* bibliography.

had once served to defend the town. On my return, I proceeded to pay my respects to my good friend the judge, and he kindly invited me to dinner. Our party consisted of his wife, daughter, and her husband, who had lately arrived on a visit to his father-in-law. They could not be said to be polished in their manners, but there was a simplicity and good nature in all they said and did, that amply compensated for any violation of those conventional rules which we are pleased to dignify with the title of good manners. The judge has a collection of curiosities, among which is a tiny ivory figure standing in a basket supported by four small columns,[1] having been found near the site of the ancient Sybaris; he had also a number of silver and bronze coins of different epochs, all found in this quarter. Our conversation naturally turned on the miracle of Ajeta, and I now see clearly how the idea of manna was suggested to the monks. This substance is furnished in large quantities by Calabria, and forms the chief item of its foreign commerce. It is got from two kinds of ash, *Ornus Europæa* and *Traxinus rotundifolia*, which grow abundantly in this part of Italy. It is procured in two different ways, chiefly by an incision made into the bark of the ash-tree, from which flows a stream of juice, which the heat of the sun hardens, and which is then collected by the inhabitants. The juice is at first transparent, but when exposed a short time to the air acquires that colour which we find it to have in chemists' shops. When collected in this way, it is called by the Calabrese *forᶎata* (forced), but it sometimes flows naturally, even appears on the leaves of the trees, and is found in large patches on the ground. What is still more extraordinary, they assert it rains manna at times, and I can bear witness to having seen something of the kind. Yesterday, when there were no clouds, I was surprised to observe a number of large drops fall, when I naturally exclaimed to the peasant whom I met on my way to Casaletto – 'How very strange!' but he added, quite coolly, that it was manna. I thought the man was imposing on me, as I had never heard of any such curious phenomenon, except in the case of the Israelites, and as I had great difficulty in communicating with him, I allowed the matter to pass; here, however, I find the thing stated as a fact, of which they have no doubt. We know that moisture is drawn up into the atmosphere to be again sent down in rain, and it is possible that the moisture drawn up from the extensive woods of Calabria may partake of the peculiar

1. Possibly an object of mediaeval origin.

quality of manna. I hope I may again be a witness of the phenomenon, and I shall not allow it to pass with such slight examination[1] . . .

Besides this, I find there appears suddenly at times on the leaves of plants a kind of glutinous substance of a sweetish flavour, which stops their growth, and is otherwise injurious. They speak of these leaves as *foglie ammannate*, and even *vino ammanato*, when the grapes have a bitterish taste from this dewy substance covering them. It appears more particularly on a shrub, which grows abundantly in their hedges, called *fusaggine* or *fusaro*, because spindles are usually made of it. It is the *Spindelbaum* of the Germans. During the continuance of great heat, they speak also of a kind of dew falling, which they call *sinobbica*. Something, indeed, of the same kind is mentioned by Ælian (*H.A.* xv. 7); he says that in India honey is rained on the pastures, and that the milk of the animals that are fed where it falls is remarkable for its sweetness . . .

I had frequently observed a small purse suspended round the necks of children. I find that it is intended to guard against the glance of an envious eye, which is a subject of constant dread to the inhabitants of this country. I believe that this superstition extends through all ranks, from the king on the throne to the meanest of the *lazzaroni*. As soon as a child is born, this purse, containing the reliques of some saint, is suspended to its neck, being the peculiar manufacture of the Capuchins, who refuse any recompense for it. They are, however, well repaid by the grateful mother, when the purveyor of the monastery passes her door. I have often met jolly-looking friars driving a well-loaded mule, and it seems that the same custom now prevails here, as in merry England in ancient times, of collecting donations of provisions for the monastery from the neighbouring inhabitants. It is then that the mother is expected to recollect the favour conferred on her child by the Capuchins. It is curious to observe how unwilling they are to have their children gazed on by strangers from this cause, and how quickly they convey them away from your sight, if they observe that you stop to admire them. With us, parents are gratified to hear their children praised for their personal appearance; with them, it gives great annoyance. They are always in dread of a particular squint of the eyes called *jetta-*

1. When motoring in this same part of the country, and under a cloudless sky, I was astonished to see drops of a colourless liquid appear on the windscreen: these were very sticky and difficult to remove.

tura, which some possess, and to which they ascribe all kinds of cala-mities. If their eye meets that of such a person, they are sure to anticipate some misfortune, unless they have taken some immediate steps to neutralise the effect; and you will be amused to hear with what ease this may be accomplished, but it must be done at once. They have only to point their fore and little fingers towards the person; they must take care that it be not seen, else they offend the *jettatore* in a way not to be appeased, and whatever power he may possess, they may expect that he will use it against them. Another way to prevent any evil consequence is to spit in the direction of the person who possesses the evil eye; but the most usual method is to insert the thumb under the forefinger, and keep it in the direction of the *jettatore*. There are several scions of noble families at Naples who have this unfortunate squint, and they are very generally shunned by their countrymen. I have often asked those whom I found believers in this superstitious notion what instances they could produce in which they had been sufferers, and they were al-ways ready with such disasters as a sprained ankle, the death of a favourite hound or tabby-cat, the breaking of some beautiful piece of china, which they had allowed to fall at the moment the *jettatore* entered.

I find that the belief in witches is very common here, called *fat-tucchiere*, and, of course, they ascribe to them all the power which the ignorant in our own country imagine to belong to such beings. They are frequently consulted by the fair lady, who wishes to secure the constancy of her lover, and with such assistance she has no doubts of success. These old women are believed to have a particular aversion to the young and beautiful of their own sex, and whenever any ill-ness, of which there is no apparent cause, befalls them, they are sure to ascribe it to the cantrips of some witch. A Neopolitan girl once told me a story of this kind, in which she had taken a very active part. Her sister had begun to droop, and was becoming weaker and weaker every day, when some of the neighbours suspected that her illness was caused by a *fattura* (a spell), and suggested that some means should be taken to discover the author. All the reputed witches of the neighbourhood were visited, and in the house of one of them they found a sheep's head filled with pins, to which they chose to ascribe all the mischief. Partly by menaces and partly by bribes, they prevailed on the old woman to undo the spell; but, lest she should again have recourse to it, my informant waited on the most powerful *Fattucchiere* in Naples, who dwells in the St Giles of that city, called the Vicaria, and prevailed on her to employ one of her strongest spells to protect her sister. This had the desired effect, for a fairer or more healthy lass is not at present to be seen in Naples. It is curious that they have the same superstition as we have respecting witches riding on broomsticks, and there is a certain night on which they all assemble under some tree at Benevento for the same purpose... Two works have been published on this subject, which I could not procure. They are: Pietro Peperno, *De Nuce Beneventana*, and Abate Zumica, on the same subject.

The police are said to have made some attempt to suppress witchcraft, though it may be believed without success. The old woman, called *janara* by the Neapolitans, may be consulted at the Chiesa dei Santi Apostoli every Monday morning, as regularly as you can in the summer season have your fortune told on Blackheath on Sunday. I have often heard them say, 'Fly from these old wretches of women'. They believe that the witches have no power on the Fridays of March, and therefore a person ... 'born on a Friday of March', is very lucky, as he cannot be bewitched, and the reason is that they believe that our Saviour was crucified on a Friday of this month. If they use the word *sabato*, 'Saturday', they consider this word, if they pronounce it at a proper moment, a great preservation against witches.

Another strange superstition here is in evil sprits, called *maghe*, who are entrusted with immense treasure, which they are willing to surrender on some extravagant conditions. The Grotto of Pozzuoli at Naples is well known to be haunted by such a spirit, and he has offered to give up his hoards of gold and silver to any one, who shall present a new-born babe to him. There is a report at Naples, that the King is not quite exempt from the superstitious notions of his subjects, and as his treasury is seldom overflowing, they say that he made an attempt, through two of his friends, to fill it by means of this spirit, but the condition was too extravagant for even His Majesty to fulfil.

They seem to have no superstition respecting the shades of the departed revisiting their former haunts, unless we consider the *monaciello*, or little Monk, to be of this kind. He is usually an attendant of old palaces, and of course causes much annoyance. The Villa Gallo[1] at Naples is said to be haunted by one of these gentlemen; and one of

1. This villa has been demolished and a block of flats built on the site.

my friends, who occupied it during the summer season, had much difficulty in procuring any attendance from his servants after nightfall. They never could be induced to move except in pairs, and some of them stoutly maintained that they had seen the *monaciello*. This beneficent household demon may be propitiated by food, which they expect to see converted into gold; and hence, when anyone has had a sudden increase of fortune, they say, *Forse avrà il monaciello in casa*, 'perhaps he has had the little Monk in his house'; but he must not boast of such supernatural gifts, else they vanish as they come.

You are constantly told in Italy by a servant, when any favourite article is lost or damaged, that it is the spirit that has done the mischief. While seated in the drawing-room one morning, the *major-domo* was employed in arranging some china in the next chamber, when a cup was heard to fall, and when he was asked what he was about, he very gravely came forward and told us that the cup had been thrown down by *lo spirito*.

Nurses still retain the custom of frightening children by what they call *mammone*, which is generally made to assume the exaggerated figure of some animal. This is, no doubt, the Mormon, or Lupus, handed down from ancient times. To stop the cries of the child, the nurses used to threaten to give it up to the wolf. You may recollect the fable of Æsop, entitled the 'Old Woman and the Wolf'. She says: 'Cease your crying; if you don't, this very moment, I shall give you up to the wolf.' At Capo di Monte, the nurse made it assume the form of a bird; here again we have the *strix*, the horned owl, of which Ovid (*Fast.* vi. 135) says ... 'They fly by night, and search for children requiring the assistance of their nurse.'

They frighten children, also, with the *maramao* or *parasacco* – malicious demons, to whom they threaten to give them up.

It was in conversation on such subjects that several hours passed pleasantly enough; but what had delighted me most is a discovery which I have accidentally made on a classical subject. Our conversation happened to turn on the fig-tree, and I inquired if he had ever heard of double figs. I find from the judge that they are by no means uncommon, being called *ficaccette*, or *accocchiatelle*. In Naples it seems that they are sold in the streets by people, who hawk them about, calling out, *accocchiatelle e mmosce*. From his description they are the fruit of the *ficus carica*, of which I spoke before, as being a very fine species of

Cilento; they are split in two, and then two figs are squeezed together, with the skin of both figs outermost. They have a peculiar appearance when thus put together, being called by the Sicilians *chiappe di fichi*, from their resemblance to the *chiappa*, 'breech' . . . Pliny also alludes to it (xx. 23, 2) . . . 'Diocles administered to the dropsical garlic in the double fig to clear the bowels.' . . . [Ramage here discourses on the splitting of figs.]

Figs are still used by the epicure to produce the diseased enlargement of the liver, which was considered so great a delicacy by the Romans Horace (*Sat.* ii. 8, 88). It was called *ficatum*, and curiously enough the Italian word for liver is *fegato*, evidently a corruption of the old Latin word *ficatum* . . . Of course we still have here the ficedula feeding on the fig as of old, now called the *beccafico*, the 'fig-pecker', a tiny bird of most exquisite flavour, as I have often found at Naples; so small, indeed, and with such soft bones, that the whole is masticated without difficulty . . .

I was struck by a remark which the judge made to his son-in-law, respecting a friend, of whom they were speaking. He said, *A mangiato di pane con loglio* – 'he has eaten bread mixed with darnel', and by that he meant that he was *melancolico*, a little cracked in the head. I found that they have an idea that this effect is caused by eating bread which has been so mixed . . .

I was sorry to part with my good friend and his family. The judge was full of intelligence on many subjects – as fine a specimen of the well-informed Italian gentleman as could be found; but still he was a proof of the truth of what Voltaire remarks (*Essai sur les Mœurs*, ch. lxxxii.) – 'Every man is the creature of the age in which he lives; very few are able to raise themselves above the ideas of their times.' He could not get rid of some of the superstitious notions of those among whom he lived; but referring to Lo Monaco, who, I had tried to convince him, must be making a fool of the whole province, he said solemnly as we parted, *Dominaddio non paga lo sabbato* – 'The Lord God does not pay his accounts every Saturday night', a very expressive proverb, which the Italians use when they mean that he will by-and-by pay with accumulated interest . . .

I need not tell you, who are so well acquainted with the various phases of human nature, that it is dangerous for a layman to poach on ecclesiastical preserves. Lo Monaco had, indeed, taken a true gauge of the superstitious nature of the lower orders of his countrymen, but he had forgotten that he had to contend with a large corporation like the Roman Church, that would not allow itself to be thus brought into ridicule with impunity. Not many miles distant were the monks of St Biagio, who had from time immemorial been imposing on the people in the same way, and we may imagine the dismay that they felt when they heard of the success which was attending Lo Monaco's miracle. I do not doubt that they made serious representations at Rome on the impropriety of allowing a layman to interfere in a matter which belonged more peculiarly to the Church, and you will hear hereafter of the close of thè farce . . .

IX

Y o u have heard that I was detained at Scalea yesterday by the unfavourable state of the weather. Towards evening there seemed some prospects of a change, and it was agreed that I should be called by one of the boatmen, if they determined to start . . . Accordingly, a little after midnight I was roused, and proceeded at once to the house of the captain of the guard, under whose command, as the boat was carrying government despatches, it was placed . . .

It was a beautiful and calm night, lighted only by the stars of heaven rolling in their appointed course above us. All was silent, except the regular and measured sound of the oars as they propelled us forward, or when the boatmen beguiled thir labour by joining in some wild and melancholy air of their country. The effect must have been striking to those, if any such there were, who happened to be passing along the shore. The music was of a wilder and bolder strain than that which I have ever heard in the vicinity of Venice or along the coasts of the Adriatic; and when the whole joined in chorus, the sound came back to us re-echoed from the shore. These men were scarcely conscious of fatigue, as they rowed to music. Wondrous is the strength of cheerfulness . . . As the dawn approached it became intensely cold, and as my dress was suited for the heat of mid-day, you can believe that I found it little protection at this hour. Still time passed on, and the sun at last rose, shaded slightly by the mists of the night, though its appearance predicted that cold was not that of which we should have long to complain. I could not help thinking of the beautiful description by Dante (*Purgatorio*, xxx. 22) of the rising sun . . .

It was indeed such a morning as that which suggested Dante's description, but a short time served to dissipate the roseate hues, and the unclouded splendour of the sun threatened soon to drive away all the fancies of the poet. There was a slight swell from the south-west, which proved an annoyance to our captain, whose acquaintance with the sea was of a very limited kind, and I observed that he cast many a longing look to the land. At last he directed that the boat should be turned to the shore, and proposed that we should walk along the coast, that he might have some respite from his sufferings. The air was still cool, and though every step sunk deeply into the sand, the change was not unpleasant. It had, however, nearly brought our forward movements to a speedy close, as we fell in with a party of custom-house officers, who regarded us with much suspicion . . . My appearance at last attracted attention, and, to prevent any unnecessary rudeness, I presented my passport, which completely changed their demeanour towards us. They pressed me strongly to accompany them to their village, called Belvedere,[1] about three miles from the coast, and which they assured me was one of the most beautiful spots in Italy, as its name implied. I saw, however, that the captain did not relish this proposal, as my name was entered in his papers, and he would have to give an account of me when he reached Paola. One of the officers offered to remedy this matter by inserting a statement in his papers that I had left at Belvedere. Still I saw that the captain might get into difficulties with the authorities, who might imagine that I had been cast into the sea, and I did not think it a gentlemanly act to throw any suspicions on my friend the captain. After we had walked several miles the sun began to be too oppressive, and we then had recourse to the boat. The mountains appeared rising to a great height in the interior. The loftiest is called Mondea, and from its top I am told that the Tuscan and Ionian seas are clearly to be distinguished, and that Sicily may be seen when the horizon is unclouded . . .

A slight breeze sprang up, when I roused the whole party, and within a few seconds we were all on board, the sails set, and the boat scudding at a considerable rate through the water. It was a change as sudden and as complete as in any artificial phantasmagoria you have

1. Belvedere Marittimo.

ever seen. A dead calm again succeeded, and the oar was again had recourse to. We saw a number of small villages on the heights, generally at a distance of three or four miles from the coast, so placed to guard against the piratical incursions of the Turks, from whose attacks they have only become safe within the last thirty years. One of the villages was called Albanese,[1] from a colony of Albanians who settled here in the time of the famous Scanderbeg, about AD 1460; and I understand that there are many villages of this people scattered throughout the kingdom of Naples, retaining the language and customs of their ancestors. I hope that I may be able to visit some of these people; I regret, however, that I shall not have the opportunity of examining Guardia, said to be a colony of French Protestants from Provence. They are no longer, indeed, members of the Reformed Church, though they are said still to speak the language of the Troubadours ... They resisted all attempts to change their faith, till superior numbers overwhelmed them; and after the massacre of all those who were able to bear arms, the survivors were compelled to conform to the Papal authority ...

Exactly as the sun began to descend behind the horizon, we entered the small harbour of Paola with flying colours, or, to speak more humbly, streamers. It was soon noised abroad that an Englishman had arrived, when I was surprised to be addressed in broken English by one of the custom-house officers, who had served on board our fleet when we occupied Sicily. I entreated his assistance to enable me to avoid all difficulty with the police, and I at once got clear by the kindness of the *sotto-intendente*, to whom my guide conducted me. Among my packet of letters was one for Don Francesco Ziccari, a gentleman of Paola, who has received me with the utmost kindness.

My host pressed me so kindly to remain a day with him to recover from my fatigues, that I yielded without much hesitation, more particularly as I understood that I should the following morning have the protection of a body of soldiers in passing a mountain ridge, which might otherwise prove dangerous from the numerous bandits that are known to frequent it. The money collected at the custom-house of Paola is to be forwarded to Cosenza, the capital of the province, and I consider myself lucky in being able to take advantage of the convoy. I have no doubt, from everything that I hear, that I am approaching a

1. S. Caterina Albanese.

dangerous part of the country; travelling, however, in the quiet un-assuming way I am doing, I think there are a good many chances in my favour, and if I am robbed, I have taken care that they shall not be great gainers. The danger of which I am most in dread is, lest finding me to be an Englishman, and having exaggerated notions of the riches of that nation, they should demand a ransom, which might prove a serious inconvenience. Still, you know that there is no great good to be gained without incurring some danger, and, as I am of a hopeful dis-position and not easily turned aside from any plan which I have formed, I shall not be deterred from proceeding forward unless I am fully satis-field that I have no chance of escaping.

The ridge of the Apennines has now again approached close to the shore, as I found along the coast at Maratea, and rises about five thou-sand feet, with a very precipitous declivity. At the foot of it lies Paola, which has the appearance of a thriving city, and I believe that this arises from a new road which connects it with the fertile valley of Cosenza, for the produce of which it serves as an outlet. It is chiefly, however, celebrated as the birthplace of a saint, Francis di Paola, who founded the order of the monks called Minimi, 1474, and of whom the inhabi-tants are naturally proud. The monastery, erected 1626, about a mile from the city, is in a picturesque situation, at the mouth of a beautiful glen – a position which reminded me forcibly of Drumlanrig Castle, the princely seat of the Duke of Buccleuch, in Dumfries-shire. Beneath flows a small stream called Patyco, which is evidently derived from that of the ancient city Patycus,[1] believed to have been placed in this vicinity, though it was of little note, being mentioned by only one Greek geographer. This monastery rivals in size that of La Cava, without having any pretensions to architectural beauty, pillars in front being of the Corinthian order, with Ionic capitals sadly defective in their proportions. The French confiscated its revenues, and when the present family was restored, the monastery was re-established with diminished splendour. The monks, twenty-six in number, speak with great horror of the French, and I was amused to hear them give as an instance of their sacrilege the destruction of some pigeons, which are considered sacred to St Francis. I inquired if the breed had become extinct, but they told me that no sooner had they again taken possession of their monastery than the pigeons made their appearance in their old

1. As yet unidentified but believed to be near Paola.

haunts, aware, it would seem, that their friends had returned.[1] They had contrived to conceal the silver statue of St Francis from the marauding hands of the French, and it is now exhibited in a small shrine, where I found a priest performing mass to one solitary woman, the exhibitions of whose grief were truly painful, and strongly contrasted with the unmoved countenance of the priest . . .

In the portico of the monastery are many rude representations of the numerous miracles which had been performed by St Francis. Among others, they point out a fountain, which, like Moses, he had caused to spring forth from the rock, and whose waters are considered by the peasants as a remedy for every sort of disease . . .

My companion I found to be highly intelligent, and, among other things, I collected from him the peculiar customs observed on the death of an individual. It is first announced by the screams of the women, and in former times by the strange custom of opening and shutting their windows with great violence, so much so that the shutters were usually torn from their hinges. The body is then placed with due solemnity with the feet towards the door, while the men sit in silence, the women beating their breasts and throwing handfuls of hair over the body. The priests are then admitted to sing psalms and offer up prayers for the deceased while the bells of the church are tolled. In Naples the body is attended to the grave or vault by the secular clergy and a deputation of five different confraternities, who follow with tapers in their hands. These confraternities consist of men who have made vows to attend funerals, and who imagine that they may in this way procure forgiveness of their sins. A white linen robe conceals them entirely from the knowledge of their fellow-citizens, as there is no part seen except their eyes peering through two small holes. On reaching the church the body is placed in the middle, with a brazier near it, on which incense is burnt. The Requiem is then sung, and the body is left in the hands of the priests. During three days the friends continue to receive visits of condolence, and custom compels them to be seated on the bare floor, and as no fire is lighted in the house for several days, their friends furnish them with food. In the room of the deceased a lamp is kept burning; and if the disease was consumption, the law compels them to destroy everything touched by the deceased, and to fumigate the house.

1. A large flock of white doves was very much in evidence when I visited this sanctuary in May 1962.

An unmarried girl is crowned with flowers at burial. After the death of a relative the men do not shave their beards for a month. If a stranger dies, women are hired to attend his funeral and wail over the dead.

On our return from the monastery we met a woman of Guardia decked out in her gala dress; a red petticoat appeared beneath a blue gown, which was bordered with crimson. The sleeves of black velvet were attached to the body of the dress by means of laces, which allowed under-garments to be seen between the elbow and shoulder; her head was tastefully adorned with a white handkerchief. I find, on more minute examination, that these French Protestants had settled here at an earlier period than I had imagined; it is said towards the middle of the sixteenth century. I found an old volume on Calabria (*Della Calabria illustrata Opera varia Istorica* del R. P. Giovanni Fiore, predicatore Capuccino da Cropani, 1691) in my host's library, and it is there stated that the inhabitants are *oltramontani*, and as having introduced the new opinions of Luther, spreading the infection to several villages around. Attempts were made to convince them of their errors, but as they continued obdurate, the viceroy of the kingdom of Naples, Duke Alcala, sent, in 1561, troops to bring them to their senses . . .

The 1st of May, *La Majuma*, is celebrated with much ceremony in this part of Italy. Their doors and windows are ornamented with green boughs . . . and garlands . . . of flowers, while the streets are traversed by youthful musicians . . .

At Christmas, I find that there is the same exchange of presents as with us, and that they have a large cake, to which they have given the name of *San Martino*, because they implore the aid of this saint when they pray for abundance. The civic guard go about singing, and demand a *strena* – a present. They also make *paste fritte* in oil and honey, as the Romans used to offer to Janus.

At Easter, servants present eggs to their masters, which they call *coluri*; eggs made up in round balls of paste are called *San Martino*. On the festival of St Luke, the 18th of October, they have at table a dish called *coccia*, composed of wheat or maize, boiled and mixed with chestnuts, then eaten with milk.

It is curious that they should have some superstitious notions which prevail with us; they are in terror if they sit down thirteen at table, if they spill the salt, if the candle falls, or if the light is extinguished. One of their proverbs is *Allegrezza di venerdì, pianto di domenica* – 'Joy on Friday, weeping on Sunday' . . .

The higher classes of women amuse themselves with embroidery, while the lower spin with a hand-spindle, twisting it with great dexterity as they walk along. Others of them are employed in working *pezzuole*, a kind of network or lace to ornament the fronts of shirts . . . It is worked on a frame filled with feathers, which they call *piumaccio*. The articles are called *pezzili, frisi*, or *puntani*. Paola and Lecce are famed for this kind of manufacture.

The peasant receives for a day's work one *carlino* (fourpence of our money) and a meal.

The father of my host had been a man of some literary attainments, and had written a work on the antiquities of Paola, which had never been given to the world. I spent some hours very pleasantly in looking over it; its information, however, was of too minute and local a nature to interest any one except his fellow-citizens. He had investigated one point, which is of some importance to those interested in the ancient geography of Italy. The city of Temesa,[1] or Tempsa, mentioned by Homer (*Odyss*. i. 184), was placed by him about twenty miles south of Paola, near a promontory called Mesa, which he considered an abbreviation of the name of the ancient city. There some ruins are still seen, and near it he says that there appears to have been some mines. Ovid (*Met.*. xv. 706), (*Fast*. v. 441), refers to them . . .

I spent a delightful evening with my host, who had assembled a large number of his friends to meet me. Many of them were intelligent, and showed a knowledge of England and its institutions which surprised me. We had an interesting conversation on the eventful history of Italy . . .

The inhabitants of this country have not much of religion, such as we understand by that word, but they are far more devout than we are. They have been brought up in the school of slavery, and yet talk to them of liberty, and if they feel they are safe in showing their real sentiments, they spring up in the greatest ecstasy. They are like their own Vesuvius, which after appearing to have slumbered for many years, bursts forth suddenly, more terrible than ever, and causes the whole land to tremble. I can see that there is a reign of terror everywhere – I do not allude to brigands, but to the repression exercised by government

1. Not yet identified, *see* bibliography.

against intellect and against all who show a desire to improve their minds. The ecclesiastical authorities rule supreme, and the Jesuits, as I found in Naples, have got hold of the education of the people. The high nobility, more particularly, favour their pretensions. I got acquainted with their professors at Naples, and found them men of great learning, distinguished for erudition, and first-rate teachers, as far as I could judge from the pupils they turned out. Yet we know that their system is retrograde, strictly scholastic, and incapable of elevating the moral level of humanity, and, wherever they have been allowed to use their influence, they have repressed the energies of the mind of man. Like to those phosphorescent fireflies which appeared the other evening as we whiled away our time at Velia, their teaching is brilliant and reflects light, but there is no heat . . .

X

NEXT morning at daybreak I left Paola, and placed myself at the foot of the mountain to wait for the party of soldiers who were proceeding to Cosenza. I had taken the precaution of hiring a mule, as I understood that the fatigue of ascending the mountain would be excessive, though a good road with many windings has been constructed along the face of it. I did not wait long before I saw two mules and a party of about thirty soldiers approaching. I directed my muleteer to proceed forward, while I lingered behind to admire the beauty of the scenery . . . The morning was still cool, the air was redolent of perfumed herbs, while the chorus of birds, so seldom heard in the part of Italy to which I have been accustomed, re-echoed along the sides of the mountain as I climbed slowly up on my bobtailed mule. The lark rose high in the air, and warbled her notes as she ascended . . .

As we approached the top, nature assumed a wilder appearance; trees and plants of a colder climate began to show themselves. The beech and oak were growing most luxuriantly, and had acquired a large size, but there was one spot where a tremendous storm had cleared the face of the mountain of every tree which had once covered it. Some were torn up by the roots, others were broken across, showing the enormous force which nature had here employed. It was not merely a few trees, but the devastation extended for upwards of a mile, till a curve in the direction of the hill had broken the force of the tempest. I had never seen such a wonderful exhibition of the force of nature. As we approached the top, I pushed rapidly forward, that I might have time to look around. On reaching it, I was startled to see a party of armed men under the trees, and expected to be at once in the midst of a bloody mêlée. One of the soldiers, however, relieved my alarm by stating that it was a body of men sent to meet us at the most dangerous point. It was a spot well adapted for the purpose of attack, as the soldiers would reach it worn out by the fatigue of the ascent. There was scarcely any level ground on the top; the descent became now much more gradual, and the eye wandered across a broad valley to the lofty and dark mountains of the Sila. It was in this vicinity that the brigands seized, some years ago, an Austrian general (the Austrians were then in possession of the kingdom), who was second in command, and carried him off to their fastnesses . . .

At last we reached the small village of San Fili, and I saw at once that I had got among a race of men different from any which I had hitherto met in Italy. They were small and well built, with a dark expression of countenance by no means pleasing. Their hair was coarse and black, often frizzed like that of negroes, though generally perfectly straight. They were evidently of a wild and lawless character, and I found afterwards that they were believed to be principally supported by the pillage of the neighbouring country. The men were dressed in blue jackets and breeches, while their conical-shaped hat was tastefully adorned with ribands of various colours. The women had all strongly-marked features, very unprepossessing in appearance. In their costume there was nothing to attract the attention except a piece of triangular pasteboard, which was placed in front to support the breast, called *pettiglia*, and a leathern apron (*faldale*), beautifully ornamented with various devices; but what struck me forcibly was the surprising regularity and dazzling whiteness of their teeth.

At the village of San Fili the soldiers intended to remain till the heat had abated; I felt, however, unwilling to lose the remainder of the day, and started at once for Cosenza. After descending about six miles, we reached the great public road leading to Naples, and then proceeded up a beautiful valley, through which flowed the river Crati, the ancient Crathis. It was well cultivated; indeed, I may say, the only extensive piece of country in a state of cultivation since I left Naples. The produce is chiefly wheat and maize, but fruit trees also abounded: pears, apples, orange and citron trees, alternated with each other. It might evidently be made to be a land flowing with milk and honey; but when I tell you that no one dare issue forth except in arms and in company, you will agree with me that your Welsh mountains and my Highland glens, with all their barrenness, are preferable places of abode.

Cosenza is situated at the top of this valley, where the hills rise to a considerable height on both sides, and, consequently, at this period of the year, a residence in it is not particularly pleasant from the stifling heat. The Prince of Satriano had been kind enough to furnish me with a letter to Cavaliere di Caria, the royal governor of the province, and ... I proceeded to the palace of his excellency, by whom I was received with more attention than I had any right to expect, or even than I could have wished ... and am now lodged in the house of the highest functionary of the province. He is a gentleman of great talents, and possesses much information on a variety of subjects.

I had not yet determined in what direction I should proceed from Cosenza; some facts, however, communicated to me by my host have deterred me from putting one part of my plan in execution. There is a village called Acri in the mountains of La Sila, about twenty miles north-east of Cosenza, which I had some idea of visiting, as it is the site of an ancient town, though of no great note, and I thought I should there see a true specimen of the real Calabrese mountaineer ... [Ramage goes on to relate the Governor's reasons for dissuading him from visiting Acri on account of the 'audacious' brigands].

I am sorry that my project of visiting the dense forests of La Sila has thus been nipped in the bud, and that I must be satisfied with the Pisgah view which I am here able to obtain. It is a high table-land, forty miles long, and from sixteen to twenty miles broad, extending through the greatest part of Calabria Citra, and even into the more southern province called Calabria Ultra II. Its highest peaks are clothed with magnificent firs (*Pinus sylvestris*), and the lower ones with oak, beeches, and elms, affording excellent pasturage in summer for large herds of cattle ... The forests of Sila furnished timber for the navies of antiquity (*Strabo*, vi. p. 261), and the Neapolitan government still make use of them for the same purpose, though it is said that they are becoming much less productive from the wastefulness and improvidence with which they are managed. Corigliano is the principal depôt for the timber felled in the province, and also for the manna trade and liquorice factories.

Giving up my intention of visiting the table-land of La Sila, I have determined to advance southwards, though I fear, from the ominous looks of his excellency when I inquired if I could proceed to the south with safety, that there is no part of his province much more free from brigands than another. Towards evening, I strolled through the capital of Higher Calabria, and found more appearance of wealth and comfort than anything I had yet observed since I had left Naples. Not a single beggar annoyed me, though there were many poor people around. The streets are narrow, as all Italian towns are, to protect them from the direct rays of the sun, though it must cause the interior of their houses to be stifling from want of ventilation. It is intersected by the river Bussento, over which are two good bridges. The Tribunale, or palace of justice, is a building of considerable pretensions; and an old castle, now used as a barrack, stands on a very commanding position. I sauntered through the castle by permission of the commanding officer, finding, however, nothing worthy of remark, except that I observed that the descendants of the ancient Romans, who are now its inmates, are equally lovers of poetry as in former times. I saw a well-known line of Dante scribbled on the wall (*Inferno*, v. 103) . . .

I was curious to see the burial place of Alaric, the celebrated King of the Goths, who died here AD 410; and as he was afraid, from the cruelties he had committed on the inhabitants, that his dead body would be abused, he gave directions that the river Bussento should be diverted from its course at its confluence with the Crati, and his body having been there buried, the river was again allowed to flow in its old channel. The peasants have an idea that large treasures were buried with the body, and I believe that various unsuccessful attempts have been made to recover them.[1] I visited the spot where the two rivers met, a picturesque burying-ground, but I did not see any reason to suppose that the river Bussento had ever been diverted from its present course . . .

I am sorry to say that I find it impossible to understand the language of the Calabrese peasant, and my Italian is equally unintelligible to him. The Calabrese dialect is peculiar; I am not, however, sufficiently versed in it to decide whether it may not be the pronunciation rather than

1. A short time ago another attempt was made to discover this burial place but it met with no success.

the roots of the language, in which it differs from the pure Italian. Several books have been published in it, and I believe that there used to be a society to promote the cultivation of Calabrese literature; but the political troubles have put an end to every association that had the slightest tendency to enlighten the community . . .

I have been anxious to get acquainted with what is being done in regard to the education of the country, but it is not easy to do so. The authorities are not willing to say much on the subject; they maintain that the law is perfectly sufficient for the purpose, if it could be carried out, which it seems difficult to do. It appears that every parish is obliged to support a schoolmaster; but as they generally took part in the late unsuccessful insurrection, few of them have been allowed to retain their situations. An order has been lately issued, forbidding the election of any one except a priest, and it is said that many parishes have, on this account, refused to proceed to an election. While I was residing at Sorrento, last year, I visited one of these schools, and found that the branches of education taught in the higher-class academy by four masters were grammar, arithmetic, algebra, and navigation; but the small number of hours devoted to study precluded the possibility of any progress being made in what they professed to teach. I hear that in Murat's time the attendance at the primary schools alone amounted to 120,000 children; at present, I cannot hear that these primary schools can be said to be in existence at all. Every difficulty is thrown in their way, and the government seems well satisfied that ignorance should be the predominating feature of their people. I inquired whether private individuals were permitted to open schools on their own account; few of such are to be found, and where they are allowed, as in Naples, they are subject to such strict regulations and so severe a surveillance, that the government plainly makes it to be known that it regards all such establishments with no favour. It is curious that in respect to elementary instruction Naples presents better opportunities for the instruction of young girls than for boys. The establishment of Miracle,[1] founded by Murat for girls of noble birth, has acquired a well-deserved reputation.

I had seen nothing but mules since I entered the province, and I inquired of his excellency where were the spirited horses of Calabria, of

1. S. Maria dei Miracole was a Franciscan Monastery until 1808 and is now the R. Liceo Ginnasio Femminile.

which I had often heard. He ordered his groom to bring out a few good specimens: they were small, high-spirited, and of a compact build; but he allowed that their numbers were rapidly diminishing, as mules were gradually taking their place. He told me of another species, which is becoming rare, called *Riccio*, or curled. It differs little from those that were before me, except in the hair, which assumes a frizzled appearance when it is bushy and long, and is like scales when it is smooth and short. I have seen no oxen or sheep; these are pastured, particularly the latter, in great numbers on the grassy slopes of La Sila, to which the wealthier inhabitants of Cosenza migrate for the summer months, as this city is reckoned unwholesome from the heat. Though his excellency was unwilling to allow it, I have heard from others that the only way they are able to secure their safety is to pay *black mail* to the heads of some band of brigands, who secure them from all others.

Cosenza has a small theatre, to which I accompanied his excellency, and heard some of Rossini's music respectably performed. It was crowded by the fair ladies of Calabria. I am ungallant enough to confess that I was not particularly struck by their personal appearance . . .

XI

I DO not mean to conceal from you that I have some misgivings as to the wisdom of my present proceedings, and feel considerable alarm from the reports that have reached me from all quarters respecting the unsettled state of the country. Be assured, however, that I shall take every precaution that prudence may dictate, except giving up my onward movement. Indeed, I do not see that it makes much difference in which direction I turn my steps, as all seem equally dangerous.

I took leave of his excellency this morning at an early hour, with many entreaties on his part to be very cautious; if I met with misfortune, I might rest assured that he would attend to any representation I might forward to him . . . His excellency seemed evidently to consider that it was a foolhardy undertaking, and that no good would come of it. He begged me at least to take a muleteer, and not attempt to travel on foot. To this, however, I was averse, and gave as a reason that such a mode of travelling indicated the possession of money, whereas a traveller on foot drew no attention . . .

I wandered at least ten miles along the great road, bordered in the immediate vicinity of Cosenza with white mulberry-trees growing in great luxuriance, and with the lofty Cocuzzolo overhanging me to the west. Here and there were patches of cultivated ground, and in the distance I saw villages perched on the declivities of the mountains. The first I reached was Rogliano, situated on a lofty hill, which commanded a magnificent view of the picturesque country around. Here I paid my respects to Don Giuseppe Politi, the judge of the district, who showed me great civility, and invited me to remain to dinner. I spent several pleasant hours with him, and had some interesting conversation respecting the state of the country. The people are generally in wretched poverty, and he seems to think that it is increasing. They live chiefly on bread made from chestnuts, which are gathered in the extensive forests of La Sila, and in winter they migrate to Sicily in search of food, though I could not make out how they could procure it there more easily than in Calabria. With all their poverty, I was amused to hear that these peasants have generally two families – one which they leave to face the winter's storm in Calabria, and another in the more sunny clime of Sicily; at least so I was told by my host. Rogliano had been destroyed in the earthquake of 1638, which caused greater damage to this part of Calabria than that of 1783. My host spoke in high terms of the mode of agriculture pursued in this part of the province. I confess that nothing met my eye this morning, as I laboured through the burning sun, to induce me, who had been accustomed to the heavy crops of Mid-Lothian, to suppose that they were in any way distinguished above their neighbours. He considered the wine to be good; to me it had a peculiar flavour which was not agreeable.

In talking of the religious habits of the Calabrese, he acknowledged that they possessed peculiar ideas respecting the mode of worshipping their Madonnas. If they do not obtain their wishes, they enclose the shrine of the Madonna as if in prison, and upbraid her in no measured language, in hopes that she may be shamed out of her conduct, and be induced to grant their prayers. It is in these remote parts of Italy that the customs of their Pagan ancestors have been preserved in their greatest purity . . .

My host was fond of horticulture, and pointed out a shrub, which he called *giurgiulea*, possessing the peculiar property of increasing the milk of ladies who are nursing. There is more likelihood that this plant may have such an effect than that some Madonna, of whom he spoke, should assist the childbirth labours of the ladies of Calabria . . .

I find that they have the custom here of allowing the beard to grow for a month after the death of a relative, and that they show their grief also by wearing their linen unwashed and unchanged till it is worn away by filth. This custom, however, I suspect, is observed by many who are not mourning for the death of a friend. I remarked also round the necks of the children small pieces of rock-salt, which they imagine to have some power of guarding against the effect of an evil eye. The young women employ for the same purpose a small silver frog, called *granula*, probably a corruption of *ranula*, and some of them, which I examined, were executed with much taste.

When the judge heard that I was determined to proceed ten miles farther to the village Diano, he offered to give me a letter to his colleague, who might otherwise throw some difficulties in my way, as he was a testy old gentleman, and always glad to have an opportunity of exercising his authority. Of course I accepted his kind offer gratefully, and, having thanked him for his hospitable entertainment, bade him an affectionate farewell. The heat was even greater than I had yet experienced, and it required to muster up all my energies to continue my course along a dusty road. My directions were to proceed forward to Carpanzano, and there inquire my way to Diano. For six miles I met not a single individual, and saw no human habitation till I at last reached a few huts, which I found to be Carpanzano. Here I was informed that Diano was four miles distant from the great public road, and that the country through which I must pass was thickly wooded. I confess that I felt somewhat startled at this intelligence – not so much from the chance of meeting brigands, as lest I should be benighted in the wood. I was told that there was a small footpath that would lead me to it, and if I did not stray, I would have no difficulty in reaching Diano. Shutting my eyes to all consequences, I left the public road, and plunged into a narrow and deep glen, with a crystal stream running along the bottom. With all my anxiety, I could not help stopping to admire the beauty of the scenery. The banks of the glen were thickly wooded with fine oaks and chestnut-trees, while many flowers, the names of which I knew not, were in luxuriant blossom, and perfumed the air. The heat of the day had now abated, and the birds were singing in joyful chorus, preventing that feeling of loneliness which perfect silence is calculated to produce. The footpath ran along the side of the stream, and, on turning a corner, I lighted suddenly in the midst of a party of young Calabrese damsels, who were employed in washing. They were surprised at my sudden appearance, but we had much difficulty in understanding each other. They were the daughters of a miller, whose house I saw at a short distance. From them I received some further directions respecting my road, and then began to mount a rugged declivity. The country continued to be covered with wood. I saw no one, nor did I meet with a single habitation, till I reached the summit of a ridge, from which I looked down on a thickly wooded valley. As I sauntered along, I was much struck by finding here and there little boxes stuck up against the trees, in which a Madonna was placed, and where the peasant might offer up his prayers. There is evidently much more of the appearance of religion here than with us. You may call it mere superstition; still there is a recognition of a Supreme Being, though in an imperfect form, and you meet with it in all places. With us it is confined to stated places and stated times; in Italy you are reminded wherever you go. I know not how to account for this devotion of the Italians to the worship of the Virgin Mary, but it strikes an ultra-Protestant from Scotland very forcibly ...

On reaching the summit of the ridge, I saw in the valley several villages; which of them was Diano I knew not. At a short distance I observed a large building, which I had no doubt must be a monastery, and proceeding to it began to hammer at the door with great violence; no attention, however, was paid to my summons. While I was thus employed, and considering what further steps I should take, a peasant-girl passed, from whom I tried to discover whether it was inhabited; it was vain, as I could not understand a syllable she said. I contrived, however, to convey to her that I wished to proceed to Diano, which she pointed out to me. On reaching the village, I found the judge employed in teaching a little child to read, and having presented my letter, inquired respecting the state of the country, and whether I ran any risk of falling into the hands of brigands. He acknowledged that it was dangerous to travel without a guard, and offered to send with me to-morrow two of the *guardia urbana*, a kind of rural police. To this proposal, however, I refused to accede, as I do not believe that these police officers would be of the slightest use, if I got into danger. I feel that it would only be drawing the attention of the country to me, and thereby make it more certain that I should be waylaid. The judge wrote a note, and giving it to a servant, told me to accompany him to a house, where I should be accommodated with a bed. On our way, I could not help pausing to listen to the beautiful notes of the nightingales, as they answered each other . . . You may imagine my annoyance when I found by my reception that the note of the judge was nothing else than a kind of billet on the householder . . . [Ramage then asked to be taken to the clergyman 'as a person in whom I might repose confidence'. He was received with much 'genuine kindness'.] . . . and whether it was the agreeable nature of my conversation, or more likely some excellent wine, which we consumed in considerable quantity, we became at last great friends. It was long past midnight ere we closed our bacchanalian orgies, and he ended by stating that he was happy to have made my acquaintance . . . [Ramage took a guide the next morning to conduct him to Nocera Terinese. He 'descended into the channel of the Savuto, the ancient Sabbatus, which rises in the table-land of La Sila from a fissure in the hill at a spot called La Fontano del Labro'. He 'crept along slowly for several hours' till he came to a deep glen – here the guide proposed they should re-cross the river to avoid the mouth of the glen where brigands might be lurking. They ascended the bank which was covered with thick brushwood, and which Ramage found alarming by the 'number of vipers and serpents that we disturbed while basking in the sun'. After some time he left the river and struck across country to the 'miserable village' of San Mango d'Aquino where he parted from his guide and went on alone to Nocera.]

It is prettily situated on the declivity of a hill, and near it flows the river Savuto, falling into the sea about two miles below Nocera. This is the first interruption in that mountain ridge which I had crossed at Paola. The valley is about one mile in breadth, when the mountains again rise suddenly to a considerable height, and are wooded to the top. It is one of the most romantic spots that I ever beheld; and as I now felt perfectly safe, I lay down under the shade of a tree, and enjoyed in undisturbed quiet the beauties of nature.

It was necessary, however, that I should take some steps to procure a lodging, and I accordingly entered Nocera, where I found the people crowding to church to wait on the bishop, who was visiting this part of his diocese for the purpose of confession. It is said that many of the priests employ this power to discover the political sentiments of their people, and convey the information to government. All those who neglect this sacred ordinance of the Church are reported to the police, and taken under their surveillance, as likely to be disaffected to government.

I went forward with the crowd into the church, though I saw many inquisitive eyes upon me, and resolved to act like Naaman in the Temple of Rimmon, bowing my head that I might excite no uproar among the people. This was neither the place nor the time to show my heretical opinions. The church was small, and closely packed by the Calabrese of the lower orders. On entering, there was the holy water, which on this great occasion was sprinkled by an attendant priest, as you crossed the threshold, but in general you must apply it with your own hands. This custom, as you well know, is a remnant of Paganism, like many others of the Romish Church ...

We had on this solemn occasion high mass, *Messa Cantata*, as it is called, when the priest, standing in front of the altar, sprinkles the holy water towards the congregation before he proceeds to the performance of the service. The Romans seem to have had something of the same kind when they were performing sacrifice, if Propertius (iv. 6, 7) gives a correct account ...

Is there not the same idea in the Romish Church respecting the wine, which they confine to the priests? The bishop was a venerable old man, who went through his duties with great dignity, performing the *Sacrifizio della Messa* very impressively. When the Host (*Hostia*), the wafer or consecreated bit of bread, was raised, the whole congregation prostrated themselves on the floor, as far as the crowd would permit, with unaffected piety; and yet, with Cicero (*De Nat. Deor.*, iii. 16), I could not help saying ... 'Do you think that there was ever a man so mad as to take that on which he feeds as a god?' And yet this is the distinguishing article of faith in the creed of Rome. Of course we had incense without stint, and this hot day the odour was most grateful; it may be, too, that it is good in a sanitary point of view, otherwise the smell from this weltering mass around me would have been overpowering. It is only a continuation of an ancient custom ...

The altar was lighted up with a profusion of wax-lights and lamps in beautiful figures, as is always the case on grand occasions. What can be the meaning of this? Are we to go for its explanation to Plato,

(Athen. 442A [*Com. Att.* frag. ed. Kock. i, p. 648]) . . . who says . . . 'Evil spirits love not the smell of lamps'.

We know that evil spirits are one of the bugbears of the Italians, and it is not unlikely that they have on this account continued a custom which they found prevailing in Pagan times.

The congregation consisted principally of women, and what astonished me was the small number of the more respectable class. The men seemed to be principally peasants, but the cause of this was afterwards satisfactorily explained. At the close of the service the bishop began a discourse on the merits of some saint, in whom I did not feel sufficient interest to induce me to remain, more particularly as I had still to search for my night's lodgings. I slipped away as quietly as I could, and proceeded to wait on the syndic, though I expected to have found him at church. He received me with the utmost kindness, and at once requested that I would do him the honour to spend the night in his house, promising next morning to accompany me to the ruins of Terina. It was soon noised abroad that an Englishman had arrived, when all the principal inhabitants did me the honour to wait on me, and I found myself again transformed into a personage of great importance. No British subject had ever set foot within their territory in the memory of man, and it was not, therefore, surprising that I should be an object of curiosity.

I found the syndic and all the respectable inhabitants in great excitement against the bishop and the ecclesiastical authorities, of whom they spoke in most disrespectful terms. It was the power of bearing arms that had created the turmoil, and it arose in this way. The syndic and his council had been directed to make out a list of those whom they considered trustworthy, which had been sent to the royal governor of the province. He had referred it to the ecclesiastical authorities, with orders to purge it of all who had been *legionarii soldati*, 'soldiers in the army of Murat', *carbonari*, *settari*, 'sectaries' – all, in fact, who had a black mark against their name for any political delinquency. They had only got the list lately returned, and you may imagine their great indignation when they found fifty of the richest and most influential men excluded, and none left except the poorest. They could scarcely credit their eyes, and were still more confounded when they found the syndic's name scored out. Here was the bishop to-day, and they ought to proceed to church to make confession, but they declared, as they were already under the suspicion of government, and arising principally from the information furnished by the bishop, they were resolved to set him at defiance, and had absented themselves from confession, as they did not think that they could be worse in the eyes of government than they were.

They had appointed no schoolmaster at Nocera because they could not find an individual among the clergy fit for the situation, and it was needless to fix upon a layman, as he was always rejected by the secret influence of the clergy ...

In the evening I paid a visit to the Capuchin monastery, and was introduced to an aged monk who had spent upwards of fifty years at this retired spot. He was regarded by the inhabitants as a learned astronomer, and the poor old man was kind enough to give me a lecture on the solar system, with which I could have very well dispensed; politeness to himself and friends induced me to express myself much gratified. I was not, however, sorry to get away, and, on my return to the house of my host, found a good supper prepared, chiefly of fish in various forms. I found that the river Savuto was a good fishing stream, and my host was addicted to the gentle craft, though he did not dare to penetrate far into the country, on account of its dangerous state. Mullets of a good size are caught at its mouth, and sword-fish in the months of July and August, with a kind of net which they call *indovinola*. We had a small fish – *minuselle* – which, though tiny in form, were of exquisite flavour. We had also a dish of quails, which are sometimes caught in great numbers at this period of the year. They call it 'quail fishing'. The peasantry kill large quantities of eels and trout in the mountain streams with lime, or with the juice of certain plants, *succo di certe pianticelle*, which have the effect of stupifying them.

There must have been an ancient city Nuceria, but whether this is the site may be doubtful, as I could hear of no remains in the immediate vicinity ... Nuceria is not mentioned by any ancient author, though its existence is clearly established by its coins, which have the Greek inscription NOΥΚΡΙΝΩΝ. They have on the obverse a head of Apollo crowned with laurel, and on the reverse a lion's head ...

XII

WHATEVER may be the vices of the Italians, I think you will allow that they are not deficient in hospitality and kindness to strangers. I should be inclined to say that their virtues were their own, and that the defects of their character were mainly caused by their system of government. Everything is done to repress their energies and to keep their minds in an obscure twilight, not altogether forbidding the cultivation of their intellect, but preventing, as far as possible, all benefit to be derived from mental pursuits. The clergy and the lawyers are the two classes that monopolise whatever learning is possessed by the nation. The interests of the former are intimately bound up with the maintenance of the power of the present royal family, and of course the distribution of patronage must secure the allegiance of a considerable portion of the latter. Still it was found, in the late attempts to establish a more liberal form of government, that the lawyers were by no means unwilling to have a wider arena for the display of their talents, and many of them were able members of the House of Deputies. On the other hand, the clergy were, with few exceptions, opposed to change, dreading lest the remnant of their property left by the French should be confiscated. I can perceive, by the tone of conversation held by the various classes, that the clergy have lost the respect of the educated part of the community, and that whatever calamities befall them will not be regretted. While I was at Naples, I made myself acquainted with the university course of study, and in that course nothing was left out that could be desired. Theology, jurisprudence, moral philosophy, literature, medicine, natural philosophy, and mathematics, were all on the programme; all these chairs were worthily represented; but when I began to inquire when and where the lectures were delivered, I saw that my inquiry was considered an impertinence, and that most of the programme was a mere myth. Jurisprudence and its concomitant subjects might lead the youth to Naples to debate on the various forms of political government, and what might not result from such a discussion? Yet Greek and Latin occupied a large portion of time, and some were malicious enough to maintain that this was done not without due calculation. In devoting so much time to the study of the classical

H   89

languages, it was thought that they would serve as a sort of bugbear to frighten the youth from entering upon a course of study which was so indefinitely prolonged.

I left Nocera at an early hour this morning with my friendly host, and proceeded down the banks of the Savuto, passing groves of mulberries, which were growing in great abundance. Nocera had at one time been the seat of a considerable manufacture of silk; like everything else in the kingdom, it had dwindled to nothing. The ruins of the ancient city Terina[1] are found about three miles from Nocera, close to the sea, at a spot called Torre del Piano. It had been placed at the extreme point of a hill, which has the appearance of having been levelled by artificial means; little, however, remains of the ancient city, except a few bricks scattered here and there, and the foundations of some buildings. The aqueduct, which had conveyed water to it from the Savuto, is still seen in some parts in tolerable preservation. This city must have been of considerable importance, as it gave name to the gulf on which it stood; which fact we learn from Thucydides (vi. 104) . . .

I met several shepherds at breakfast on excellent curds, and I was not sorry to partake of their hospitality. I bought a few coins and terracotta figures that had been found in this vicinity. The variety and beauty of the silver coins of Terina prove the importance of the town, and belong, for the most part, to the best period of Greek art. There is usually a winged female figure on the reverse, which is probably intended for the Siren Ligeia, who is reported to have been buried on a rocky islet, which was pointed out to me, and is known as Pietra della Nave . . . I parted from my host amidst the ruins of Terina, and proceeded with a guide on my way to Nicastro. Our direct road would have been across the mountains and through the country which I had avoided yesterday; the longer and safer course was preferable. The ridge of the Apennines runs along about a mile from the shore, rising to no considerable height, and wooded to the summit. After walking a few miles, I was surprised to come upon a house whose neat and comfortable look was a striking contrast to the uninhabited appearance of the coast around. With us it would have been an unpardonable rudeness to have intruded on a gentleman to whom you had no introduction; strangers, however, are so seldom seen on this remote coast, that I

1. As yet unidentified, but possibly on the sea near Sant' Eufemia, *see* bibliography.

did not doubt of a favourable reception. On approaching the house, which was surrounded by many of those plants which only grow with us under protection, I was met by two young ladies, whose manners at once showed that they had been accustomed to what the world calls good society. You may imagine how much surprised they were at my appearance, and still more so when I addressed them in French, and inquired for their father. They invited me into the house, and their father, Don Michele Procida, soon afterwards came forward, and, on entering into conversation with them, I found that they had resided a considerable time in France. He has a large property here, which he visits occasionally with his family, spending the greater part of his time at Naples. They had never heard of any one travelling through Calabria in the unprotected state in which I have been proceeding, and they could scarcely imagine it possible that I could have escaped. The old gentleman pressed me to pass the remainder of the day with him, and the young ladies joined their entreaties with such hearty good will, that, I do assure you, it required all my natural stoicism to keep to my original intentions. I feel, however, the heat increasing every day, and I am anxious to get my face turned towards the north. With unfeigned regret, therefore, I bade them farewell, and proceeded on my course along the coast. No words can describe to you its desolate appearance, and the reflexion of the sun's rays from the heated sand gave me some idea of the difficulties of travelling in the deserts of Africa. For a distance of upwards of ten miles we passed only a single house, and here we were able to procure a flask of miserable wine . . . After a few more miles the ridge of the Apennines ended abruptly, and an extensive plain stretched before me. The isthmus, which separates the two seas here, is narrow, being not much more than thirty miles, and it is said that Dionysius the elder proposed to erect a fortification across to defend the southern part of Italy from the wild Bruttians; the Greek cities, however, were unwilling that this should be done, and Dionysius was obliged to abandon his proposed plan.

We now left the coast, and proceeded into the interior, reaching the small village of S. Biagio,[1] which is celebrated for its sulphureous waters, considered a cure for many diseases. Here I wished to dine, but there was no *locanda*. The shopkeeper, however, of the village undertook to furnish me with dinner, and I tried to get some rest by stretching myself

1. ? Sambiase.

on a hard bench. Meanwhile the inhabitants collected round the door, and jostled each other to get a peep at me. To think of sleep was useless, unless I could eject a large body of the inhabitants, who showed much anxiety to question me on many points respecting England. The Thames Tunnel they had heard of, and that seemed to give them a higher idea of the power and riches of England than any fact in her history with which they were acquainted. One classical gentleman exclaimed that it surpassed any work which their Roman ancestors had executed, and that nothing which the Greeks had done could be at all compared with it, ranking, he said, with the Pyramids of Egypt.

The hills round Nicastro ... are covered with immense groves of olive-trees, and the balsamic odours which were exhaled from the orange and lemon trees in this neighbourhood, might have led me to believe that I had come upon 'Araby the blest'. The olives rise to the height of forest-trees, but the oil is of a bad flavour,[1] and used only in manufactories. The income of the proprietors is mostly derived from this source, and would be large if they could find an outlet for their produce. As it is, they complain of great difficulty in meeting the demands of government. At the present moment the circulating medium has been almost entirely abstracted by the Austrian soldiers, who have been in the occupation of the country for the last few years. The Austrian soldiers are kept under strict discipline, and are in general a prudent, saving race of men. They have not expended in the Neapolitan territory a single farthing they could avoid, carrying off the greater part of their pay in silver to their own country ...

I dismissed my guide at S. Biagio, and proceeded forward to Nicastro, which I found to be situated in the post-road, which I had left three days ago at Carpanzano. Observing the sign of *La Gran Bretagna*, I thought that I could not do less than honour it with my company, and I found it really a very respectable inn. Nicastro is a large, well-built town, highly romantic in its appearance, from the woody hills with which it is surrounded, and the lofty towers of an old castle that commands it. This is the castle in which Henry, eldest son of the Emperor Frederick II, was confined for having embraced the Guelph party against his father. Nothing could be more beautiful than the valley through which I passed after leaving S. Biagio. The ground was strewed with flowers, and hedges of laurels, myrtles, and pomegranates, made

1. In 1962, I noticed that the oil in this neighbourhood had not a good flavour.

it a very paradise. The foliage gave an agreeable shade, and afforded shelter to thousands of singing-birds. In the evening I ascended the hill above the town, from which there is a most charming view – a vast horizon bounded by the sea and illumined by the setting sun, whose rays tinged the bay of St Euphemia. The *Sinus Terinæus*, which I have already mentioned, was a picture of the most enchanting description, and I regretted when the shades of evening forced me to retire . . .

This morning I left Nicastro at daybreak, and passed through the plains . . . The plain extends for upwards of twenty miles, is low and marshy, being traversed by the river Lamato, the ancient Lametes, which overflows its banks in the winter season. I had hired a mule this morning to convey me to Maida, though it was no great distance, as I was told that I should find some difficulty in fording the river. Except in the immediate vicinity of Nicastro the country was uncultivated, serving, however, for pasture to large herds of buffaloes and wild horses. The few peasants whom we passed had a sickly appearance, and showed evident marks of being subject to the pestilential effluvia of the marshes . . . Maida, situated on a hill overlooking the plain, contains about three thousand inhabitants, and though it would require little to unite the village by a good road to the main trunk which penetrates the country, I found that no attempt had been made to do so, and I had to climb by a narrow and rugged path, which could only be safely passed by the sure-footed mules of Calabria. Being situated almost equidistant from two seas, and in that part of Calabria which is least mountainous, it enjoys a free current of air that renders a sojourn here delightful at this season of the year. I reached Maida at an early hour, and as I had a letter of introduction to the judge of the district, I waited on him, and was received with great kindness.

Having explained the objects I had in view, I expressed myself desirous of conversing with any of the inhabitants, whom he might consider likely to give me information respecting the peculiar customs or antiquities of Maida. He kindly promised to attend to my request, and a short time afterwards begged me to follow him, when you may imagine my surprise at being ushered into a kind of court-house, where he had assembled all the respectable inhabitants of the village to meet me. The judge introduced me to them, when I rose, and, addressing them in the best Italian I could muster, expressed myself delighted to make their acquaintance, stating how much pleasure I had received from my solitary tour through this remote but beautiful part of Italy, and how much gratitude I felt for the hospitality and genuine kindness I had uniformly met from all classes, both rich and poor. One of them rose and said that he was expressing the sentiments of his friends around him, when he intimated his surprise that I should undergo all this danger and fatigue for what they considered such a very inadequate object. To that I said that I would answer in the very beautiful language of one of the noblest poets in the world, their own Horace (*Epist.* i. ii. 17), and whose poems many of them, no doubt, knew by heart ... I repeated the words with our Scotch accent, and one of them immediately remarked, that we must pronounce the Latin language as they did, as he understood the passage perfectly from my distinct enunciation. He said that he was afraid that the Italians had changed places with the *Ultimi Britanni*, and that high civilisation had passed from Italy to Great Britain, which now occupied the noble position in the world which their ancestors had maintained in former times. To this I could only say, while acknowledging the compliment, that I trusted there was a good time coming, and that no one would rejoice more than the inhabitants of the British Isles to hear a rustling in the dead bones of their country. I passed, however, from this dangerous subject to the peculiar features of Maida and its vicinity. There are salt springs above the village; but what I thought to be of more value, seams of coal, antimony, and alabaster are found in the neighbourhood, which will, no doubt, hereafter be turned to account ... [Here follows a discussion on local legal problems.]

As soon as the judge had transacted his business, he proposed that we should proceed to examine an ancient castle, and the ruins of the church of St Constantine. The castle has no appearance of being of an earlier date than the thirteenth century, and if a Roman station, called by geographers Ad Turres, ever existed at this spot, all vestiges of it have long since disappeared. None of the inhabitants had ever heard of any antiquities being discovered in this vicinity. The church – now called Constantine – to which they attached much interest, had been nearly destroyed by the famous earthquake of 1783, and it still remained as the earthquake had left it. It is said that the Emperor Constantine, on his way to found his eastern empire, stopped at this village and consecrated a pagan temple, which he found on this spot to the worship of the true God.

94

After dinner I proposed, while my host was enjoying his siesta, to visit the small village of Vena, a few miles from Maida, which I had learnt was an Albanian colony; and though my host thought the heat was so great as ought to deter me, I started, with one of the armed police as my guide ... We did not meet a single individual till we approached the village. The inhabitants were attending evening mass, so that I had a good opportunity of examining the costumes of the peasantry, and their external appearance. The chapel was small, and crowded principally by women, so devoutly engaged in prayer that even the presence of a stranger did not attract their attention. Their features were more distinctly oval than those of Italian women, and they had high cheek-bones, so as to remind me forcibly of my own countrywomen. I observed none striking for their personal charms, but there was a modesty and simplicity particularly pleasing. Their gowns were richly embroidered, the colours being generally bright blue or purple. Their hair was fantastically arranged, so as to tower above their head like an ancient helmet. Lord Broughton, in his *Travels in Albania in 1809 and 1810* (Chapter xii.), says, 'The dress of their women is very fantastical, and different in different villages. Those of Cesarades were chiefly clothed in red cotton (I never observed the colour elsewhere), and their heads were covered with a shawl, so disposed as to look like a helmet, with a crest and clasp under the ears.' This helmet-like appearance of their hair was particularly striking. They had a perfect acquaintance with the Italian language, though they employed the Albanian in conversation with each other. I have much difficulty in discovering any of their peculiar customs, as it has seldom occurred to them that they differ from the rest of the world; but on inquiring whether their marriage ceremonies varied in any respect from that observed by the other Italians, one of them mentioned the following custom: 'It is a dance called Valle, which must precede the ceremony. The women unite in a ring, clasping the hands of each other, and, with a flag carried in front, proceed dancing and singing the war-songs of their country, when they were fighting with the Turks. This takes place as they are conveying the young bride to her husband's house.' They still use the Greek rite at marriage. There are two crowns prepared for the bride and bridegroom, which, after being blessed, are placed on their heads, and then on the pillows of the bed. The armed Pyrrhic dance, they say, is still known to them under

95

the name of *Albanese,* or *Zamico.* These Albanians settled in the kingdom of Naples in the fifteenth century, at the time that their own country was overrun by the Turks, preferring to be exiles rather than give up the religion of their fathers. They at that time belonged to the Greek Church; but it is long since they submitted to the authority of the Pope, and I do not hear that any force was used to bring about the change . . . [Since 'the day was fast drawing to a close', Ramage returned to Maida for the night.]

XIII

I HAVE invariably abstained from expressing any opinion respecting the political administration of the Neapolitan government, unless circumstances naturally led to the subject, and I have not then concealed the sentiments which a British subject usually holds respecting the advantages of a constitutional form of government, guarding myself, at the same time, against giving an opinion whether it would be suited for the present state of this people. I have observed the same rule in respect to religion, though, when I am asked to state what objections I have to the Roman Catholic Church, I have never hesitated to point out those doctrines and that part of her government from which I dissented. I have thus endeavoured to steer a middle course, not wishing to intrude my own opinions on others, and, at the same time, having no desire that there should be any concealment respecting them. Following this rule very strictly, you will be surprised, in my account of this day's proceedings, to hear that I was on the point of being arrested for using what my opponent was pleased to call language defamatory of the Holy Catholic Church.

I started at daybreak on a good stout mule on my way to visit Pizzo, the spot where the brave but unfortunate Murat met his fate. The country continued to exhibit a very uncultivated appearance, being at first covered with marshes, though the scenery was in many parts magnificent; the mountains were wooded to the top, and till I approached the sea I traversed a forest of oaks and cork-trees. It is from these woods that my guide told me the brigands issue on unprotected travellers, and he pointed to several rude crosses, which had been erected where murders were committed . . .

No brigands, however, made their appearance, and I cannot help feeling somewhat callous to the alarming reports with which the inhabitants are constantly assailing me. The road, running along a natural platform for many miles, was delightfully shaded by lofty trees, and occasionally we had glimpses of the sea, slightly rippled by a breeze, which reached us sufficiently to cool the air. I cannot conceive a more beautiful scene than that through which I passed. At last I reached Pizzo, which stands close to the sea, a short distance from the post road, and when I entered the principal *locanda*, I was surprised to be addressed in French by a person who was seated at one of the tables. I made no concealment as to my object or my country, entering freely into conversation with him. He artfully led me to the subject of religion, and, believing that I was conversing with a person unconnected with the country, I made no secret of my opinions respecting the ignorance of the clergy, and the superstitious character of the people. You may judge of my surprise and indignation when, on rising from dinner, he coolly said that the sentiments which I had expressed on these subjects were of a kind that he, as lieutenant of gendarmes, should find it his duty to put me under arrest. The heat of the day had caused him to sit undressed, so that I was not aware that he was one of the officers belonging to government. I saw at once that he was an unprincipled bully, and I determined to meet him without flinching, thinking it likely that he would be afraid to put his threat in execution if he found that I was not so unprotected as my present appearance might have led him to believe. I told him that I had imagined that I had been addressing a French gentleman; I found, however, that I had been conversing with a person who had acted the dishonourable part of entrapping me into conversation on a subject on which I had no desire to speak, and was then going to take advantage of my candour to curry favour with his government for zeal in its cause. My arrest could only inconvenience me for a short time, as I had letters to all the chief magistrates in his district from the most influential men in Naples, and their guarantee for my honour would, I trust, bear down any statement which he could bring against me. I should take care, at the same time, that his conduct should, through the English minister at Naples, be represented in the proper quarter for animadversion, and I should demand his dismissal as satisfaction for my unjust imprisonment. I told him that I was aware of instances in which Englishmen had been treated by

Neapolitans in the way that he threatened, but I also knew that these very men were afterwards placed by their government at the disposal of those Englishmen for punishment. At the same time I pulled out a letter, and asked if he could read the address. He acknowledged that it was to the royal governor of his province. I showed him another to the supreme judge. I saw at once by his confusion and cowed look that I had judged rightly of my man, and I now dared him to put his threat into execution. His tone was completely changed, and he assured me, in a humble manner, that he had no intention to exert his authority, though others in his place might possibly have done so. He showed a desire to make up for the annoyance he had given me, and I thought it impolitic to take any further notice of what had taken place. Though I showed a bold front on the emergency, I did not feel sure that I might not have been considered to have broken the law technically by my line of argument, as the penal code contains this enactment: 'Whoever teaches against the Catholic doctrine in order to change it, shall be banished from the kingdom for life.' I am quite certain that any faltering on my part would have ensured my arrest, which would have been very annoying, and I resolved in my own mind that I should be still more cautious for the future, and steer clear of such a pitfall.

Hearing that I was anxious to visit the spot where Murat had fallen, the lieutenant offered to accompany me, and to employ his official authority to obtain from the gaoler some account of his last moments. As I thought that I might, perhaps, have some difficulty in getting admittance to the prison, I accepted his offer, though I had no confidence in his honour, and imagined that this kindness might only be a pretence to get me within the walls of the prison without exciting the attention of the inhabitants . . .

You may have read a detailed account of Murat's trial and condemnation, but you may find it interesting to hear the statement of the gaoler, who evidently considered himself the most important personage in the transaction. It was on a Sunday morning, October 8, 1815, that two small vessels were seen to approach Pizzo without attracting much attention from the inhabitants, who were employed at the time in hearing mass. Murat and thirty of his followers landed immediately, without a single question being asked, and proceeded to the publib square, where he found the legionary soldiers on duty in that very uniform which he had himself bestowed upon them. He exclaimed, 'Ah, my brave legionaries, you still wear my uniform'; and, naming one whom he recognised, he said, 'Do you not know me, your king, Joachim Murat?' To this one of them answered, 'Ferdinand is our king, by whom we are paid.' Meanwhile, a crowd of people had collected round him, and he urged them to cry, *Viva Gioacchino Murat!* and to pull down the flag which was displayed on the castle, calling it a *mappino*, a 'rag'. This word is Neapolitan, and is used to signify the towel made use of in the kitchen by the cook to clean her dishes, and was, no doubt, used by Murat in contempt. It is derived from the Latin, *mappa*. When no one offered to do so, he upbraided them as a mere band of brigands and traitors to their sovereign. As no one seemed willing to bring forward the horses for which he called, he inquired for the road to Monteleone, the chief city in the vicinity, and began to mount the hill to the post-road.

In the meantime a person had proceeded to give information to the commanding officer that Murat had landed, and was haranguing the soldiers in the public square. The result was soon known, and the direction in which he was proceeding. The officer immediately ordered a party of men to hurry forward to the point, where the road from Pizzo joined that to Monteleone, while he himself followed in the direction that Murat had taken. Murat had reached the heights where the two roads meet, when an officer stepped forward, and said, 'I arrest you in the name of King Ferdinand as a traitor.' Murat's men immediately prepared to resist, and had levelled their guns, when Murat called out to them not to fire, while the officer opposed to him ordered his men to aim at Murat, yet not one shot took effect. It is difficult to account for Murat's indecision at this moment, as no one who has read his history can doubt that he was brave to a fault, but instead of making any resistance, he fled down a precipitous bank and reached the shore. In all prints that you may have seen of him, you will find him represented with long cavalry boots and enormous spurs. He was dressed in this way at the time, and as he attempted to leap into a fisherman's boat, his spurs got entangled in a net and held him fast till his opponents got up, when he was taken prisoner. Then began one of those disgraceful scenes which have only too often taken place when the tide of popular favour has turned against some unfortunate wretch. A few years before, the inhabitants of Pizzo would have crouched before his chariot-wheels; now, they heaped on him every species of indignity. They spat in his face, they tore his clothes, and even plucked the hair from his head and whiskers. I am ashamed to say that the women were more savage than the men, and if the soldiers had not come up and rescued him from their hands, his life would have been sacrificed to their fury. He was carried to the castle, and thrust into a low and dirty dungeon, into which I entered. A telegraphic despatch was sent to the commander of the forces in the district, General Nunziante, who hurried forward without delay, with all the troops he could collect, and took military possession of Pizzo. The ex-king was placed at his disposal, and he had no longer any reason to complain of his treatment. Everything was granted that was consistent with his safe custody, and it is only justice to the military officers whose duty it was to act against him, to state that from them he received no treatment unworthy of a high station which he had once held. On Thursday morning orders were received from government to proceed to his trial, and a military commission of twelve persons was formed in order that all legal forms might be complied with. He was even allowed to employ in his defence, if he chose, a person who is called the advocate of the poor. There could be no doubt that he had forfeited his life by an attempt to excite rebellion; every government must possess the power to punish by the extreme penalty of the law any one who shall attempt to depose it. The exact grounds, however, of his condemnation arose, I believe, from his contravention of a law which he had himself enacted. By the quarantine laws, death is the penalty incurred by any one who shall land in the kingdom of Naples from a vessel that has not received *pratique* – that is to say, which has not remained in harbour a certain time under the surveillance of the officers of health. The object, you know, is to guard against the introduction of the plague from the East, and the penalty was one which he had himself sanctioned. This, I believe, was the technical grounds of his condemnation, but even without this he must have fallen a victim to his want of success. After the examination of some witnesses, and no attempt of defence being made by Murat, the military commission retired for a short time to consider its verdict, soon, however, returning, when the president, General Nunziante, addressed Murat somewhat to the following effect: 'General Murat, our consciences are clear; you are condemned to death by your own law, and you must die. If you wish a confessor, you shall have one summoned immediately.' He requested that a confessor should be sent for, adding, that he could not believe that Ferdinand would confirm his condemnation; but there was to be no forgiveness for him; orders had already been given that the law should immediately take effect. It is said that General Nunziante was so deeply affected at the part he was obliged to act, that he retired from the room, and did not again make his appearance. While he was waiting for the confessor, Murat said, 'Officers, you have done your duty,' and at the same time requested that paper should be furnished him that he might write a few lines to his wife. He then presented the note to the officers, who pledged their honour that it should reach its destination. He was then asked where he wished to die, being led into a small courtyard within the castle. He paced up and down for a few minutes, exclaiming, *Dove è il mio destino* – 'Where is my fate?' when suddenly stopping at a spot which was nearly a foot higher than the rest of the courtyard, and facing round, exclaimed, *Ecco il mio destino* – 'Behold the fated spot.' He then addressed the officers to the following effect: 'Officers, I have commanded in many battles; I should wish to give the word of command for the last time, if you can grant me that request.' Permission having been given, he called out, in a clear and firm voice: 'Soldiers, form line,' when six drew themselves up about ten feet from him. 'Prepare arms, present' – and having in his possession a gold repeater with his wife's miniature upon it, he drew it from his pocket, and as he raised it to his lips, called out – 'Fire!' He fell back against a door, and as he appeared to struggle, three soldiers, who had been placed on a roof above, fired a volley at his head, which put him out of pain. Thus perished the brave Murat, whose fate we may indeed regret, but its justice we can scarcely deny. His body was placed in a common coffin, and conveyed without ceremony to the church by the clergy. He was buried in the vault set apart for the poor, which, however, has been closed since that period. I was shown the small room where the council was held, and two low-roofed dungeons in which Murate and his companions were imprisoned. The door against which he fell appears still stained with his blood. I then proceeded to the church where the bones of the hero were laid. It was small and neat, and on remarking that it seemed to be of late date, I was told that Murat himself had contributed funds for its erection. It appears that he had shown considerable favour to this village of Pizzo, and it was probably from a recollection of this that he selected Pizzo for his foolhardy attempt. In the middle of the church a small stone, with an iron ring by which it was raised, was shown as the entrance to the vault; and, suspended to the roof, the small banner which was to have led him to fortune waved mournfully over his tomb.

This was a painful story to listen to, and I could have wished to have been left to my own reflection, but the lieutenant stuck to me, wishing, no doubt, to obliterate any bad impressions he might have left on my mind. As he intended to proceed next morning to Cantanzaro, he sent for a muleteer, with whom he tried to make a bargain; failing to make one to his own satisfaction, he threatened the poor man with castigation, and summoned the syndic to his presence. He employed the same haughty, overbearing manner with which he had begun to treat me, and I remarked in French that he was surely adopting a wrong method to gain his point. He assured me, however, that if he did not keep the whole district in awe of his authority, he might at once give up his command, as nothing but strong measures suited their wild and ferocious tempers. He maintained that they were all brigands, or connected intimately with them. He said that it was not unusual to hear the reproach addressed at other places to its natives on the slightest altercation: *Tu sei del Pizzo e questo basta* – 'Thou art a native of Pizzo and that is enough'. He threatened to report the whole village to government, if the magistrate did not furnish him with a horse at his own rating. The poor syndic showed evident symptoms of terror, and stated that his excellency should be obeyed. This title is always given when they wish to propitiate the favour of the individual whom they address, and sounds in my ears as if they were a down-trodden race. It is like 'your honour' of the Irish. This lieutenant is a native of the Roman States, and had been long in the service of the Austrian government in the north of Italy. He came down with the army of occupation, and has been retained by the Neopolitan government. He is, I should suppose, a fair specimen of the Italian soldier of fortune of the present day, living at the expense of both king and people. This is the force which the government is anxious to augment, as it fears to put arms in the hands of its own subjects. There are now nearly four thousand Swiss troops in the vicinity of Naples, who are intended for the personal defence of the royal family; such a force however, must be galling to the feelings of the natives, and, like all mercenary bodies of men, they treat the inhabitants in a rude, overbearing manner ...

I made inquiries for ancient remains, as some geographers place an ancient city, Napetia,[1] at Pizzo, giving the name of Napetinus to the Gulf of Euphemia, known also as Terinæus. No one had ever heard of any antiquities having been found here. They pointed out a valley called Trentacappelli, where marble of various colours is dug up, white, black, and yellow; and one of the inhabitants, who seemed to know something of geology, said that fossil remains were very plentiful in this neighbourhood. The rocks are calcareous, and this may very well be the case. Pizzo is prettily situated, with a harbour of some size, though it is much exposed ...

I would have willingly remained at Pizzo for the night, but the company of the lieutenant became so thoroughly distasteful to me, and I could in no way shake him off except by positive rudeness, which I did not choose to use, that I preferred the fatigue of a walk of six miles, as far as Monteleone[2] ... The ascent from Pizzo to Monteleone is long and steep, with terraces rising above one another, which are cultivated in the form of gardens. There are many streams at present with little water, though sufficient to irrigate the ground and produce vegetables of all kinds. It was long after sunset when I presented myself at the palace of the Marquis Gagliardi, by whom I have been received with the utmost kindness. He is one of the most influential proprietors in this part of Italy, and prefers to spend his time in the improvement of his property to a useless life in the city of Naples. His manners are those of a polished gentleman, and the marchioness is a lady, who would be an acquisition to the most brilliant court circle.

Another day of great excitement has closed, and though I feel thoroughly worn out, I have been amply repaid for all the fatigue I have undergone.

XIV

I DETERMINED to spend a day with my kind host at Monteleone, and examine the beauties of the surrounding district. The city is built upon a hill of considerable height, which commands a wide view of the country, extending from the bay of St Euphemia, along the shore of which I have been passing for the last few days, to that of Gioia[3] and

1. Perhaps Lametinoi. (T. J. Dunbabin. *The Western Greeks*, p. 162).
2. Monteleone re-assumed its Roman name of Vibo Valentia in 1928.
3. Gioia Tauro.

the Apennines. A magnificent spectacle strikes the eye all around, and the view is crowned in the distance by the bluish smoke of Etna. A castle, surrounded by fine trees, gives it a commanding appearance; and at a short distance lofty mountains, covered with forests, secure it from the cold winds of the north. It is, indeed, a lovely spot ... Monteleone, containing about seven thousand inhabitants, was the capital of a province till within the last few years, when the district was divided. Reggio and Catanzaro are now the seats of government, and in consequence of this arrangement the streets of Monteleone have a more deserted and gloomy appearance than you are prepared to expect from the size and respectability of the houses.

It is the site of an ancient Greek city called Hippo,[1] said to have been founded about 388 BC, by a colony from Locri; however, as the position is eminently fitted by nature for such a purpose, we can scarcely imagine that it was left unoccupied till so late a period ... A few years later we find it a bone of contention between Dionysius the elder of Syracuse and the Carthaginians, by the former of whom the inhabitants were transferred to Syracuse. Subsequently it fell, with all the other Greek cities, into the hands of the Bruttii, who were the native inhabitants of this part of Italy. After the conclusion of the second Punic war the Romans sent a colony, 194 BC, and changed its name to Vibo Valentia, when it seems to have become a city of great importance, being called by Cicero, who resided here previous to his quitting Italy at the time of his exile, 'an illustrious and noble municipal town'. The beautiful gulf, on which I was looking, had also witnessed an engagement between the fleets of Pompey and Cæsar (Cæsar, *Bell. Civ.* iii. 101). Strabo (vi. 256) mentions a grove and meadow remarkable for its beauty in its vicinity; and there was a magnificent temple[2] to the goddess Proserpine, in whose honour the women used at her festival to gather flowers and to twine garlands. I was, of course, anxious to find out if there were any remains of this temple; but they have a tradition that it was entirely obliterated by Roger, Count of Sicily, in the eleventh century, who, from the desire to enjoy the odour of sanctity, transferred all the marble pillars and hewn stones to the Cathedral Church of Mileto, twenty or thirty miles to the south of Monteleone.

1. Hipponion.
2. This temple, fifth century B C, has been excavated and is preserved in a public park, *see* bibliography.

The plains here are famed for the variety and beauty of the flowers with which they are covered; and hence the Greek colonists of Hipponium maintained it to be the place from which Proserpine was carried off. I find that the festival of the Madonna is now celebrated very much in the same way as we may suppose that of Proserpine was in ancient times ... There is more particularly a *festa* of St Luke, in the middle of June, when they erect columns, round which they twine flowers. The remains of the ancient walls are still to be seen in the direction of the "telegraph," of a construction similar to those I found at Pæstum, being of immense square masses of stone placed on each other without mortar. In some stones are holes bored, into which strong bars of iron are supposed to have been introduced. An Italian geographer asserts that the circumference of the walls was eight miles; but though Hipponium was an important city, this is, probably, an exaggerated statement. At the Porta di Piazza there are some sepulchral inscriptions in the Roman character, built into the wall of a house; and it is strange that no Greek inscriptions should have been preserved, except the epigraph of the medals and coins. At the church of St Leoluca, the patron saint of Monteleone, there is a mosaic pavement in good preservation, though it is of coarse design; and at a spot where they have been lately levelling the ground for the passage of the post-road, they have exposed the remains of a brick building, the original use of which it is impossible to determine. The church of the Capuchins contains a tolerable painting of Salvator Rosa's brother; and in that dedicated to St Leoluca there is a marble statue of the Madonna of considerable pretensions.

The Canonico Iorio, a gentleman of high literary acquirements, and well known to all English travellers who have visited Naples, was kind enough to furnish me with a letter of introduction to Signor Capialbi,[1] one of the most intelligent and best educated gentlemen in the south of Italy, and whose family has been long distinguished for its love of literature. He possesses a museum of antiquities of considerable value, containing many rare coins, medals, and vases; but he had much cause to deplore the visit of the French, who deprived him of a great portion of his collection, and when they evacuated the country they were irrecoverably lost to him.

1. Count Vito Capialbi (1790–1853). The Palazzo Capialbi now houses the archæological museum and Capialbi's library.

During the morning I paid a visit to the Collegio Vibonese, the exterior of which prepared me for a flourishing establishment. However, only the higher classes are able to send their children to this seminary, and out of a population of seven thousand only twenty-four pupils could be mustered . . .

I observe by the last census that there are 27,612 priests, 8455 monks, 8185 nuns, 20 archbishops, and 73 bishops. What could they have been before the French turned so many adrift! In 1807, about two hundred and fifty convents were dissolved; only a few hospices, and the monasteries of Monte Cassino, La Cava, and Monte Vergine, were retained, though much diminished in numbers and yearly income. The mendicant monks, from whom the state could derive nothing, were suffered to remain, and therefore you hear of my meeting the Capuchins in various parts of the country. Of late years, however, many converts and religious foundations have been restored, and some of my liberal friends maintain that the ambition and arrogance of the clergy are again becoming intolerable . . .

In the afternoon I rode down to the village of Bivona, on the shore, which is considered to have been the ancient port of Monteleone. If it were so, it possessed a poor harbour, though we must recollect that the vessels of the ancients could be drawn up on the beach. There was much more protection at Pizzo. It was evident, however, that an attempt had been made to construct a port, as the remains are of a very massive style.

I was present at mass this evening, and everywhere I can see that the Calabrese are urgent in their demands on Heaven. If drought desolate their fields, and no attention is paid to their prayers, it is said that they proceed to put the statues of their most revered saints in prison, hoping that this humiliation may make their intercession more effective . . .

I inquired whether the feudal system still subsisted here in all its strictness, but I find that the French put an end to it in a great measure, and it has never recovered its former power. Before the French occupied Calabria, the rich and powerful barons exercised a despotic sway . . . feudalism being never, as far as I can understand, seen in a more odious and disgusting form. Those who have read *I Promessi Sposi* of Manzoni, may have some idea of the miserable state in which the country was kept . . . The great barons, however, have deserted their property in the provinces, leaving it to be managed by agents, and lead an idle, useless life, dangling about the court at Naples. They have country-houses along the shores of the bay, and alternate all the year between the opera and the *dolce far niente* of their country-houses.

I am now on the spot which suffered so much from the earthquake in 1783, destroying many thousands of the inhabitants, yet it is astonishing how tranquilly the mind can contemplate danger when it has once been accustomed to it ...

I left Monteleone this morning before daybreak, with a muleteer, to proceed to Casal Nuovo[1] ... We proceeded along the post-road which leads to Reggio; being only lately constructed, it was in a very rough and unfinished state. As we receded from Monteleone, the country again began to assume the same desolate appearance which has so forcibly struck me in every part of my tour. When I use the appellation of desolate, I merely mean that man has left Nature to herself, and that he makes no use of those advantages which she offers to him.

We met with an old man carrying a quantity of *ricotte*, a kind of curdled goat's milk, and on finding that he was conveying it to a neighbouring village to market, I became the purchaser of the greater part of it, that I might lose no portion of the coolness of the morning by delaying to breakfast. How often I have longed for a good substantial Scotch breakfast with 'Finnon haddies', salmon, and all the other et ceteras! The Italians are sadly ignorant on many points, but I am sometimes inclined to think, when I am hungry in the morning, that they display their ignorance in nothing more lamentably than in not knowing how excellent a thing a good breakfast is.

Our route lay along the banks of the river Mesima, the ancient Medma or Mesma, till we approached a forest, which I found to be called Rosarno ... [Ramage took a cross-country route through the forest until he descended into the channel of a river called Vocale. He thereafter proceeded for 'many miles' until he came to the village of San Fili (unidentified) in a gorge in the mountains.] ... and as I had been upwards of seven hours astride of my mule, it was necessary to have some rest. My muleteer, however, maintained that we were only a few miles from Casal Nuovo, and I agreed that we should continue on our journey. We entered upon a plain, which is said to be nearly thirty miles in extent, and is thickly covered with olive-trees. It reaches

1. Casal Nuovo became known as Cittanova in 1852.

between the rivers Mesima and Muro,[1] and might be made one of the most fertile spots in Italy. These olive-trees are different in form from those to which I have been accustomed in other parts of Italy; instead of the knotted, hollow trunk, the stems were tall and straight, the branches not twisted into fantastic shapes, but smooth, and at equal distances from each other. The ground beneath was covered with beautiful ferns, through which paths are cut, and I believe that the ferns are moved every year, as it would otherwise injure the roots of the olive-trees. They are always very anxious respecting this crop, as it is apt to fail for various reasons. It is very much like our own apple-trees in Scotland, whose blossoms are often blighted by the dry east wind. So here the flowers of the olive-tree are liable to early destruction from cold dry winds, or else from too much damp, and even after the fruit is set and far advanced a heavy shower of rain may utterly destroy it. They speak also of a glutinous fluid appearing upon the olive like a blight after the continuation of a south-west wind, which they believe to bring some poisonous vapour from Mount Etna, and this causes the olive to rot off the branch. After having passed upwards of eight hours on muleback, it may be easily conceived that I hailed with pleasure the small village of Casal Nuovo, where I meant to spend the night. The Marquis of Gagliardi had been kind enough to recommend me to the care of a gentleman who was agent on his estates here, and nothing could exceed his attention to me.

I was now on the central spot where the earthquake of 1783 had been felt most severely, when the greater part of the village had been swallowed up. The houses are now built principally of wood, as few months pass without a shock more or less severe being felt, and yet they speak of the insecurity of their situation with the utmost nonchalance. About a week ago they had felt a severer shock than had taken place for many years before, and they had thought it prudent to spend the night in the open air. Several of the inhabitants were old enough to have a very vivid recollection of what had taken place in 1783, and shuddered at the thought of what they had witnessed. They said that the appearance of the sky gave warning of some fearful catastrophe impending; close, dark mists hung heavily over the surface of the plain; the atmosphere appeared in some places so red hot that they would not have been surprised to see it burst into flames; even the waters of the

1. River Marro.

river had a turbid colour, and a strong sulphurous smell was diffused around. The violent shocks began on the 5th of February, 1783, and continued to the 28th of May. It was on the 5th of February that Casal Nuovo more particularly suffered, when the greater proportion of the inhabitants were crushed under the ruins of the houses . . .

I have been surprised to hear the bitterness with which the inhabitants speak of their countrymen in other parts of Italy, even of those of another province. Imagine a Lancashire man looking upon a man of Yorkshire as scarcely belonging to the same country, and you will have some idea of the feelings that prevail here. It is this that will always render it difficult to unite Italy into one homogeneous nation, and make it anything else than a 'geographical expression'. When they come to understand the meaning of the word patriotism, and the sacrifices it imposes; when they shall be persuaded that their country can only be freed by subordinating their individual interests to those of the national unity – it is then only that Italy will be ripe for freedom . . .

I suspect that we must attribute much to the enervating effects of the climate. A three years' residence has enabled me to understand that it requires much mental energy to withstand its weakening influences. . .

XV

BEFORE I left Naples I had fixed on Gerace as the most southern point of Italy that I cared to visit . . . as it stands not far from the site of Locri, the most southern of the celebrated cities of Magna Græcia. I have now only to continue my course northwards along the coast for two hundred miles, and I shall visit the site of every ancient city that was famous in former times in this part of the world . . . You will recollect that I started from Naples on Tuesday, the 29th of April, and I have reached Gerace on Sunday, the 18th of May, having not loitered much on my journey.

Casal Nuovo stands at the foot of that ridge of the Apennines which terminates near Reggio, opposite to Sicily. It rises to a considerable height, though I found that I should have no difficulty in crossing it, mounted on one of the surefooted ponies of the country. This passage of the mountains is called Il Passo del Mercante, and, as you will not be surprised to hear, is beset with brigands. I found that the Marquis of Gagliardi had, with a degree of kindness for which I feel deeply grateful to him, given directions to his agent that several of his tenants should be sent, fully armed, to accompany me across this dangerous pass. I could have willingly dispensed with this attendance, and, indeed, made strong remonstrances against it; my kind host, however, pleaded so strongly his master's imperative orders that I had nothing for it but to submit ... My guard consisted of four men, of whom two were mounted on horseback and two were on foot ... As for myself, my only weapon of defence, if weapon it could be called, was my dilapidated umbrella, which I fear the Italian brigand would not be inclined to consider very formidable. If we met them, however, I intended to flourish it in the way we sometimes alarm cattle; and as they are probably unacquainted with such an article, they might imagine it some deadly weapon of war, and take to flight.

As soon as we left the village our ascent of the mountain began, and continued for upwards of three hours without intermission through a thick wood. Occasionally there was an open glade, and then the eye stretched across an extensive plain to the sea, which lay unruffled in the distance, studded with small islands,[1] among which was Stromboli, sending up without ceasing volumes of smoke ... As we approached the top a very different scene awaited us, for we got enveloped in so thick a mist that I could have thought myself suddenly transported to my native hills; at last we reached a region where a fearful tempest of thunder and lightning was raging. The wind blew a hurricane, and rain fell in torrents. The climate had completely changed, and I had now to complain of being nearly frozen. I cared little for myself, but my papers and maps stood a good chance of being completely spoiled. I avoided this, however, by transferring them to my companions, who were all furnished with long Calabrese black cloaks, descending to their heels. We were now traversing the territory of the brigands, and though I could not be persuaded that there was the slightest danger from man amidst so fearful a manifestation of the powers of nature, my companions thought otherwise, and took those precautions which their experience of such scenes dictated. Strict silence was enjoined, though I considered this very needless, as the brigands must have had very quick ears to hear even the loudest trumpet amidst the roar of the thunder,

1. The Æolian Islands.

as it ran echoing along the mountain's side. One of my guards preceded us by a few yards, and, with his finger on the trigger, kept a sharp look-out on every tree and bush which we passed, while my other companions seemed to be equally on the alert . . . On the summit there was a small piece of table-land, which I was surprised to find partly cultivated, and the grain was just beginning to make its appearance . . . Here the wind blew with such terrific fury that it was dangerous to remain on horseback, and we all dismounted, prepared to throw ourselves on the ground to avoid being swept away. I thought of the havoc I had witnessed near Paola, and of the wish that had crossed my mind, that I had been present to see Nature in all her terrors, and it seemed as if I were going to be gratified more speedily than I had then imagined . . .

Our descent was by a far steeper path than that by which we had mounted, and it was not long before we had left the storm above us . . . As we gradually issued from the dark clouds with which we had been surrounded, the eye rested on the wide expanse of the Ionian sea, with its whitish-blue colour, which not a breath of wind seemed to have ruffled, and on which the sun was shining brightly. We reached a small village, Agnana, consisting of only a few houses in the gorge of the mountains, and whose inhabitants were said to act as spies to the brigands, and to warn them if an unprotected traveller attempted to cross the mountain. Here we got some coarse bread, cheese, and execrable wine. About a mile below this village all danger was declared to be at an end, and, though we were still many miles from Gerace, my guard thought they might return to Casal Nuovo. I wished to pay them for the trouble they had taken, but they refused to accept anything, saying that they were only too happy to be of use to any friend of the Marquis of Gagliardi; and here I took a farewell of my companions, and proceeded on my solitary way, allowing my muleteer to return, that he might have the protection of my guard in recrossing the mountains. I was not sorry to be left alone, as I felt little inclined to keep up a conversation with those with whom I had so few ideas in common. I know not whether the scenes through which I had just passed might not have imparted a feeling of melancholy to the mind, and made everything appear less joyous than it would otherwise have done, but I suffered an oppression of spirits, for which I could not account. Though the sun shone brightly, and not a drop of rain had fallen where I now stood, there was a gloom and melancholy around which pressed heavily on the spirits. The Apennines run here nearly parallel to the shore, and at the distance of about four miles from it. As far as the eye can reach, the intermediate space is intersected by numerous undulating ridges, which run down to the shore, and allow of no plain of any extent. At some distance stood the village of Gerace, on a high point, and the gloomy and dark appearance of its houses seemed well to harmonise with the deserted aspect of the surrounding country. I can scarcely tell in what this eastern side of the Apennines differed from the western, for there was loneliness in both, but it was more striking here. The sides of the hills had no marks of cultivation, and even the footpath along which I was proceeding seemed seldom to be trodden. In fact, I could have imagined myself in the midst of an uninhabited country, if I had not seen the castle of Gerace towering in the distance. After some time I reached Gerace, and inquired for the *sotto-intendente*, to whose care I was recommended by my kind friend the Marquis of Gagliardi. A respectable house was pointed out as his residence, and on entering it I was introduced to an old gentleman of a mild and benevolent countenance, who received me in the kindest manner. I dare say that I was a spectacle well suited to call forth a feeling of compassion, as I had been thoroughly drenched in the mountains, and I must have looked jaded and worn out. His excellency's clothes were scarcely suited to my spare figure, but I was glad of any change, however ridiculous might be my appearance.

I am now at last in that part of Italy which I have long wished to visit. It has been sometimes asked why it should have been called Magna Græcia, and various ingenious reasons have been suggested, but the one which is most obvious is probably nearest to the truth – that it was from the importance and power of the Greek colonies, which had at a very early period extended over the whole of this part of the country. The name, indeed, does not seem to have had any very definite application, including sometimes even the island of Sicily, yet it was more usual to restrict it to the portion of Italy lying between Locri and Tarentum. It thus contained eight republics, which were generally independent of each other – Locri, Caulonia, Scyllacium, Croton, Sybaris, Heracleia, Metapontum, and Tarentum. Many other smaller cities might be enumerated, which were included under the appellation of Magna Græcia; these, however, were the most important. The

LOCRI

shore, of which they had taken possession, was well provided with
spacious bays and gulfs, its fertile plains were watered by numerous
streams, and its climate could not be excelled. Everything, therefore,
concurred to raise it to as high a degree of perfection as nature could
possibly reach without the assistance of art . . .

Of the Greek cities in this part of Italy, the oldest was Locri,[1] the
ruins of which are found at no great distance from Gerace. It is said
that it was founded principally by a colony of slaves, who, during the
absence of their masters, had carried off their wives. Whatever may be
the truth of this tradition, its citizens became in later times famed for
their riches and importance, which they owed in a great measure to
the wisdom of their code of laws conferred on them by Zaleucus. Their
prosperity was injured by what at first appeared calculated to promote
their interests. They became intimately connected with Dionysius the
elder, who married the daughter of one of its principal citizens, and in
consequence of this alliance the city fell into the hands of his son
Dionysius, who tyrannised over it in a manner that can scarcely be
credited. From that time the prosperity of the city gradually declined,
and after it became part of the Roman Empire, it sank into insignificance.

Such was the city the site of which I proceeded, in company with a
friend of my host, this morning to visit, and found it to be upwards of
four miles distant from Gerace, close to the shore. Its ancient walls
can be traced nearly round its whole circumference. A portion of them
to the south are in a tolerable state of preservation, and show that they
were constructed of large blocks of calcareous limestone, in which the
country around abounds. For half a mile on the side next the sea the
remains of the wall are visible, so that the sea seems to have undergone
no change in this part of the coast for the last two thousand years. The
site of the city occupied a space of ground about two miles in length
by less than a mile in breadth, extending from the sea-coast, at what is
called Torre di Gerace, to the rising ground leading to the Apennines.
From the slopes of these hills the city extended towards the sea, and
had its harbour, if harbour it can be called, at the mouth of the little
river St Ilario. A French nobleman, the Duc de Luynes, was here a few
days ago, and caused the foundation of a building of considerable size
to be excavated. The basement is constructed of massive blocks of
limestone, placed over each other without mortar, and close by are

1. For reports of excavations on this site, see bibliography.

113

scattered pieces of immense columns of the same material, which had no doubt decorated the building. It is situated outside the walls, on the brow of a hill of no great height, yet so as to overlook any building lying between it and the sea. All the intervening space is covered with fragments of ancient buildings, of which only one at the north-east corner would appear, from the immense blocks of stone for its foundation, to have been of considerable size. I examined with care every spot close to the shore for the site of the Temple of Proserpine,[1] which Strabo mentions as the richest and most magnificent that Italy possessed, but not a vestige of it can be seen, if it is necessary to suppose that it was close to the shore. We know that it suffered severely from Pyrrhus, but we can scarely imagine that its foundations should not still exist. It may possibly be the building which I have just mentioned as having fragments of pillars lying around. There is a hill called Epopis, mentioned by ancient geographers, on which the citadel of Locri was situated. I vainly tried to determine which of several ridges ought to be considered the spot where it stood. There is no hill of a very decided character, though several ridges run down to within a quarter of a mile of the sea. There are three small hills, on one or other of which may have been the fortress; three ruined forts are now seen on them, called Castellaccio, Mantelle, and Sietta.[2] Some have thought that Gerace was the ancient Epopis: this is impossible, as it is at least four miles from the site of these ruins; and, besides, no ancient remains have been discovered in its immediate vicinity. There are, indeed, a few ancient marble pillars in the cathedral and a single inscription; these, however, could easily have been transported from the shore, and we know that this has been often done elsewhere. I have not the slightest doubt that Locri was situated on this site, and did not include Gerace, which had its origin in the Middle Ages, when the inhabitants took up their residence at some distance from the sea, that they might be in some degree beyond the reach of piratical corsairs. As I was not pressed for time, I wandered away towards the mountains, and stumbled on what must have been the remains of an aqueduct, which had to penetrate through a rock for a considerable distance . . .

1. The temple of Persephone is now thought to have been on the hill Mannella, see P. Zancani Montuoro, 'Il Tempio di Persefone a Locri' (Rendiconti della Reale Accademia dei Lincei, Serie VIII, vol. XIV, fasc. 5–6, May–June, 1959).

2. Castellace, Mannella, and Abbadessa

Having satisfied my curiosity respecting the ruins of Locri, I proceeded on my return to Gerace, passing through a grove of olive-trees and a vineyard, where that peculiar species of vine, from which the *vino greco* is procured, was trained to a trellis-work five or six feet in height. In the vicinity of Naples the vines are trained from tree to tree; it is seldom the case here. We passed also a few mulberry-trees, which supply food for the silkworm, and I find that the manufacture of silk is pursued with considerable success. I expressed a wish to see their cocoons (*bacche di seta*), but I observed from their answer that they were averse to the proposal, and I afterwards found the cause of the refusal to be not particularly flattering to me. They are afraid to expose the silkworm to the gaze of a stranger lest an ill-omened look should destroy them. I am thus subject to the imputation of a *jettatore*, of whom I have already spoken. They have, however, a mode of neutralising the effect of the evil eye by making use of incense, together with palms that have been blessed on Easter Sunday; olives, too, that have been blessed have the same effect, if they are burned in the room where a *jettatore* has been. This superstition respecting the evil eye is found everywhere throughout Italy, and seems to be applicable to everything . . . [Ramage here elaborates on this superstition quoting from the Classics.]

I was curious to see the contents of the little purse made by the Capuchins, and suspended round the necks of the children, but I found the matter was regarded in too serious a light by mothers to venture on such an examination . . . It would have been strange if they had been found to contain a representation of the membrane virile, which we know was suspended round the necks of the Roman children . . .

In this province there are seventy-two cultivators of the silkworm, but the only silk manufactory on a large scale that I can hear of is at San Leucio, near Naples. It is supported by government, who supply it with children from the poorhouse, called Albergo dei Poveri, paying at the same time fourpence a day for every child thus employed. In the plains of Sorrento I found, on inquiry, that there were nearly three hundred persons employed in the manufacture of silk stockings, but they could not compete in colour or fineness with the workmanship of France or England; in strength of material they were far superior . . .

In respect to linen they have made but little progress, if I may judge from the tablecloths and sheets which I have had an opportunity of examining. They are generally coarse and ill bleached. The village of La Cava, near Salerno, has been most successful in its manufacture of linen, and employs about fourteen hundred and sixteen individuals.

I had often heard it positively asserted by some of my learned Neapolitan friends that there were several villages in the remote parts of Calabria whose inhabitants had preserved the ancient Greek language, without much change, from the period when the whole of this coast was colonised by the Greeks. Bova, about twenty miles to the south of Gerace, was said to be one of them; and you will not be surprised that I was anxious to solve the problem, when it was so nearly within my reach. I had determined to visit it, if I could receive no satisfactory information at Gerace. I made my intention known to my host, when he stated that there were two muleteers from Bova in Gerace at that moment, and he immediately gave directions that they should wait upon me. I have been studying Romaic for the last six months, under one of the few Greeks who survived the fatal siege of Missalonghi, and it occurred to me that they might understand this modernised Greek. They had no difficulty in conversing, though my pronunciation sounded somewhat strange in their ears. In respect to their origin, they understood that they had come from beyond seas a few centuries ago, and I have no doubt that it was a colony of Greeks, that had emigrated from the Morea at the same time that the Albanians came over. Their language appeared, with some slight variations, to be much the same as that now spoken in the Morea ... [Ramage gives a list of words in modern use which he considers to be preserved from Ancient Greek.]

On my return from the ruins of Locri I visited the cathedral of Gerace, which I found to have suffered severely from the earthquake of 1783, being rendered useless for public worship. The ancient columns of which I spoke, as probably brought from the Temple of Proserpine on the shore, are of white marble, fluted, with the exception of three, which are *verde-antique*, coarse red limestone, and granite. The capitals are of inferior workmanship, and can scarcely be supposed to have originally surmounted them. The great altar remains untouched, but it is in the crypt that divine service is now celebrated ... [Inscription.]

XVI

WHATEVER fault we may find with this people for their superstition and ignorance, there is a lovableness in their character which I am not utilitarian enough in my philosophy to resist. Amidst such superstition there is also a great deal of genuine piety and humble submission to the severest strokes of Providence, and I sometimes wish that my own countrymen were equally attentive to the performance of their religious duties. My worthy host was a good specimen of the higher class of Italians, of amiable character, strict in his devotions, and though firmly attached to the doctrines of the Roman Catholic religion, tolerant to those, like myself, who differed from him in opinion. I had an interesting conversation with him on the subject of religion ... [Ramage records this in detail. He left Gerace at daybreak the next day and proceeds along the coast via Roccella to Castel Vetere.]

The small village of Castel Vetere[1] was seen at some distance on the summit of a hill, which seemed perpendicular on all sides; but its gloomy appearance served only to increase the melancholy feelings which the scenery around was calculated to excite. The rock on which Castel Vetere stands is ascended by a winding path, and before the invention of artillery might have sustained a considerable siege. I was received with kindness by the friends of the *sotto-intendente*, and the day passed quickly away in very agreeable conversation. I found here Baron Musco, a gentleman well acquainted with the English language, and who had spent much time in the society of the English. He is now residing on his property, and showed me some valuable gold rings and bracelets which had been found in some sepulchres at Gioiosa,[2] in this vicinity. On one of the rings were the letters P H V, without any device to determine to what epoch it belonged.

Caulon, or Caulonia, one of the earliest Greek colonies founded on these shores, stood somewhere in the neighbourhood. It was destroyed by Dionysius the Elder, 389 BC, and its inhabitants removed to

1. The modern town of Caulonia. Up to 1860, it was known as Castel Vetere from the Byzantine – Norman Castle which crowned the summit of the precipitous rock on which the village was situated.

2. Gioiosa Ionico.

Syracuse; it must again, however, have risen from its ruins, as we find it espousing the cause of Pyrrhus, and subsequently attacked by the Romans during the second Punic war. It is said to have stood on an elevated situation, which would suit very well with Castel Vetere, if it were not stated at the same time that it was near the sea, while Castel Vetere is at least four miles distant. Besides, no ancient remains, cameos, or coins have been discovered here, while at a place called Calamona, about one mile from the sea and three from Castel Vetere, many sepulchres are visible, and coins of various Greek colonies have been found there. Near this spot, on a hill called Foca, are the remains of buildings, and from a personal inspection of the ground I should be inclined to place the site of the ancient Caulonia[1] there. When I visited it the site was covered with the prickly pear, and hedged round by the gigantic aloe. Beneath it stretches a plain nearly two miles in breadth, through which flows the small stream Alaro,[2] which there is little doubt is the ancient Sagras. It was on the banks of this river that the inhabitants of Croton sustained a memorable defeat from the Locrians; and so extraordinary was the result that it gave rise to a proverbial expression, 'more true than the event that happened at the Sagras'. In talking to the inhabitants of the country, I could hear of no other level piece of ground within twenty miles where two large armies could be drawn up. There is a spot in the plain called 'Sanguinaro', which may be considered a corruption of *sanguinarius*, the Latin word for 'bloody'.

During our conversation, the Baron Musco said of a child belonging to one of his friends in Naples, that it was *un fanciullo della Madonna*, – 'a child of the Madonna'; and on inquiring what he meant, he said that it was a custom of this country, when a woman loses her child in birth, to take a foundling and bring it up in its stead; this is called taking a child from the Madonna.

This morning, mounting my mule, I proceeded on my journey, undecided whether I should seek Squillace by the sea-coast or try to reach it through the mountains. I crept slowly through the plain of the Sagras, and then leaving the sea crossed a hilly country for several miles. On either side of me I saw small villages perched on heights. Intending to visit the iron mines worked by government here, I

1. An early fifth-century doric temple was excavated at Monasterace near Punta Stilo by P. Orsi many years ago and further excavations on this site are now (1962) being conducted by the Italian authorities. *See* bibliography.   2. Stilaro.

received from my friends of Castel Vetere a letter of introduction to the overseer, Capitano Natzi, who resided at a village called Pazzano. Being disappointed in finding him, I pushed forward to the mines, which were about three miles in the mountains. My road lay up a deep glen, with the mountains rising on both sides to a great height, and thickly covered with wood. The scenery was most magnificent, and I determined to bid defiance to the brigands and penetrate through these passes. On reaching the mines by a road which was kept in a good state of repair, I could perceive no appearance of any human being, but after much hallooing a little boy came forward. I proposed to accompany him into the mine, though we had no light, as I found that the workmen were now employed in the shaft. He attempted to frighten me by extraordinary stories of a spirit who haunted the mine, and had a great antipathy to strangers. To this I of course paid no attention, but tying a strong cord round his arm to prevent his escape, I ordered him to precede me, and threatened summary punishment if he dared to play any trick. As we were proceeding to enter, one of the head workmen came up, and I then found no further difficulty. There are four shafts, of which only one is productive. The vein is three to four feet in breadth, and I found that they had penetrated about half a mile into the mountain, and that the vein is descending.

The southern part of Italy is rich in mines, which were worked in former times. In the vicinity of Locri there were four silver mines, and in the district of Caulon there were several at Bivonica, Argentaria, Fiumara, and Stilo. In the territory of Amantea, at Monte Cocuzzo, there were mines of rubies and emeralds, but no attempt has been made in the present day to derive any advantage from them. The government claims the possession of all the mineral riches of the kingdom, and one of its greatest errors is that it will neither itself attempt to explore, nor give permission to others to do so.

The miners recommended that I should keep along the coast. I was so charmed, however, with the appearance of the mountains and the coolness of the air, that I resolved to face the brigands. Accordingly I proceeded to ascend the mountain-range, which was covered with magnificent oaks, beeches, and gloomy pines, that had borne the blast of many a winter. Every step presented new beauties, and opened to the eye fresh objects of admiration. There was a wildness in the scenery, and a gloom in the darkly-wooded mountains, that overpowered the mind. All was silent save the sound of some distant waterfall, or the low moaning of the breeze through the aged forest. At times the piercing scream of the eagle startled the ear, or some wild goat would dart away to its secret recess. I afterwards heard that the woods abounded in foxes, weasels, polecats, squirrels, and even wolves are scattered over them. While I was thus quietly admiring the beauties of nature I was alarmed at the appearance of a large body of armed men, reclining under the trees. The gleam of their muskets first attracted my eye, and I soon perceived by a movement among them that my approach was not unobserved. Several ponies and mules were quietly grazing beside them, while panniers and cloaks lay scattered on the ground. I cannot say that I did not begin to repent having allowed my admiration of scenery to lead me into this dangerous rencontre. I had sufficient time, before I reached them, to recall to my recollection all the barbarities that the brigands of the mountains are accused of having committed. As I approached the spot where they were assembled, a person, who seemed by his dress and superior bearing to be the Robin Hood of the party, stepped forward, and relieved me from all anxiety by addressing me in French. He said that he saw by my appearance that I was a foreigner, and requested me to join their party at dinner, an invitation which I was noways loth to accept. I found that they belonged to the iron-foundry at Mongiana, and were employed in marking trees to be cut down for charcoal. They were guarded by a body of wild-looking peasantry, whom I should not have cared to encounter in my solitary ride. They told me I had only to proceed a few miles farther to reach Mongiana, the village where the foundry was situated, but that I had acted with great foolhardiness in advancing into this part of Calabria without a guard. They never ventured beyond their village unless protected by a body of armed men, nor does it appear that they were safe from attack even then, as is well illustrated by the following story which they told me: 'A short time ago, when the government ordered all the arms in the country to be collected in the capital of each province, a band of twelve brigands had marched through some village in the vicinity, and proceeding to the house of the curate had carried him off to their fastnesses, regardless of the excommunications of the Church. They fixed on a large sum for his ransom, and despatched a shepherd to convey the information to the village. As the curate was beloved by his parishioners the money was collected, and the poor clergyman released from his unpleasant thraldom.' This may give you some idea what degree of security there is in travelling through this country, and I confess that I shall not be sorry when I have left it.

In the distance, my companions pointed to a village called Fabrizia, the inhabitants of which are said to be of a ruder and wilder character than their neighbours. If a father be slain, and the years of his son preclude immediate vengeance, the bloody shirt is preserved as a memorial, and is presented to the son when he arrives at the age of manhood. It is thus that the feuds between rival families never cease, but are transmitted from one generation to another. When the only son of a family dies here, the father and mother tinge their under-clothing with *legnuolo*, and wear them till they are destroyed by age.

I found the iron-foundry of Mongiana to be of considerable size, but foolishly erected at a great distance from the mines ... On leaving Mongiana, I proceeded across a level plain several miles in extent, which had none of the characteristics of an Italian climate. The fields were covered with green grass, or the grain was just springing up, while the coolness of the air made me feel that I was less warmly clothed than the climate required. It was a miniature table-land on the top of the Apennines, which I could perceive grew narrower as the mountains proceeded to the south, till they became nearly perpendicular at the spot where I had crossed them near Gerace. The temperature is very cold during the winter season, and snow continues more or less from the end of November till the beginning of April. Crowds of peasants were returning from the fair of Serra.[1] They were much taller, and of a more masculine frame of body, than the inhabitants of the sea-coast, and their women rivalled them in strength and height.

Having reached the small village of Serra, I found it to consist principally of wooden houses of the most miserable description. The frequent earthquakes to which they are subject render it the only material to which they can have recourse with any degree of safety ...

There are several small churches built, like the houses, principally of wood; the belfries have a strange appearance from this circumstance. At no great distance are the ruins of the monastery of St Stefano del Bosco, the most ancient of the Carthusian establishments in the kingdom, having been founded by St Bruno himself, and where his remains are deposited. It was levelled to the ground in less than three minutes by

1. Serra S. Bruno.

the earthquake of 1783, and all its magnificence passed away like as if had never been.

... This morning I continued on foot my course to the north without a guide, passing through the village of Spadola, famed in this quarter for its cheese, yet still more wretched in appearance than Serra; and as I had heard that it contained a church called Santa Maria Sopra Minerva, I was desirous to ascertain whether there were any ancient remains. Velleius Paterculus (i. 15) mentions that Minervium was colonised at the same time with Scyllacium. I waited on the clergyman, whom I found in a hut nearly devoid of furniture, and you may imagine that he stared when he was made acquainted with the reason that had induced me to call upon him. No one had ever visited his village on the same errand, and I might have spared myself the trouble for any information that I gained ...

All the villages through which I passed were equally miserable, though the country was beautiful, and the scenery of a different kind from that which I had traversed yesterday. The descent was gradual, and the mountains had less of an Alpine character. There were magnificent chestnuts and oaks, while the hedges were formed of the holly, the sweet-briar, and woodbine. I was struck by the abundant crop of wild strawberries, and the cherry-orchards in full bearing; indeed, along this coast I found this fruit most delicious. When I reached San Vito,[1] I determined to strike again into the mountains, that I might visit the black-lead mine at Olivadi, said to be the only mine of this material in Italy ...

On my way to Squillace, I passed through a wood of oaks and chestnut-trees, of the largest size I had yet seen. One of the oaks was twenty feet in circumference, at the distance of three feet from the ground, and a chestnut-tree exceeded thirty-five feet ... After passing through the village of Palormiti, I came within sight of Squillace, situated on a rising ground about three miles from the sea, and I was glad when I got safely within its walls. I have been received with much kindness by a friend of the *sotto-intendente* of Gerace, who seemed to take pleasure in showing me whatever is worthy of my attention.

Squillace is a city of considerable importance, and, with the exception of Cosenza, has more appearance of commercial activity than any I have

1. San Vito s. Ionico.

yet visited. The ancient Scyllacium[1] was situated nearer to the sea, where the ruins of the monastery Vivariense are found. This monastery was built by Cassiodorus, a native of this place, secretary and intimate friend of Theodoric, King of the Goths, towards the end of the fifth century. Cassiodorus spent the latter years of his life within its walls, and close to it the inhabitants point out a fountain, which they call Fontana di Cassiodoro. The remains of the monastery prove that it must have covered a large space of ground. From an inscription that has been found, it appears that the Emperor Antoninus had contributed a considerable sum of money from his treasury to convey water from a distant spring. Three noble arches of this aqueduct are still to be seen at a spot called Simari, and if a more minute examination was made than my time allowed, I have no doubt that it might be traced from a considerable distance ... Another curious inscription in the Greek language has been found here, which shows that Greek games were celebrated in this city to a late period of the empire.[2]

Squillace was at one time under the Patriarch of Constantinople; it has long since submitted to the authority of the Pope. One part of the town is called Quartiere de'Giudei, showing that the Jews had formerly occupied a portion of it. The ruins of the castle are picturesque, and the cathedral, which is a building of some pretensions, possesses holy reliques, valuable in the eyes of the superstitious devotee, such as a small fragment of the holy cross, and a portion of the hair of the Virgin Mary and of Mary Magdalene. They were shown to me as of the most sacred character, and I have no doubt that it was expected that I should show them some honour, but I made no sign.

On inquiring whether the bay of Squillace was still subject to sudden storms, as I knew from a passage in Virgil (_Æn._ iii. 553) it had been in former times, I was told that they had long since ceased, and as this appeared a curious natural phenomenon, of which I was of course sceptical, I inquired if they could at all account for the change. They told me that the storms had been caused by a set of evil spirits, who had

1. Skylletion is still unidentified, but thought to be near Squillace, _see_ bibliography.
2. Mr Peter Fraser kindly informs me that this inscription is in fact Attic (_IG_ ii[2]. 1192), and was recognised as such by Boeckh in _CIG_ i (1828), no. 287. There is no indication how or when it reached South Italy, and its presence there is remarkable.

taken up their abode in a grotto close to the village Stallati,[1] but they had been put to flight by a band of angels, who had wafted the body of the holy Saint Gregory to this grotto, to whom it is now consecrated. The evil spirits have never since made their appearance, and the storms that infested the bay no longer bring disaster on the mariner. I went down to the shore, but there is no harbour or anchoring-place except when wind is off land. The water is said to be very deep close to the shore, and consequently there is no shelter in case of vessels finding themselves on a lee shore with a strong gale of wind. I decline, therefore, to believe that the coast of the bay of Squillace is more safe than it was in former times.

Feudal habits and customs still maintain their ground in this remote part of the world, and I find that every village possesses its noble families, who pride themselves on the purity of their blood. Feudal enactments, which have no longer the force of law, still exercise an influence over the customs of the people. There used to be a particular dress for each class in society, and severe penalties were enacted against the use of swallow-tailed coats by any person who could not satisfactorily prove his title to nobility. Though this law is no longer in force, the different ranks are still to be distinguished by their dress, and in the costume of the women it is still more marked.

On leaving Squillace this morning I descended into the eastern part of the plain which I had crossed about ten days ago between Nicastro and Maida. About twenty miles before me rose once more the lofty mountains of the Sila in all their gloom, and with no pleasing associations connected with them. The road lay through extensive fields of wheat and Indian corn, with groves of mulberry-trees as food for their silkworms. I had been informed that I should pass the remains of an ancient temple at a spot called Roccelletta,[2] close to the shore; I was a little disappointed to find it a large building of the Middle Ages, of which it was impossible to determine the use. At all events, it was neither of Roman nor Greek construction, and the tradition is that it was destroyed a few centuries ago by the Turks, who used to keep all this part of Italy in a constant state of terror. It is here, however, that geographers place Castra Hannibalis, and here possibly it might have

1. Staletti.
2. Roccelletta D. Vescovo di Squillace. This church, after the cathedral at Gerace, is the largest in Calabria: the date of its foundation has been much discussed.

been, but I could find not a vestige of ancient remains . . . There was an
appearance of industry and activity, announcing my approach to a
provincial capital; but on entering Catanzaro the exterior of the houses
did not impress me with a high idea of its opulence, and the opportunity I have since enjoyed of examining the interior of some of them has
fully confirmed my first impressions. It contains several shops, which
had a respectable appearance, and seemed to be well filled even with
English cloth. Indeed, I have been much surprised to observe in every
part of Calabria that neither the cutlery nor the cloth of England have
failed to penetrate into the country in defiance of the fiscal regulations
of government, while there is the greatest abundance of sugar and coffee
supplied by the contraband trade. The immense extent of coast renders
it nearly impossible to prevent smuggling, and the officer stationed at
each tower,[1] who starves on eightpence a day, can scarcely be expected
to possess sufficient resolution to withstand a bribe; and even if it were
so, it would be no difficult matter to elude him. Malta, the Ionian
Islands, and Gibraltar serve as an entrepôt for our goods, and from
them the inhabitants of Calabria are furnished with many comforts at
a cheaper rate than the fiscal regulations would allow them. The higher
authorities even are said to connive at this infraction of the law.

I had a letter to the royal governor of the province, but learning that
he was in bad health, I forwarded the letter, and took up my abode at
the *Giglio d'Oro* . . . I inquired if there were any booksellers' shops in
Catanzaro, as I have lost a copy of Horace which I had brought with
me, and which I wished to replace. Their answers in the affirmative
delighted me; I was disappointed, however, when I found that it contained nothing but prayer-books in Latin, and such catechisms as the
following: 'Question. Define monarchy. Answer. It is a power which
is born of God, and created by the hands of man. Q. But are not kings
sometimes tyrants? A. That is a calumny of foolish and silly men.
Wrongs never proceed from kings, but arise from the corruption and
malice of human nature. Q. Can the people be its own legislator, or
originate political reforms? A. Danton, Robespierre, St Just, and the
National Convention, of impious memory, show how far that is possible.
Q. Why were our ancestors more fortunate, or less unfortunate, than
we are? A. Because they preferred their petitions to their princes for
everything, and thus only obtained things that were useful and just.

1. Customs officials still have their barracks in converted towers.

Q. What is the most glorious attribute of the Neapolitans? A. 'To be faithful to their king.' Such is a specimen of the silly nonsense to which the government grants its protection, and the kind of learning which it would wish to diffuse among the people.

XVII

AFTER resting for some hours at Catanzaro I determined to visit Tiriolo, a village nine miles distant, picturesquely situated on a declivity of the Apennines, from which I could look down on the Tuscan and Ionian seas at the same time, and from which the water flows into both seas. It was the post-road to Naples from the capital of the province, and yet the path was only intended for mules. The inhabitants of Tiriolo are a race of sturdy mountaineers, and its women were particularly striking for their Amazonian figures. Their dress adds to their masculine appearance, and I confess that I felt no inclination to do anything to excite their indignation. I met several who were carrying water on their head, and I could not but admire the magnificence of their form.[1] They had their gown tucked up so completely behind them that it could scarcely be observed, while a piece of red cloth, employed as a petticoat, was carelessly wrapped round them, and as it opened displayed a snow-white chemise reaching to their knees. They wore neither shoes nor stockings, and from the appearance of the lower extremities I imagine that they are as great a luxury as to my own countrywomen in former times. The men were clothed in a loose mantle, and wore the conical-shaped hat which is the usual protection for the head in the south of Italy.

It is curious that we should have no account of any ancient city being placed at this spot, though many coins have been discovered; and what is more strange, a bronze tablet was found in 1640, on which is inscribed a decree of the Roman senate, 186 BC, against a society devoted to the worship of Bacchus, which had excited their alarm from the licentious and profligate character of its devotees. This decree is

1. In 1962, I seldom remember seeing water carried in any other way; and not only water. Women always leave their hands quite free except when they may have a child in their arms, but with the water jar or any other bundle on their head at the same time. On several occasions I observed women carrying large baskets on their heads with a lusty child inside the basket.

alluded to by Livy (xxxix. 18), and it is surprising that a copy of it should be found in this remote part of Italy. The tablet has by some means been transferred to the Royal Museum of Vienna, where I have seen it.[1] The position of the ancient city is considerably below the present village, and at this spot the peasants are continually picking up valuable coins and cameos. I ascended to the summit of a lofty hill behind the village, from which Mount Ætna and Stromboli can easily be distinguished when the horizon is unclouded. Though my view was not so extensive, I was amply repaid for the fatigue of the ascent. I was standing on the last of that lofty range of mountains, which, shooting out from the Alps, runs down through the centre of Italy, and here sinks abruptly nearly to a level with the sea. The plains of Maida and Catanzaro lay before me, and beyond them the mountains again rose with the same abruptness, and continued their course to the extreme point of Italy. To the north my view was confined by mountains towering one above another; to the east my eye rested on a point of and which I knew to form the promontory of Capo della Colonna, the site of an ancient temple, which I am on my way to visit . . .

On entering the locanda I was addressed by a gentleman who had heard of my arrival, and who was kind enough to show me a manuscript history of Tiriolo, giving a minute account of all the ancient remains that have been discovered in this vicinity. It was written by the clergyman of the parish, and was a curious instance of diligence devoted to a small subject. There is scarcely a village of Italy that does not contain a topographer, and it is amusing to observe what importance the most trivial facts assume in their descriptions . . .

Having fully satisfied my curiosity at Tiriolo, I hastened back to Catanzaro, and had scarcely reached my inn when one of the officers of government waited on me, to express the regret of the governor that he was unable to receive me, at the same time requesting to know in what way his authority could forward my objects. He told me that there was a museum belonging to Signor Ferraro, which might be worthy of my attention, and the governor had deputed him to introduce me. I visited the collection, and found it to consist of many coins, cameos, and other curiosities, which, however, had not been arranged . . .

[Ramage records the Inscription on the Tiriolo Tablet.]

This morning I mounted my mule long before the dawn appeared in

1. Dessau, *Inscr. Lat. Sel.* 18.

the east, that I might make some progress before the heat of the day became overwhelming . . .

At daybreak a few muleteers passed me on their way to Catanzaro, having panniers well filled with cheese and fruit. It is in this way it is said that they introduce smuggled goods. The cherries along this coast are the largest and most delicious I have ever tasted,[1] and on them I made my breakfast as I jogged along. In a distance of fifteen miles there was only one *locanda*, which was closed, as its master was engaged reaping at a considerable distance. The water which I could procure was quite warm, and I have never suffered more from heat than in my ride to-day. The grain is already nearly all cut, and to-day I witnessed what I had not before seen, the mode which they employ to separate the grain from the stalks. They use horses for the purpose of treading it out. I saw a peasant driving eight horses round in a small circle, four abreast, and under them was spread the corn.

The thrashing-floor was a raised place in the field, open on all sides to the wind. It was covered with clay, which was very hard, and had evidently been smoothed by a roller. In fact, we had here Virgil's directions (*Georg*. i. 178) exactly followed out at a distance of two thousand years . . .

My road lay along the coast for nearly twenty miles . . .

This confined plain, with scarcely a breath of wind, stretched for upwards of seven miles, when I reached a nearly perpendicular ridge, at the summit of which the small village of Cutro is placed. I was obliged to take refuge in the miserable *locanda*, and felt so thoroughly knocked up that I resolved to give up my intention of proceeding forward to Cotrone.[2] A pretty fair modicum of wine, however, revived my spirits, and, after resting a couple of hours, I again proceeded on my journey. The country became better cultivated as I approached the city of Cotrone, and it was with feelings of great delight that I beheld its castle as I issued from the small valley of the Æsarus. This river, which is the scene of some of the most beautiful bucolics of Theocritus, I found to be less picturesque than I was prepared to expect, but it is curious how much our feelings influence our opinions even of external objects, and it may be that my jaded spirits made me unable to appreciate the beauties of the Æsarus.

1. I found myself in complete agreement with Ramage.
2. Now usually known as Crotone.

Cotrone is a walled town, and, as I entered its gates, I was prepared to be pulled up by the sentinel; however, I passed unchallenged. It was evening, and the public square was crowded. The descendants of that Milo, whose feats of strength are among the wonders of our boyish days, stood before me. It was in vain that I looked round to discover the athletic forms and brawny muscles of former times. The stare of solid ignorance, the look of unintelligent curiosity, were the only striking features in the character of the modern inhabitants of Cotrone. Yet nature is still unchanged; the same mountain protects its harbours from the storms of the south; the soil of the surrounding country would yield as abundant crops as it ever did in former times. To support the physical powers of the human body, nature is as lavish in her gifts as she was two thousand years ago. It is the mind that is degenerated, the intellectual powers that seem to be extinct. The walls of the city once encircled a space of twelve miles, now they scarcely form a circuit of one mile, and the inhabitants have abundant room within the precincts of the ancient fortress.

As I alighted in the public square, I seemed to be an object of curiosity to the inhabitants, who were enjoying the cool of the evening at the door of the principal coffee-house. My muleteer discovered a house where I could be furnished with a bed, and, though it was not particularly clean, I had little doubt that I should sleep soundly. As I had no letter to any of the inhabitants of Cotrone . . . I thought it my wisest plan, though much tired, to present myself before the chief magistrate of the city. This person, I found, was called Baron Brancaccio, and from his rank I imagined that I should find gentlemanlike behaviour. The entrance to his house did not prepossess me in favour of its interior . . . [Ramage met only with discourtesy and unhelpfulness and decided to return to the inn.]

. . . The shades of evening had already set in when I entered the eating-house, a low-roofed chamber, the gloom of which was only heightened by a few glimmering lamps. I stopped an instant on the threshold, and threw a hurried glance over the inmates of the apartment. It was furnished with several long benches of the rudest construction, and the tables consisted of a single plank supported by four pieces of wood, from which the bark had not been stripped. In one corner sat a sailor supping on a dish of salad, not apparently of the most inviting sort, and throwing many a wistful eye on a flask of wine which he had just emptied. In another part of the chamber lay a peasant of the lowest class, who rose as I entered, and paid his bill with four *grani*, or two-pence English. The landlady offered me maccaroni and *treglia*, a kind of fish plentiful on the coasts of the Mediterranean, and if she and her cooking utensils had been a little more cleanly, I should have found little fault with her supper. The wine was detestable, and yet what could be expected, as my whole expenses only amounted to eightpence.

Cotrone is the site of the ancient Croto, one of the most celebrated of the republics of Magna Græcia, founded as early as 710 BC; and flourishing for five hundred years. It was the residence of Pythagoras and of many of his most distinguished disciples, being indebted to the principles and doctrines inculcated by them for much of the eminence to which it rose. Its youth was remarkable for that robustness of frame which is requisite to ensure success in athletic exercises, and it was a common saying that the least able of the wrestlers of Croto was superior to the first of the other Greeks. The conquest of Sybaris was a brilliant epoch in its history, but from this period the inhabitants became enervated by luxury and love of pleasure. The city extended on both sides of the river Æsarus, of which not a vestige can now be seen in that direction. Time has obliterated every trace, and I found vine-yards and corn-fields where lofty buildings once stood. It is said the harbour which now exists was formed of the stones of old buildings, and this is by no means improbable, though the stones are small and have no appearance of having been used for any other purpose. The old harbour is supposed to have been at the mouth of the Æsarus, and the present town is thought to have been the ancient fortress of Croto. About six miles from Croto, on the promontory of Lacinium, stood a temple of Juno, which was scarcely inferior in celebrity to the city for the magnificence of its decorations, and the veneration with which it was regarded.

At daybreak I issued from the gate of Cotrone to visit the ruins of this temple, situated on the promontory, now called Capo della Colonna, from the pillars that once adorned it, but which have all disappeared except one ... I passed along a barren, uninhabited coast, and as I approached the point the hills gradually became less high, till they at last entirely disappeared, and a level plain of about a mile in extent lay before me. A single column rose in the distance, a monument of distant ages, the connecting link between the past and the present ... There was nothing but this solitary column to remind me that I was approaching a spot rich in historical recollections. One or two ill-constructed houses, the summer residence of some of the more opulent inhabitants of Cotrone, and a ruined watch-tower, were the only indications of human existence. There was also a small chapel, dedicated to the worship of the Madonna del Capo, who now occupies the place of the pagan goddess. The painting of the Madonna was exhibited to me with much reverence by an old man, to whom the care of the chapel is entrusted. I thought of the famous Helen painted by Zeuxis which had once adorned the temple of Juno, and sighed to think that the Virgin Mary was represented by such a daub . . .

I was only a few days too late to witness the celebration of the festival of the Madonna, which is observed with great ceremony by the inhabitants of Cotrone, and at which a fair is held on the plain . . .

The temple stood on the extreme point of a narrow tongue of land, where the view must have been confined to the clear blue sky above, and to the darkly rolling ocean beneath. The castellated towers of Croto and the lofty mountains of the Sila were objects of interest, but their beauty was lost in the distance. Far off, near Cape Rizzuto, a rocky islet was visible to the south,[1] which is believed to represent Ogygia, the island of Calypso, so beautifully described by Homer. I could have wished to visit it; there was no boat, however, at my command. A few yards below the lofty column the waves dashed lazily against the rock, which for ages had withstood their ceaseless roar, and now was cut into a thousand fantastic shapes. The founders of this temple seem to have built for eternity, so massive are the stones of its foundation. On one side, which is most perfect, five rows of stones, ten feet in length, had supported this magnificent edifice. Above this a thick wall of brick, no doubt of a later date, had been raised, the unbroken masses of which lie in various directions. Towards the sea a portion continues still entire, and reaches a height of nearly thirty feet. The column, which seems to be about thirty feet in height, and which gives name to the cape, is of the Doric order, being fluted and broader at the base than at the capital. It is supported on a pediment of four rows of stones, placed on each other without mortar. The length of the temple on the western side, which is most perfect, is upwards of four hundred feet. Scarcely any attempt has been made to clear away

1. Le Castella. This island is crowned by a large castle of the Aragon period.

the earth, so that the true dimensions cannot exactly be made out ...

On my return to Cotrone I visited the harbour, which contained only a few boats and feluccas; nor could any vessel of a large size enter from the accumulation of sand at its mouth. I then strolled through the streets, and found the houses small and dirty. I attempted to enter the castle, within which there is said to be several ancient inscriptions. This, however, was a vain attempt, as the sentinel stepped forward and said that I could not advance without the permission of his commanding officer. As he was confined by sickness, I was unable to satisfy my curiosity, and retired to my lodgings, where I meant to remain for the rest of the day to recover from my fatigue. Here, however, an enemy attacked me in a way that made me speedily evacuate Cotrone. I found my room possessed by legions of flies, brought out by the mid-day sun, and I could invent no method by which I could obtain a moment's rest. I found that it was one of the peculiar plagues of Cotrone at this period of the year, and to me they were far more annoying than the mosquito – no very agreeable companion, I can assure you. This attack determined me at once to leave Cotrone, and proceed forward to Strongoli, which was at least twelve miles distant ...

I passed several bands of reapers, who attacked my muleteer with volleys of clownish raillery, the wit of which I am sorry I was unable to understand. It was answered with great good humour, and a quick succession of sarcastic repartee passed between them as long as we continued in sight ...

The language of these reapers sounded strange to me; and, indeed, in this part of Italy it is curious to observe the varieties of dialect and even distinct languages that are spoken ...

The coast along which I passed exhibited the same uncultivated appearance as yesterday, having large salt-pools here and there; and, after having struck into the interior for five or six miles, I reached the largest river I had yet seen, called Neto, the ancient Neæthus. It was navigable in the time of Strabo for several miles, but its mouth has long been barred by sand-banks. I crossed it without much difficulty, with my muleteer behind me, though in winter it would require a boat to pass it in safety ... Strongoli now began to appear at some distance on the summit of a hill, and I rejoiced to think that my day's labour was drawing to an end, though I was ignorant as to my night's lodgings.

The day was fast coming to a close as I ascended the steep hill on which Strongoli is situated, clinging with difficulty to the uncomfortable saddle of my mule. I entered a half-ruined village, and proceeded at once to the house of the judge to procure me shelter for the night. His daughters invited me to enter, while they despatched a messenger for their father. I was shown into a small but neat apartment, where I found three handsome girls, assisting each other at their toilette, who seemed not in the least disconcerted by my intrusion. Their manners were simple and pleasing; their father requested me to accept a bed in his house, and when I hesitated, from an unwillingness to intrude upon him, the young ladies joined with such evident good will in urging the request, that I could not refuse. They have spent the greater part of their life in Naples, and they consider their residence here to be a kind of exile. How strongly contrasted is my reception here to what met me last night in Cotrone!

As I found that there were some remains of antiquity in the vicinity of the village, I proceeded at once to visit them. The village itself presents nothing remarkable, having never recovered from the severe treatment it had received from the Turks. It is supposed to be the site of Petilia,[1] dating its origin from the time of the Trojan war, if geographers can be believed, but it is chiefly remarkable for the long and obstinate resistance it made to Hannibal in the second Punic war. Philoctetes is said to have been its founder, and, as a proof of this, the inhabitants of Strongoli point out the ruins of an ancient edifice, and call it the Temple of Philoctetes. Here they are constantly discovering coins, bronze figures, and terracotta lamps. Near their cathedral, which is large and handsome, lie several fragments of pillars of cipollino marble, with some sepulchral inscriptions, that have been already copied . . .

One of the respectable inhabitants is in the possession of a considerable collection of valuable coins; there was one beautiful medallion that arrested my attention more particularly, but it looked so new, that I suspected it to be of modern date. On one side is a warrior in the act of offering incense on an altar, with an ancient galley in the distance. The inscription is in well-formed letters:

EXSOLVVNT GRATES CAESAR ET IMPERIUM

1. This site has not yet been excavated, but is thought to be near Strongoli, *see* p. 17, n. 1 and *see* bibliography.

On the reverse is a warrior seated on the banks of a stream, with some buildings in the distance, and the inscription,

HAC TANDEM MARS AD THERMAS ABLVISSEM.[1]

... [After passing some time in conversation in the public square, Ramage returned to his host to find] ... an excellent supper prepared, and a few of the inhabitants invited to meet me. The sparkling eyes, however, of the younger sister proved the most attractive object of the company, and induced me to prolong our social meeting to the 'wee sma' hours ayont the twal''. They gave me a pressing invitation to spend at least part of the following day with them; there are many reasons, however, why I must press forward.

XVIII

BEFORE the stars had disappeared I was descending by a narrow and rugged footpath from the village of Strongoli ... [and] as the sun rose, I was ascending the rising ground on which the village of Cirò was placed, and passing several patches of Indian corn and small vineyards. A plain of several miles in extent lay towards the sea, where herds of wild ponies were seen galloping through the brushwood. A promontory, on which an ancient Temple of Apollo[2] is said to have been situated, appeared at some distance, and I would have been strongly tempted to visit the spot if I had not known that it had been examined by Swinburne towards the end of last century, when no remains were visible. It is now called Capo della Alice, a corruption possibly of Alæus, the appellation given to Apollo here. The small village Cirò is walled, though its fortifications seem in so ruinous a state that little resistance could be made to a hostile attack. There was nothing within to induce me to enter, though it is believed to be the site of Crimisa, which, like Petilia, was founded by Philoctetes ...

The oaken gates of Cirò were now open, and a few of its inhabitants were idling with some girls washing linen at the fountain outside the

1. Professor Jocelyn Toynbee has kindly allowed me to state that she much doubts whether this medallion could be of genuine antiquity.

2. The fifth-century doric temple of Apollo Alaios was excavated many years ago by P. Orsi, and the city of Crimisa is probably nearby, see bibliography.

walls. I have been particularly struck by the number of women I have observed in field labour; and on calling the attention of one of the natives to the circumstance, he acknowledged that the women were more industrious, and performed more labour, than their husbands. The education of women of the lower ranks is entirely neglected, and I believe that, even in the higher classes, it is not uncommon to find that they are unable to write. Their manners, however, are pleasing from their simplicity, and I was often astonished to observe with what perfect nonchalance they talked on subjects which are not usually introduced by us in presence of ladies, and I felt at times rather out of countenance, while they evidently were not aware that they were doing anything of which they need feel ashamed. You will understand how matters are in respect to marriage, when I tell you that the law enjoins no marriage to take place before the bridegroom is fourteen and the bride twelve years of age. The ceremony must be contracted in the sight of the Church, if it is to have civil validity either for the parties themselves or for the children. There is, however, a civil act (*atto civile*), for the execution of which civil officers are appointed, but it limits its provisions concerning marriage to the civil and political effects, leaving all the duties that religion imposes untouched and unchanged. Separation may be obtained, but there can be no complete divorce. The husband may prefer a complaint for adultery, and the guilty wife is confined from three months to two years in a house of correction. The adulterer is fined from fifty to five hundred ducats.

Leaving the young damsels at Cirò, I continued to advance for several hours through thick groves of olive-trees, without, however, meeting a human being. It is this want of population scattered over the country that weighs down the spirits; the inhabitants are collected in villages along the heights at some distance from the shores, and you may wander for several hours without seeing any one. On this part of the coast a ridge of hills, of moderate height, runs along parallel to the shore, and at no great distance, the summits of which are covered principally with that species of ash which produces the manna, being larger in leaf than our ash, though it grows to no great height. At last I reached the small village of Cariati, which gives title to one of the most respectable families of Naples . . .

Cariati is a wretched village, containing not more than a thousand inhabitants, with a church of Gothic architecture, and surrounded by walls in the last state of dilapidation. It has been often plundered by Turkish corsairs, has suffered from the hordes of brigands, and was nearly destroyed by the French in 1806.

I rested at Cariati for a short time, till the insects became so annoying that I was fairly driven out, and I determined to push on four hours longer to Rossano. As the day drew towards a close I entered a beautiful wood of olive-trees, and as I was thoroughly tired of the jolting of my mule, I alighted and walked leisurely forward. It was a lovely scene, and I was willing to linger as long as daylight would allow; but my muleteer quickly put an end to my meditations, by assuring me that we were now in a very dangerous wood, called Nierto, where robberies were constantly committed, and that it would be our wisest plan to move forward as rapidly as possible. He pointed to the brow of a hill about half a mile distant, and said that he had observed four men running rapidly along, as if they intended to reach a defile before us, which we must necessarily pass.

At this moment we reached an opening in the wood, with a cross, to mark where a murder had been committed, and at the same time I was able to get a glimpse of the hill, where I could perceive three or four men proceeding with great speed, as my muleteer had asserted, while my imagination bodied forth the glance of rifles in their hands. Not a moment was to be lost, as they were already nearer to the defile than we were, but we had in our favour the speed of the mule. I mounted without a moment's delay, and my muleteer leaped up behind. The mule was excellent, and moved forward at a rapid rate under its heavy load. Our opponents evidently saw our intention of getting before them, as they increased their speed as soon as we commenced our operations. The wood in many parts was thick, and the windings of the path rendered it impossible to see many yards before us. To an unconcerned spectator it would have been an amusing race; to me, however, it was of too serious import to allow of anything but feelings of the deepest anxiety. I felt, truly, that death or captivity hung in the balance. I placed a few pieces of gold in my hand, that I might have a chance of saving a small remnant of my purse. The muleteer said that one half-hour would enable us to reach the defile at the rate we were proceeding, and, if we passed it in safety, we might expect to reach Rossano without further molestation. Fortunately we gained the race, and when we

5 Mill at Amalfi, *top*
Pizzo and the Gulf of S.Eufemia

6 Pizzo, where Murat was assassinated, *top*
The Rock of Scylla

passed the dangerous spot, without seeing a single individual, I was tempted to toss up my hat and cry huzza for the victory . . .

The hills on both sides of this defile rose to a considerable height, more particularly to the left, on the side on which my enemies were approaching, and every moment I expected to hear the report of a rifle, as they would look down upon us while we were galloping through. I know not whether it may not be one of those defiles of which Procopius, speaks, when he mentions Roscianum, the village Rossano, towards which I was proceeding . . .

Another half-hour placed me in the village of Rossano, where I proceeded to the house of the judge, to whom the Prince of Satriano had furnished me with a letter. I confess that I did not like the appearance of the inhabitants as I passed through the streets of Rossano, and was sadly disappointed when I found that the judge was performing his duties in some other part of his district. I left the letter, and proceeded to search for a lodging. The first *locanda* that I entered was so miserable, and the landlady so forbidding in looks, that I shuddered at the idea of passing the night under her roof . . . [After searching for a better lodging, Ramage received a message from the judge's wife inviting him to stay with them.] The old lady received me with great kindness, but was in perfect horror at the idea of my proceeding to-morrow without a guard: and as all her friends concurred with her that the country was unsafe, I agreed, rather to get rid of their importunities than from personal fears, to wait on the lieutenant of gendarmes and request that he would send a couple of men with me. On proceeding to the guard-house, judge of my surprise on being introduced to my old plague, the lieutenant, who had threatened to arrest me at Pizzo. He professed himself glad to see me, and ordered his servant to produce wine. I stated at once the object of my visit, and inquired if he thought there was any real danger. He assured me that there was no doubt about it, but that he durst not send two men, as it would be only sacrificing their lives as well as my own. He would send half a dozen, if I would remain one day longer at Rossano. It would appear that to-morrow is the birthday – name-day, or some such thing, of the king – and therefore a holiday to all the troops. I thanked the lieutenant for his offer, and said that I should inform him to-morrow if I intended to accept it, though I had no such intention. However, he has induced me to give up one part of my plan – a visit to Lungobucco, in the Sila, where a lead mine has been lately opened by a company of English capitalists. It would be vain to hope to escape if I proceeded in that direction.

In this vicinity I hear of nothing but robberies and murders, and they hold up their hands in amazement that I should have ventured to approach Rossano, except under a strong guard. The principal proprietors are completely blockaded, and dare not move a step beyond the precincts of the village, unless in company with others, and strongly armed . . .

While I was seated at the window in conversation with the lieutenant, the funeral of an old man passed; he was stretched at length on an uncovered bier, with a book in his hand, and followed by a number of women dressed in black dominoes, with white handkerchiefs over their heads. I met at the house of my hostess an intelligent Albanian priest, Don Angelo Masci, and I find that they have a college at Bisignano, a small village a short distance from Rossano. They originally belonged to the Greek Church, but have long ago conformed to the Latin. Their library contains several manuscripts in the Albanian language, and, among others, a grammar written by one of the professors, and a volume of native songs collected by a person called Varibobba . . .

Signor Masci accompanied me to the house of a canon of the church of Rossano, who possessed a manuscript[1] of the Gospels of St Matthew and St Mark in Greek characters, illuminated with small figures at the beginning of each chapter. It is in excellent preservation, and must be of an early date, though I could not discover how it had come into his possession. I intend to proceed to-morrow to Cassano, in the vicinity of which stood the ancient city Sybaris; yet it is a hazardous undertaking. The lieutenant has told me that the whole village of Rossano, as he said of Pizzo, are a set of brigands, and as I know this to be an exaggeration, I trust to find the other statements to be equally so. At all events, I am resolved to face the danger . . .

This has been a day of great anxiety, and I cannot say that I am sorry I am now bidding adieu to Calabria, though I have every reason to be grateful for the kind and hospitable manner with which I have been

1. This very beautiful sixth-century A D, illuminated manuscript, known as the Purple Codex, can be seen on application to the custodian at the Archbishop's Palace, adjoining the Cathedral, between the hours of 9.30 a.m–noon and 4–6 p.m in winter; 5–7 p.m in summer. Also *see* N. Douglas, *Old Calabria*, pp. 117–118.

almost invariably received. Still it is harassing to be constantly in the expectation of being either robbed or murdered, and during several hours of this day I was fully prepared to encounter some such fate. Thank God, however, I have escaped, and I do not intend ever again to throw myself in the way of a Calabrese brigand.

This morning I was surprised to find that I had been unconsciously exposed to another danger during the night which had never occurred to me. A severe shock of an earthquake had taken place, and the whole inhabitants of the village had been so much alarmed that they had spent the greater part of the night in the public square, afraid of being buried in the ruins of their houses. Of course no one felt any particular interest in my safety, and I was allowed to sleep undisturbed amidst all their alarm. I have no doubt that I was entirely forgotten, and as there was no disastrous result, I am not sorry that I was allowed to remain quietly in bed . . .

My friends had procured me a muleteer, in whom, they said, I might repose entire confidence; still the old lady continued most urgent that I should remain another day, and accept a guard of gendarmes. I had, however, made up my mind to run all risks, and I left the village Rossano at daybreak. I found a party of the inhabitants, fully armed, proceeding in my direction, but, to my disappointment, they only continued with me a short distance, being on their way to Corigliano. Our road lay through a wood, principally of olive-trees, mixed with myrtles, growing in great luxuriance, and clumps of low brushwood; it was evidently a continuation of that through which I had passed yesterday. It extended for about ten miles, and I was of course anxious that no time should be unnecessarily spent in crossing it. My mule was, however, a sad contrast to the animal I had yesterday, and the muleteer seemed to take matters very coolly. I dismounted, and tried to induce the mule to go somewhat quicker; but it was true to its nature, and refused to budge beyond a snail's pace. At last I gave up the contest in sheer despair, and quietly awaited the result. When we got clear of the wood, and I saw a level plain of several miles in extent before me, I cannot sufficiently express my delight, as I have been told that my dangers would then be at an end. Here, then, I consider that I bid adieu to Calabria and its dangers; for, though it continues a little farther north, I understand that I shall hear no more of brigands.

You may ask what opinion I have formed of the country and its inhabitants. The three Calabrias have been always, in a great measure, separated from the rest of the world. In this respect the district is unique, and the manners of its people have been little influenced by intercourse with their more civilised neighbours. Enclosed by two seas, having in the middle that lofty range of mountains which I have traversed thrice in different directions, covered for several months in the year with deep snow, without sufficient roads or communications between the different divisions, they have all the productions of the north and south, ice and tropical heat, at the distance of a few miles. Recollect the sudden change of temperature I came upon in a couple of hours, when I penetrated into the mountains of Serra. In what other part of Europe will you find another country like this? Then as to the inhabitants, I met men of the highest intelligence and polish, that would have done honour to any country, and, at the same time, the mass of the population sunk in rudeness and ignorance. It is not merely rudeness, but I heard of a ferocity of character which perpetuates family feuds from generation to generation, and regards revenge as a right and a duty. They seem now to be in the state that the Highlands of Scotland were some five hundred years ago. This disposition, inherited from their heathen progenitors, has never been in any degree softened by the influence of religion, or even of the nobility and persons of note, who are generally absentees. In former times the great feudal barons, no doubt, used to live on their properties, but wholly apart from the people, on whom they had no influence, at least for good. In fact, they composed two distinct worlds. With us, the nobility live a portion of the year on their estates, and take a deep interest in every measure that is likely to benefit themselves or their tenants. Here it is quite otherwise; agents manage everything, and transmit the rents to be spent in Naples. The feudal systems subsisted in all its strictness till the beginning of this century. All the principal taxes were laid upon the lower classes, while the nobility and clergy were mostly exempted. It was a law of Joseph Bonaparte that broke up this system. He enacted that 'the feudal system and all feudal jurisdiction be abolished, and all towns, villages, hamlets be subjected to the general laws of the country'. These changes, introduced by the French, had so far taken root, that, on the restoration of the Bourbons, it was impossible to replace things on their former footing; yet some such attempts have been made, and the present government strives to secure for the nobility more favourable rights, and has confirmed the succession of fiefs which the law had done away with.[1]

I soon reached the banks of the Crati, the ancient Crathis, which you may recollect that I crossed at Cosenza on my way to the south. I had some difficulty in fording it from the depth of the stream and the rapidity with which it flows. Indeed, if we had not met with a shepherd, who piloted us across, I should inevitably have been swept away. I tried what effect its waters would have on my hair, as Euripides (*Troades*, 228) says that they have the power of giving a golden-red tinge, but, alas! no such beautiful change took place, and I am obliged to remain as nature intended me ... I inquired afterwards if any such peculiarity was known to the inhabitants to be in the waters, but they were not aware that they possessed such powers.

Grain of every kind wavered over the drier parts of this plain, and my guide said that towards the sea herds of cattle abounded, though I saw none. The marshy ground afforded shelter to wild boars and water-fowls of every species.

1. After the Second World War, the Italian Government passed a special law governing land reform in the Sila whereby land on estates exceeding 750 acres was to be expropriated against compensation. Peasants were offered land on condition that their sole means of livelihood was from agriculture. In 1950, a government scheme even more far-reaching in character was decided on, and a foundation, *Cassa per il Mezzogiorno*, was set up with a ten year plan envisaging the annual expenditure of 100,000 million lire. Along the Ionian coast, a deserted region and till lately malaria-ridden, backed by soil-eroded hills where the main four rivers alternately flooded or dried up, according to the season, dams were to be erected across the rivers Agri, Sinni, Bradano, and Tara to make possible the conservation of waters for the torrential streams farther up and their utilisation for conservancy in large areas of the surrounding country. New crops, such as fodder crops, tobacco, tomatoes, and vegetables were to be grown, and cultivation of cereals, olives, and vines was to be extended, as also the building up of the exiguous livestock population. Now, 1962, the results of this policy, which has resulted in large numbers of the local population being employed, are clearly evident. New roads, aqueducts, power-stations have been built – re-afforestation, and soil and mountain conservancy measures have been undertaken. This '*Riforma Agraria*' also applies to Basilicata and Puglia. *See* M. Grinford, *Rebuilding in Italy*. London and New York, Royal Institute for International Affairs, 1955: especially pp. 191–206; and also 'Saving South Italy', *The Times*, July 11 and 12, 1963.

XIX

A FEW miles below the spot where I crossed, the Crati is joined by another stream, the Coscile, the ancient Sybaris, having the same name as a celebrated city which stood in this vicinity. This river had the property, according to some authors, of making horses shy that drank of its waters; my muleteer knew of no such power. The exact position of the ancient city of Sybaris[1] has not yet been satisfactorily fixed, though we are told by an ancient historian (*Diod. Sic.* xii. 9) that the river Sybaris, which originally flowed into the sea by a separate mouth, had its course changed by the victorious inhabitants of Croto that it might flow through and destroy the city. It is natural, therefore, to look for its remains near the confluence of the two rivers. At the same time, you must know that it is said to have been completely destroyed 510 BC, and we can scarcely expect that much of it will have survived such a lapse of time. However, I resolved to examine the exact appearances at the confluence of the two rivers, and accordingly, as soon as I had crossed, I proceeded down the banks to that part of the plain which is called Gadella. I heard afterwards that excavations had been attempted here, but water always rises as soon as they have penetrated a few feet below the surface. I persevered till I reached the confluence, notwithstanding there was a great deal of marshy ground, and in the winter season it must be quite impassable. There was not the slightest appearance of any buildings having been at this spot, nor can I imagine that Sybaris was placed here, unless nature has completely changed the ground on which I was standing . . . I tried to get across the river Coscile, but the plain through which the river flowed was soft, and the stream ran so rapidly, that I had to creep slowly along its banks for several miles before I reached a spot where I could safely

1. In a further attempt to locate this city, excavations have recently been resumed by the Superintendent of Antiquities for Reggio Calabria, and by the *Fondazione Ing. C. M. Lerici politechnico di Milano* in collaboration with the University Museum at Philadelphia. For reports of previous excavations relative to this site *see* U. Zanotti-Bianco, 'La Campagna Archeologico del 1932 nella piana del Crati'. *Atti e Mem. Soc. Magna Crecia.* (N.S. III, 1960, pp. 7–20); and in (*N.S.* IV, pp. 7–63), P. Zancani Montuoro, 'I Ritrovamenti al "Parco del Cavallo" '. Also see *ILN*, Arch. Sect., No. 2114, 8–12–62; No. 2115, 15–12–62.

pass. I proceeded on to Cassano without encountering any further difficulties, and was received with great kindness by a friend of the judge of Rossano, Signor Cafasi. The appearance of Cassano is highly picturesque, as it rises gradually like the steps of an amphitheatre up the sides of a steep mountain, extending round the rock on which stands the ruins of the ancient baronial castle belonging to one of the noblest families of Naples, the Duke of Cassano. The town contains somewhere about five thousand inhabitants, and exhibits considerable commercial activity from the manufacture of liquorice and even cotton and silk, which are grown, spun, and wove in Cassano. At the entrance of the town there is a spot called Bocca d'Auso, from which smoke is occasionally seen to issue, and near it are some sulphureous hot springs, with baths constructed for public use by the Cassano family. It was still early in the day, and I resolved to examine a little more of the site of Sybaris on the other side of Coscile. I ordered two active little ponies, which my host offered to procure for me, and, accompanied by Signor Cafasi, started for the site of the ancient Cossa, which was said to be situated at a spot called Civita, three miles distant from Cassano. It is mentioned by Cæsar (*Bell. Civ.* iii. 22), who ... states that Milo laid siege to it, and was killed under its walls. These very walls may be imperfectly traced, and the foundations of some buildings are scattered here and there on the summit of a rising ground. What remains is very little, and shows that it had at no time been of great size. I looked round for inscriptions, but nothing of the kind could be seen. There is a tower called Torre di Milone. After I had satisfied myself as to the ruins of Cossa, we rode towards the confluence of the Coscile and Crati, keeping down the left bank. There are no remains of buildings to be seen, but there are numerous irregular hillocks, which I do not doubt would be found to be the foundations of buildings. It was quite evident to the eye that the channel of the Coscile had been changed, whether by some convulsion of nature or by the hand of man it is impossible to say. History says that it was by the hands of the inhabitants of Croto, who wished to obliterate the very existence of their enemy Sybaris. The old channel is called Abbotitura, and contains a good deal of water; and at no great distance from it is what is called Laghetto, a small lake which communicates with the sea, and which my guide told me abounded with eels, mullets, and a variety of other fish. Some have considered Laghetto as the site of the port of Sybaris, but no remains of buildings are to be seen. The *agnus castus* was growing in these marshes very luxuriantly. Both species were abundant, the larger with white and purple flowers, and the smaller with purple flowers alone. It was called *castus*, as you are aware, from its alleged anti-venereal properties, though modern naturalists, I believe, are not quite agreed on this point. At all events, the ancients were of this opinion.

I looked at the spot where Sybaris is supposed to have stood, and found it difficult to believe that it could have been selected for such a purpose. Within a couple of miles of the mouths of two rivers, it must at all times have been subject to the effluvia of much stagnant water, and, indeed, we know that it was unhealthy from a proverb among them 'that he who did not wish to die before his time ought not at Sybaris to see the sun either rise or set'.

I inquired of my intelligent host respecting the position of Thurium,[1] but its supposed site would have carried me back to the country of the brigands, and I need not tell you that it would have required a strong temptation to induce me to place myself once more within their grasp. He said that there is a spot called Turione[2] between the villages Spezzano and Terra Nuova,[3] where coins, vases, and images are frequently found in great numbers, and where he himself has seen the fragments of a marble column. This he considered to be the site of the ancient Thurium.

It was now necessary to return to Cassano, through which I strolled, visiting the Capuchin monastery, situated on a hill from which there is an excellent view of the plain through which the Crati flows, and in the distance the Ionian Sea is seen, while behind rose the lofty mountain Pollino, on which snow lies till the middle of July. The eyes stretched over a wide plain, covered here and there with patches of grain, but the greater part is uncultivated. Varro (*R.R.* i. 44) speaks of it as of surprising fertility, producing wheat a hundred-fold, and if it were reclaimed I do not doubt that nature would be as ready as in former times to reward man for his industry . . .

You may ask me why these plains, on which I was looking, should be uncultivated. It is easily explained to you, who are a political economist; they have no outlet for their surplus produce; the inhabitants can derive no benefit from their industry. This is the complaint

1. For possible identification of this site *see* p. 142, n.1.   2. Unidentified.
3. Spezzano Albanese and Terranova da Sibari.

which I have heard in every part of the country, equally from the friends as from the enemies of the present government. The very parties who are carrying on the government have exclaimed, 'Could not this sacred majesty, whom may God bless, find some means by which we could get rid of our produce? This is the only change for which we pray.'

The Capuchins are employed at the present moment in raising Angelo di Acri, who had been some hundred years ago one of their fraternity, to the rank of a saint in the Roman calendar. A hundred years must always elapse before any such attempt can be made, and it then altogether depends on the sum of money that can be raised to bribe the Papal See, or, to speak less offensively, to pay all necessary expenses, whether he shall receive the honour solicited. The question is considered in Rome, and a regular trial takes place, in which the character of the embryo saint is freely canvassed by a lawyer appointed for the purpose, who is called *Avvocato del Diavolo* – 'the Devil's Advocate'. The trial is, of course, a mere farce, if the money is forthcoming, and the objections of the advocate are considered to be the mere ebullitions of his Satanic Majesty's envious spirit. The money – about eight hundred pounds, I believe – is paid into the papal treasury, and whoever dares to call in question the high honour assigned to the individual is excommunicated by the canons of the Church. Those whose sanctity does not entitle them to this rank must rest contented with the lower dignity of Venerabile and Beato. This is one of the absurdities of Popery introduced during the dark ages of the Church, and it is strange that this pretension should not now be allowed to fall into desuetude. The number of saints in the Roman calendar is often matter of surprise; but it need not be so, when we find that this small district of Calabria has furnished ninety individuals who have been considered worthy of being canonised. Seventy have been entitled to the honour of *Beati*. Ten of the Roman pontiffs owe their birth and education to Calabria.

The quantity of holy relics possessed by this remote part of the world is astonishing. In the monastery of Belforte there is a finger of Stephen, the first Christian martyr, a piece of the Holy Cross and of the sepulchre in which our Saviour was buried; but, what is still more wonderful, there is a fragment of the rod of Aaron. At the village of Soriano there is a statue of St Dominic, which was brought, in the month of October, 1530, from Spain, and presented to a chapel here by the Virgin Mary herself. This legend somewhat resembles that of the holy shrine of Loretto.

You may recollect that I mentioned a miracle that was taking place at Ajeta,[1] and that I tried to convince the judge of Scalea that it was a gross imposition. I have just heard the end of that silly trick. It would appear that the bishop of this diocese received orders from Rome to proceed to Ajeta, and put an end to what the papal authorities had no doubt would be found to be a device of Satan. I wonder if they were aware of the monks of St Biagio practising the same imposition? You will be surprised to hear how simple was the plan adopted by Lo Monaco, and nothing can show more clearly how gullible people are in this part of the world. All that was done – and he has confessed it – was to throw the liquor over the statue, and to place basins full of the water near it, before he admitted the people. They saw the liquor still trickling down the statue, and did not doubt that the contents of the basins had been collected in this way.

I hope to reach Taranto in three days, and I am glad to hear that there is little danger of my encountering brigands. The coast is such a desert that I am told I shall have great difficulty in getting along. I understand that there is no road, and that the villages are generally situated far inland. However, I shall not allow myself to be turned aside by any common difficulty.

On consulting with my friends at Cassano, I thought that my next stage must be to the village of Roseto, and ... at daybreak, I started, with the pleasant feeling that I had now nothing to fear from brigands. The freshness of the morning was delightful; a thick fog hung over the marshy ground, where the mighty Sybaris once stretched with its luxurious inhabitants, whose indolent repose a crushed rose-leaf was sufficient to disturb. There was a fragrance in the air from the orange and citron blossoms, and the distant Ionian Sea reflected a trembling light in the mirror of its gently moved waters ... The breeze blew gently, while the morning song of the birds resounded everywhere through the leafy boughs. It was a terrestrial paradise through which I was passing ...

Immediately after leaving Cassano, I crossed a small stream, Raganello, the ancient Cylistarnus, and soon reached Francavilla,[2] a

1. See p. 57.   2. Francavilla Marittima.

wretched-looking village, though myrtles, pomegranates, figs, and oranges, showed that Nature was ready to bestow her choicest blessings. The villages still continued to be on the heights at several miles from the sea, to protect them from the Turkish corsairs, who used, as I said before, to land and carry off the inhabitants as slaves. This state of things still continued to exist within the memory of the present generation, as I found a coastguard at the village of Trebisacce, where I stopped a few hours during the heat of the day, who had been taken prisoner about thirty years ago and carried to Algiers. I was amused to find that he rather regretted his release from slavery, as he acknowledged that he used to receive plenty of excellent mutton, to which in his days of freedom he is now an entire stranger. This old fellow was a great oddity, and as I had nothing better to do, I confess I furnished him with somewhat more wine than was exactly consistent with propriety. He was a most bigoted adherent to the forms of the Romish Church, and spoke with delight of some poor young priest on whom he had brought the reproof of his bishop, because he had elevated the host once less than the rubric required. He became at last so obstreperous in his mirth that I was put to flight, and took refuge on the back of my mule. Ere long I reached the small village of Roseto, picturesquely situated amidst broken ravines, where I was received with great hospitality by a gentleman, Signor Mazzaria, to whom my host at Cassano had given me a letter. Though he is residing in this remote spot, I found him a well-educated and intelligent man, intimately acquainted more particularly with the woods and forests of the country. We cannot understand the importance of such a question, as our fuel depends not on wood to be turned into charcoal, but on mineral coal; here, however, it is a matter of serious moment, and the government has found it necessary to exercise control even over woods belonging to private individuals . . . [Ramage goes on to discuss local agricultural problems, especially governmental control of fuel and forests.]

I was warned by my friends at Roseto that little intercourse was kept up with the eastern part of Italy except by sea, and that I would find the coast for the last fifty miles in approaching Taranto so barren and ill-furnished with water that it would be no easy task to accomplish the enterprise. I have learned, however, to look with considerable scepticism on the reports of even the most intelligent Italians as to difficulties; they are so little accustomed to exertion, and the climate makes them so unwilling to move, that they cannot understand what a resolute spirit can accomplish, who refuses to introduce into his vocabulary the word 'impossible'. Onward I was resolved to go, till I knocked my head against an impenetrable wall, and you will be amused to see how gradually one difficulty after another disappeared. The coast continued of the same uninteresting character as yesterday. I passed the dry channels of several mountain streams, which evidently contained a large body of water during the winter season; at this moment not a particle could be seen. At last I reached the picturesque banks of the river Sinno, the ancient Siris, which was finely wooded, and covered with a profusion of flowers in full blossom. Nothing could exceed the beauty of this secluded spot;[1] it was a perfect paradise, and I could not help thinking that some of Ariosto's descriptions (*Orland. Fur.*, vi. 20) must have been derived from what I saw before me ...

I gazed with delight on such a scene, and thought that the vivid imagination of the poets was exceeded by the reality of nature. The wonderful beauty of the flowers has made it to be supposed that the gardens of the inhabitants of Heracleia, situated some three miles distant, must have been at this spot, and that these flowers had been introduced by them. Numerous flowering creepers hung in graceful festoons from the branches of the poplar; the underwood consisting of the lentiscus, thorn, wild vine, oleander, arbutus, the sweet bay. The dwarf oak abounds everywhere along this coast, and the liquorice plant grows wild and in great luxuriance. It was the rich plains in this neighbourhood that occasioned many wars between the inhabitants of Tarentum and Sybaris, and which induced the latter city to found Metapontum, in order that the Tarentines might be excluded from the Siritis. I have no doubt that the nature of the soil is as rich and productive as it was in those days, but there is no population to turn it to account. Since I left Roseto, I have only seen in the distance one or two small villages, perched picturesquely on conical-shaped hills at some distance from the sea, and have not encountered a single human being. The Sinno is a considerable stream even at this season of the year, and we know that, in ancient times, it is said to have been navigable for several miles into the interior. I passed it about a mile from its mouth

1. There is now a cement factory at the bridge over this river and Ramage would have found it difficult to reconcile his description of this region if he had gazed upon it in 1962.

on the back of my mule, and I am sure that at present no vessel could ascend it except a very flat-bottomed boat. I attempted to penetrate to the sea along its left bank, but I got so involved in marshy ground that I gave it up in despair. I cannot believe that any city[1] can have been situated in this direction, unless the nature of the ground has been much changed . . .

The sand, which has choked up the mouth of the river, renders the neighbourhood marshy, and, combining with the Agri, makes the whole coast for many miles a complete desert. This is a strange contrast to its former state, when its inhabitants rivalled the Sybarites in riches, as well as in the luxury and profligacy of their habits . . . [Ramage went on to Policoro: here his muleteer refused to go farther and he was unable to hire another.]

Before I proceeded, I wished to examine the site of the ancient city Heracleia,[2] situated about half a mile nearer the sea. This city was founded by the inhabitants of Tarentum after the destruction of Siris, and is chiefly remarkable as being the seat of the general council of the Greek states. The country, as I approached the ruins, was covered with thick brushwood; they are about a mile from the shore, as far as I could judge, and can be traced here and there for a quarter of a mile. There are foundations of buildings of considerable size, but, though I examined in all directions, I could see no columns to indicate the position of the temple. Here, however, have been found many coins, bronzes, and other remains of antiquity; and, within a short distance of the spot, the bronze tables,[3] commonly known as the Tabulæ Heracleenses, one of the most interesting monuments of antiquity, were found last century. They contain a long Latin inscription relating to the municipal regulations of Heracleia. This curious document is engraved on two tables of bronze, at the back of which is found a long Greek inscription of a much earlier date, but of inferior interest. The flourishing state of the arts in this town is proved by the beauty and variety of its coins. What a change from the busy scenes of former days! It is now haunted by the wild buffalo, who are reared in large numbers here, and droves of untamed horses were seen galloping through the open glades.

1. The ancient city of Siris is still unidentified, see bibliography.
2. Excavations have been undertaken in recent years at and near Policoro: this is thought to be the site of Heracleia, and see bibliography.
3. Ref. IG, 14, 645. These tables are now in the Museo Nazionale at Naples.

Having satisfied my curiosity as to the ruins of Heracleia, I left Policoro in a cart drawn by two buffaloes, which are made use of for such purposes, and passed over a level plain for a mile, when we reached a large and muddy river, which I knew to be the ancient Aciris, now the Agri. It was on the rising ground lying before me that a celebrated battle (280 BC) between Pyrrhus and the Romans is believed to have been fought. The buffaloes had no difficulty in carrying me across, but I could not have passed it on foot. In the winter it must be quite impassable, except by boat. On reaching the opposite bank, I dismounted, and walked forward slowly through a country which showed no signs of cultivation. Wearied, I threw myself down under the shade, and began to examine my map with much anxiety, to consider what probability there was that I should be able to reach Taranto along the coast. After passing Torre à Mare,[1] the coast seemed perfectly desert; and this is what everybody had told me. While I was thus employed, I was interrupted by hearing behind me, on the path along which I had passed, the sound of voices, merrily singing, and the clatter of mules' feet. Ere long three muleteers came in sight, and, when they saw me, you may imagine their astonishment to find a *forestiere*, as I am called here, in such a lonely spot. I joined them; and, inquiring whither they were bound, was delighted to hear that they were on their way to Taranto. They were to sleep at Scanzana, where I had intended to take up my abode. All my anxiety at once vanished, as I had no difficulty in making an arrangement that I should have one of their mules, stipulating that they should stop at Torre à Mare a few hours, that I might visit the ruins of Metapontum, and in every other way they were to conform to my commands. I could not have arranged matters better, and the want of a saddle, which would have annoyed me at another time, was not to be thought of except as a good joke.

I need not say that my lodgings were of the most miserable description; and indeed, if I had thought that it would turn out to be such as I eventually found, I should have spent the night in the open air, at the risk of malaria fever, which, after all, I found myself compelled to do. I ascended to my sleeping apartment, where I found two other travellers, by a ladder and a trap-door. As I intended to be up one hour before daybreak, I took a very accurate survey of the bearings of the chamber, that I might be able to pilot myself out of it; and it was well

1. Torremare.

that I had this foresight. As the bed seemed tolerably clean, I undressed, and soon fell asleep, but awoke some hours afterwards with a feeling as if I were on the point of being suffocated. I started up, and tried to get at the window, but was unsuccessful. I then contrived to get my clothes on, and, after poking about, found the trap-door, by which I cautiously descended. My movements awoke the landlord, who, imagining that he was going to be robbed, alarmed the whole house, and I began to fear that I might have some difficulty in convincing them that I had no dishonest intentions. We were all in darkness, but I bawled very loudly that I was the *inglese*, and began to swear by *Santo Diavolo, Vacco*, and all the saints in the calendar, that he had the intention of suffocating me, by placing me in his upper chamber. When he understood my complaint, he laughed heartily, and said that I had been above the *forno*, 'the oven'; and, on inquiring more minutely, I found that he was the baker for all the people in the neighbourhood, and that I had been sleeping above his oven. There is no end of adventures in this strange country; one night to be on the point of being buried by an earthquake, and next to be baked in an oven. I could not help joining in the laugh, though it was annoying to be prevented from getting that rest which the labours and fatigues of the next day rendered so necessary. I could have wished to start immediately, but it still wanted several hours of daylight. I proceeded into the courtyard, where I found the muleteers sleeping soundly beside their mules, and I sat down to wait patiently for the hour of our departure . . . [Ramage and his muleteers set off before dawn and 'at the first streak of light'.]
. . . crossed the river Basento, the ancient Casuentus, a small and muddy stream, and on approaching Torre à Mare I knew that I was in the neighbourhood of Metapontum, now marked by a single house, called Masseria di Torre à Mare . . . This Torre à Mare is about one mile and a half from the sea, and is so called from an old building of a castellated form of the Middle Ages; but the ruins of Metapontum are found at a spot called Chiesa di Sansone,[1] near the mouth of the river Bradano, the ancient Bradanus. Here are considerable remains of the foundations of buildings. I could, however, trace no appearance of walls, nor indeed any edifice so entire that its use could be ascertained. I then proceeded

1. The doric temple of Apollo Lycius, a theatre and other remains have now been excavated, and lie near the railway junction of Metaponto about 2 m. to the south of the Temple 'Tavole Palatine', *see* bibliography.

about two miles up the bank of the Bradanus, till I reached the largest remains of any ancient monument that I had seen since I left the Temples of Pæstum. It is a temple situated on a rising ground near the right bank of the Bradanus, and known as the Tavola dei Paladini.[1] There are fifteen columns still remaining, five on one side and ten on the other. It is of the Doric order of architecture, though it has not the imposing massiveness of the pillars adorning the Temples of Pæstum. My guide told me that coins were occasionally found.

Metapontum is an interesting spot as the scene of the last days of the philosopher Pythagoras, whose house was consecrated as a temple of Ceres, and whose tomb was still to be seen in the days of Cicero. There is some appearance of the remains of a temple at the Chiesa di Sansone...

I had no time to think of food, but satisfied my hunger with the coarse bread of the muleteers as I jogged along. After crossing the river Bradano ... we reached the Torre di Mattoni, situated on the shore, and our course now lay along the sandy beach for about five-and-twenty miles. The view was confined to the beautiful bay of Taranto on the one side, smooth as glass, and a lofty bank of sand on the other ... The sand-bank was tufted with juniper-bushes, and dwarf cypress, while here and there you get glimpses of pines, which prevented the eye from reaching any distance inland. The beach was covered with many specimens of very beautiful shells. The heat became excessive, as the sun beat directly upon us, till we seemed to be passing through the oven over which I had been baking this morning. I am pretty well accustomed to the heat of this climate; to-day, however, was a fearful trial, and I was now convinced that my friends were right in warning me of what I had undertaken. I felt, in the expressive words of Job (xxxvii. 18), as translated by Umbreit, that 'the pure ether was spread before me during the scorching heat as a melted mirror over the parched desert'. My umbrella was scarcely any protection, and my clothes would scarcely fit an Irish beggar. Perched on the back of my mule, which had an uneasy movement, holding my umbrella over my head as I best could, I looked forward anxiously for the first Pisgah view of Taranto. Our wine, too, was soon at an end, but our sufferings on this head arose from my own want of foresight, as I could

1. Tavole Palatine – A small, well-arranged museum was opened in 1961 beside the road a short distance from this temple, the contents of which are described in *Metaponto. Guida breve dell' Antiquarium*, 1961.

7 Reggio di Calabria and Straits of Messina, *top*
'Casa Inglese', Mount Etna

8 Crotone, *top*
  Crotone, Column of Temple of Juno Lacinia

easily have brought a sufficiency from Scanzana. No water was to be found, and the pangs of thirst I never experience so strongly before. Time, however, brings everything to an end, and at last the lofty castle of Taranto appeared in the distance. Before we entered the city we had to cross the Tara, a very considerable stream, though it seems on the map to run only a short distance inland. Here we were all glad to bathe our throbbing temples; as the water was brackish, our thirst could not be slaked. The muleteers had some hesitation about crossing this stream, as they had heard of people being carried down to the sea. After consultation, one, who could swim, agreed to make the attempt, and entered the stream with his mule, while his companions and myself looked anxiously on. We expected every moment to see the mule floundering in the water; yet he got safely across, and, following his example, we reached the other side, though not without being thoroughly drenched. Whatever might be the consequence of this sudden immersion, it was delightful for the moment, and seemed to give fresh strength ... In this dripping state I rode into the public square of Taranto, which was crowded with inhabitants, and my appearance evidently caused great amazement, as it was impossible for them to imagine how I should have got into such a state. I must have had much the appearance of a drowned rat ... I had been now quite twelve hours jogging on the back of a mule, and I need not tell you how thoroughly knocked up I felt. I proceeded straight to a man who was selling iced water, and, mingled a glass of it with rosolio, drank it off, setting at defiance all consequences. It is astonishing that my health should not have broken down under the fatigue and heat I have undergone; I have lived, however, very temperately, avoiding much wine, and, above all, I have performed daily morning and evening ablutions with my sponge. This I believe to have been the chief reason why I have escaped, as the pores are always open, and allow a free flow of perspiration.

As Taranto is a large city, I had no difficulty in finding a tolerable hotel, and here I determined to remain, rather than trouble a gentleman to whom I had a letter of introduction. In the evening I forwarded my letter to the Cavaliere d'Ayala, who sent me a kind invitation to take up my abode with him. This I declined to do, but I found him so pressing that I yielded. The advantage of being at a private house is, that you have a comfortable bed; and, indeed, I doubt if I could have accomplished all that I have done if I had been obliged to sleep at a miserable *locanda* each night. The only disadvantage is, that you are apt to be killed by kindness, and are sometimes obliged to sit conversing when you would wish to be sleeping.

Here, then, ends my examination of the more southern part of Italy, and I cannot say that I am sorry to have done with Magna Græcia, though I shall always look back with pleasure to the few weeks I have spent in it. It is painful, however, to recollect that the country, which is now nearly a desert, was once the residence of a highly civilised people, where the arts and sciences were cultivated with eminent success, and where philosophy had widely spread her humanising influences. All this has passed away, and Nature has again resumed her ancient sway. Nothing now remains of their palaces and magnificent temples except a few ruined walls, which only serve to assist the geographer in fixing the spot where the ancient city stood. The country has again returned to that state of nature from which the Greek colonies once enabled it to emerge. From Locri to Tarentum, the country which I have just traversed, the whole coast was once studded with mighty cities, whose commerce extended to every part of the known world; now we traverse a shore where a traveller finds it difficult to obtain even shelter at night, from the deadly exhalations that its barren and deserted fields send forth. The mind is at first unwilling to believe the possibility of such a change, but of its stern reality the last week has confirmed me.

The first view of the city which I had just entered was highly picturesque; it is situated on a jutting promontory, looking on one side to a magnificent bay, and having on the other a small lake called Mare Piccolo. The smiling banks of this lake appeared in the distance thickly covered with the fig, the olive, and the vine . . .

The entrance to the city is by a bridge, which extends across a small strait, uniting the Mare Piccolo and the Mare Grande.

XX

NEXT morning, the 30th of May, I was early a-foot to examine the city of Taranto. The cathedral first attracted my attention – sacred to St Cataldo, a native of Ireland, who resided, according to the tradition of the Tarentines, in their city AD 166, in the reign of the Emperor

Aurelius. It is a large and magnificent building, adorned in a grotesque manner by a number of columns of all dimensions, exhibiting almost every variety of marble known to the ancients; but the chapel of the saint is still more rich in its ornaments, and is furnished with a silver statue, to which, as usual, they ascribe many miracles. The marble pillars which adorn the cathedral are said to have been brought from the temples of Heracleia and Metapontum . . .

The people of this part of Italy maintain that they owe their first knowledge of Christianity to . . . [St Paul] . . . who landed at a spot about twenty miles south of Taranto,[1] on the shore of the bay, where he performed divine service, and where a chapel is still found sacred to St Peter. In one of the churches of Taranto he is said to have performed the first mass in Italy. I traversed the city in various directions, and found the streets narrow and gloomy, with the houses lofty and crowded together. The population is somewhere about fifteen thousand. Like Crotone, it is fully contained within the walls of the ancient fortress, or acropolis, which stood on a rocky island in front of the inner harbour. Beautiful and picturesque walks might be made along the banks of the Mare Piccolo, but the inhabitants are either too poor, or possess too little public spirit, to put in execution anything that may require exertion. It was in this direction that the ancient city was built; and in the fields you observe quantities of bricks and broken vases. Here, too, at the Monte di Chiocciole, you see a large hill of the débris of the shellfish (*murex*), from which they procured the purple that vied with the Tyrian dye. The hill is entirely composed of this shellfish, and, at the end of last century, it is said that a large vat was discovered, the plastered sides of which still exhibited purple streaks. It is long since the use of this fish to furnish a purple dye was given up; and even the method employed by the ancients to extract the colouring matter has been lost, but the shellfish still remains, and a large number of the inhabitants are employed in oyster and mussel fishing. There are two kinds of shellfish from which the purple was obtained. First, *buccina*, or *murice*, which is of small dimension; secondly, *porpora* . . . much larger. The oyster-fishery at the present time begins on St Andrew's Day, and ends at Easter; while the mussel-fishery extends from Easter to Christmas. The chief officer of the *dogana*, to whom I was introduced, keeps a strict watch over the fishing, and showed

1. ? At Bevagne between Taranto and Manduria.

me a book called *Il Libro Rosso*, in which the rules are contained. The remains of the ancient amphitheatre are seen in the gardens of the Padri Teresiani,[1] on the road leading to Lecce, and show that it must have been of a size corresponding to the magnificence of the city. When the sea is tranquil, the remains of a bridge across a narrow strait of the Mare Piccolo are still visible; this is the spot where tradition informs us Plato landed, and was received by a crowd of Tarantine philosophers. The climate is delicious; the severity of a northern winter is unknown; a perpetual spring may be said to exist. The soil of the surrounding country is still as fertile; its wine and its oil are still of the best quality. Pliny praises the lusciousness of its figs and the excellence of its walnuts; while Martial (xiii. 18) extols its strong-smelling leeks . . .

I was struck by the stately appearance of the cypress in the gardens on the banks of the Mare Piccolo, which shows that they are still the same as in the time of Cato, 171 BC . . . [who] . . . gives instructions as to the sowing of the seeds of the Tarentine cypress, while Columella (*Lib.* 5, 10) praises the luscious nature of the pears.

These productions of nature have not degenerated, and the honey, that once rivalled that of the famed Hymettus, has not yet lost its sweetness. The peculiar flavour is caused by the odiferous herbs with which the country abounds; and there is a small valley called Le Pacchie, where it is produced in greatest perfection. The sea abounds in every sort of fish, and, among the various objects on which the industry of the Tarentines is exerted, I may mention the sowing of the *chiocciole nere*, from which they derive a considerable revenue. They fix in the sea long stakes of the pine-tree, which are found in March to be covered with the young of this shellfish. In June they take the stakes out of the water, and, scraping the fish from them, throw them into the Mare Piccolo, where they are kept for two years, and on the third they are ready for market.

I paid a visit to the manufactory of the famed *lanapenna*, or *lanapesce*, a downy substance, which they obtain from a shellfish about seven inches in length; its two shells are covered with a very fine hair, which they collect and steep in fresh water for two days; it is then beat and carded like flax, when it is ready for the spinning-wheel. They make stockings, gloves, shirts, and even caps of this material.

1. These remains were formerly to be seen in what was then the Piazza Anfiteatro.

The only other place in Italy where this manufacture is said to exist is Reggio, on the Faro. I find Photius, who lived in the ninth century of the Christian era, says in his Lexicon: 'Tarentine dress: a thin and transparent garment'; no doubt referring to this peculiar manufacture. There is a castle built by Charles V[1] which commands both seas, and is flanked by enormous towers. It is occupied at present by a regiment of Sicilians, a fine body of men.[2]

I could not be at Tarentum without visiting the banks of the famed Galæsus . . . I found the stream, which is supposed to be the ancient Galæsus, about four miles distant, to be now called Le Citrezze, and near it an old church, Santa Maria de Galeso. It is a very small stream, only about twenty feet in breadth, rising not more than half a mile from the Mare Piccolo, into which it falls. Like many of these streams in Italy, it bursts at once in a considerable volume of water from the ground. I saw no sheep in its neighbourhood, nor do I believe that native geographers are correct in fixing on this small stream as the Galæsus . . . I should be much more inclined to consider another stream of which I heard, rising near the village of Martina,[3] as the celebrated Galæsus. It is said to fall into the Mare Piccolo, on the north side, and, having a course of nearly twenty miles, would have sufficient grazing for sheep, which Le Citrezze has not . . . [Ramage quotes from Strabo (VI, p. 278) as to the history of the city.] All this explains why there should be so little remaining of the ancient city.[4] I met with an old monk who had devoted much time to the examination of the antiquities of Tarentum, and he assured us that he had been able to discover little. He took me two miles out of the city to an old church, Santa Maria di Murvetre (muri veteres), and here he pointed to some slight vestiges of an ancient wall. This was all of ancient Tarentum that seemed to remain . . .

The wines which I get here have none of the fiery qualities of our port and sherry, but have much more of the hock and moselle flavour. I asked about the ponies of Saturum; they have long since disappeared, nor have the Tarentines now any horses such as they had formerly,

1. The castle was built by Ferdinand of Aragon between 1481 and 1492.
2. Now the headquarters of the *Comando della Marina*.
3. Martina Franca.
4. For reports on recent excavations of Taranto see *Guida d'Italia del Touring Club Italiano*, 'Puglia', 1962, p. 477.

when they furnished a body of light cavalry to Alexander the Great and his successors, and which are still mentioned so late as the times of the Roman Empire.

I was anxious to hear what my friend the Capuchin friar had to say respecting the *tarantismo*, a curious natural phenomenon firmly believed for several centuries by the whole of Europe. There is a spider, known to naturalists as *tarantula*, which is very abundant in this part of Italy, and the bite of which was said to produce symptoms equally severe with those of the most malignant fever, and of such a nature as to admit of being cured only by music. Some authors have even given a list of the tunes[1] which are most efficacious in restoring the *tarentolati* (for so the patients were called) to health ... The spider is the *phalangium* of Pliny, who says that it possesses a malignant poison. In some cases, and with some constitutions, my friend said that the bite caused severe convulsions. The natives of this part of Italy he considered to be, from the excessive heat and the kind of food on which they live, peculiarly subject to hysterical affections. They are fond of music, and when a number of young people join together in what we, in Scotland, call 'daffing', they become so excited, that they might well be considered to be the descendants of the priestesses of Cybele, whose maddening dances are handed down to us on ancient vases ...

My hostess wrote out with her own hand the manner in which the *pizzica*,[2] a dance peculiar to the Tarentines, was conducted, and I do not doubt that she could have shown it still more clearly, and with better effect, on the floor of the ballroom. I give you her own words, and you will see that it is not unlike an old rather vulgar Scotch dance, called the Pillow, which has been banished since quadrilles became fashionable, but which may still be seen at country kirns ... 'A lady begins a country dance alone; after a few moments she throws a handkerchief to some one whom she fancies, and invites him to dance with her. The same caprice dismisses him and invites another, and then another, till wearied she goes to rest herself. Then her last partner has the privilege of inviting other ladies. The dance continues in this way always more varied and delightful. Woe to the imprudent onlooker whom curiosity leads to watch the throwing of a handkerchief, since neither his ignorance of the mazy dance nor gravity of years is any

1. Janet Ross. *The Land of Manfred*, pp. 187–191.
2. Janet Ross, op. cit., p. 294.

excuse; custom obliges him not to refuse the invitation which he receives.' . . .

Everywhere I find the people thinking of little else than the enjoyment of the passing hour. They seem thoroughly to have imbibed the Epicurean doctrine of Horace's (*Od.* i. 11. 3) . . . I observe in this people the most shrewd and active industry not to make riches, but to live free from care.

Having seen as much of Taranto as I cared to do, I have determined to start by sea to visit the heel of the boot, Capo di Leuca, where a Temple of Minerva once stood.

[Ramage embarked for Gallipoli in an open boat loaded with shellfish at seven in the evening. He 'sat for many hours contemplating the beauty of the heavens' and 'watching phosphoric sparks that seemed to be thrown in myriads from the prow of the boat' till they 'seemed to be passing through a liquid plain of stars'. Owing to unfavourable winds they had only reached the Torre di Saturo by dawn] . . . and it was a couple of hours after sunset when we cast anchor in the harbour of Gallipoli. I was thus obliged to remain another night in an open boat to be devoured by insects, equally plentiful here as elsewhere. I tried to forget myelf in sleep; but though I was much exhausted sleep fled from my eyelids, and I passed the night in feverish discomfort. The sun at length rose, and I then found Gallipoli, the ancient Callipolis, beautifully situate on a rocky islet, connected by a long stone bridge of twelve arches with the mainland. My imprisonment was not yet at an end, as the quarantine officers did not make their appearance for two hours, when I was permitted to land.

As Gallipoli is one of the few cities in the kingdom of Naples frequented by English merchantmen, the public *albergo* was somewhat more comfortable than usual; and, after a short rest, I issued forth to examine the city. I waited on the English vice-consul and the *sotto-intendente*, to both of whom I had letters, and they received me with the utmost kindness. I can perceive, however, by the political turn they give to the conversation, that they suspect I have other objects in view than those I profess. I have no doubt that I increase their suspicions, by the perfect candour with which I express my opinions on any subject they choose to start.

The country round Gallipoli produces the best oil in Italy, which is chiefly exported to England in English vessels; but this is not the period of the year when they come. The city is built on a rocky tongue of land running a short distance into the sea, and the number of stories in some of the houses rival those of the 'auld toon' of Edinburgh. The city is separated from the continent by an artificial canal; its castle was erected by Charles I of Anjou, now, however, in a very rickety state. In respect to ancient remains, I could hear of none, and the only curiosity that I saw was a carved figure of the Impenitent Thief on the Cross in wood, whose countenance exhibited more of hardened wickedness than I imagined it possible for wood to express.[1] It was in the church of the Franciscans, which was neat and remarkably clean – not very common in these parts. The population of Gallipoli is about twelve thousand; it is a busy commercial town, trading in corn, fruits, and more particularly in oil, for which there are extensive cisterns cut in the solid limestone rock, containing the olive oil collected from all parts of Puglia. It has also manufactories of cotton stockings, muslin, and woollen goods. The date-palm grows with more luxuriance in the gardens than in any other part of Italy which I have visited.

I left Gallipoli about three o'clock, and proceeded to the south through a country by no means picturesque, but well stocked with olive-trees ... I reached Ugento, the ancient Uxentum, without difficulty, and at once waited on the syndic, and through him was introduced to the monks of the Franciscan monastery, with whom I was to remain for the night. I then visited a canon of the church, who possessed a manuscript history of Uxentum; but, finding that he dated its origin a few years after the Deluge, and drew on his imagination rather than on historical records to substantiate his account, I felt little inclination to examine it more minutely. The remains of the ancient city are about a mile from the present village, and the foundations of its walls are still to be seen in a more perfect state than those of Tarentum, which I had lately seen at Murvetre. Sepulchres are often found in this direction, and so late as 1825 one had been discovered ...

Next morning my host awoke me a little before dawn, and, after making contributions to the necessities of the monastery, I proceeded towards the Capo di Leuca, passing through a country only partially cultivated, and studded here and there with small villages. The whole of this peninsula is composed of low bare hills of limestone, particularly annoying to the eye when the sun is reflected from its white surface.

1. This carving is still to be seen in all its wickedness.

There are no regular valleys, and, of course, no rivers. This naturally occasions a scarcity of water, and, as springs are seldom found at any of the villages, it is only by piercing deeply into the rock that they can obtain a supply ... The inhabitants of Manduria, Copertino, and Nardo are often surprised by the appearance of a mirage, or *fata morgana*, such as is sometimes observed at the Straits of Messina. You know that this mirage is an optical deception, by which you imagine that you see a variety of objects in the air, as if they were reflected to you by a looking-glass. These optical deceptions take many varied shapes, and assume the most fantastic forms. Sometimes the eye is surprised by the towers and castles of a strongly fortified city; then the scene suddenly changes, when sheep, cows, and oxen are seen quietly grazing in fertile pastures. In the middle of the fifteenth century, when the country was kept in a constant state of alarm by the Turks, the whole coast from Mount Garganus, the spur of the boot to the Capo di Leuca, was roused at the same hour by the appearance of a large fleet of vessels approaching from the east. So firmly convinced were the inhabitants of its reality, that many fled into the interior, and the magistrates despatched expresses to government to communicate the danger to which they were exposed. These appearances do not continue long, but, like the vapours in which they are seen, are constantly changing their position, and assuming new forms. From this circumstance they are called by the inhabitants *mutate*. It is in the early part of the morning that they are generally seen, when the air is perfectly calm, or when the *scirocco* is beginning to blow. We read in ancient historians of men appearing fighting in the air. I have no doubt that it may be accounted for by some such optical deception as this ... [Passing through several villages, Ramage satisfied the curiosity of the local people by saying he was going to the Madonna de Finibus Terræ (the sanctuary of S. Maria di Leuca).] It is not unusual for pilgrimages to be made for this purpose.[1] I passed close to a conical-shaped hill, like the barrows that are found in the south of England. It was not less than three hundred feet high, as far as the eye could judge. I understand that there are many of these mounds in this peninsula, and they are called by the inhabitants *specole*, look-out towers, being composed sometimes of earth, as this one was, and sometimes of stones. I dismounted from my mule, and climbed to the top, from which there was a wide view of

1. This is still a place of pilgrimage.

the plain, over which I had been passing, and of the sea in all directions. It is level at the top, evidently artificial; but at what period such mounds were erected we have no records to enable us to decide. They were, no doubt, constructed by a very different race from the present, and it is curious that fabulous history should cause the giants to take refuge here from the wrath of Jupiter. May these mounds not be the workmanship of this pre-historic race?[1] On descending, I stopped a short time to rest the mule at the village of Salve, and on inquiring if they could show any ancient remains in their neighbourhood, one of the most intelligent of the inhabitants took me to an old church in the neighbourhood, called Sta. Maria di Vereto, and there I found some slight remains of ancient buildings. This is, no doubt, the Veretum of Pliny and Ptolemy. As I approached the promontory, cultivation became still more scanty, till at last it entirely ceased, and the bare limestone-rock protruded in all its ugliness. This continued for upwards of two miles, when I reached a small chapel dedicated to the Madonna di Finibus Terræ, and near it a small fort, which was a mere farce, being in a complete state of dilapidation. The old priest who officiated at the altar, and three soldiers, were seated at the door. I saluted them respectfully, and inquired if they were aware of any ancient remains in this vicinity. The Temple of Minerva was, no doubt, erected at this spot, but the only remnant that is found is a single block of pure white marble, which may have been the pedestal of a statue. To the old priest the Madonna possessed much more of interest, and I believe that I scarcely pleased him by my stoical indifference when he unveiled the features of a young girl now occupying the place of the sage Minerva. On the 1st of August her festival is celebrated, when the inhabitants of the adjoining country crowd to do her honour, and confess their sins to the worthy priest. Altogether this was an interesting spot on which I stood, as I consider, from an examination of the coast, that the temple was far more likely to have been situated here than at Castro, where it is usually placed. We must imagine that Virgil had some idea

1. I am indebted to Dottore Nevio Degrassi who informs me that these *speculae* or *specchia* are difficult to date and their function is not certain. They were probably used as watch-towers, and later, as sepulchral mounds – in the latter, bronzes and Attic vases from the sixth century B C, together with local pottery have been found. Only the very rough date from the late Bronze Age to sixth century BC, can be assumed.

of the geography of this part of Italy when he describes the approach
to it by his hero Æneas ...

This spot, where I stood, was the natural site of the temple, a little
removed from the shore, and at a considerable height above the sea.
I looked down on a natural bay of some size, extending from Point
Ristola on the west, to Capo di Leuca on the east. It must afford good
shelter to vessels in every direction except the south, and we hear from
Thucydides (*Hist.*, vi. 30, 44) that the Athenian fleet, 415 BC, on its
way to Sicily, touched at this promontory, known to the Romans
as the *Japygium*, or *Salentinum Promontorium*. I found that it was
approaching the hour when mass was to be performed, and it was, of
course, expected that I should attend. I told them that I was an Englishman, and that my principles did not admit of my joining in their form
of worship. I would stop, however, till my muleteer performed his
religious duties, and would, meanwhile, descend to the shore to admire
the works of the great God, whom we both worshipped, though under
different external forms. This pleased the old man, who could not but
see that I had some tincture of religion, and he said that he would pray
I might yet see the error of my ways; to which I replied, that I had been
taught in our heretical country that the prayers of a righteous man
availeth much. I left him to perform mass, and descended to the shore.
The chapel is not situated on the cape, but in a kind of hollow with
rising ground to the east, trending away to the point of Leuca. The
descent was easy, if it had not been for the glare of the white limestone
rock, which had at present little appearance of vegetation. It was pro-
perly called Leuca, from the Greek word λεμκός, white. The sea came
up nearly to the rocks ... I walked leisurely along about a mile, till
I reached the point which rises several hundred feet nearly perpendicular, and when I rounded the point the coast towards the north became
higher. There was no appearance of human habitation ... It was lovely
enough, and within the sea horizon not a vessel was visible ... I
climbed with some difficulty to the summit of the point of land, and had
an extensive view in all directions, stretching across the entrance of the
Bay of Tarentum, to what seemed an indistinct line of mountains in
the far-distant Calabria ... and, turning to the other side, I could
easily trace the gloomy mountains of Epirus ... [Later he went on
4 miles to Gagliano, and while food was being prepared] ... I walked
to the public square to witness a solemn procession which was on the

point of issuing from the church. It was crowded with the inhabitants. In the costume of the women there was nothing remarkable; the men wore a coarse blue jacket, and the conical-shaped hat of the south of Italy. From the church issued four silk flags, attended each by a select body of peasantry; then the priests with the host, surrounded by twenty of the *guardia urbana*; the magistrates followed, and then the men and women. When they arrived in the middle of the little square the host was elevated, when all within sight fell on their knees. I had placed myself in such a position that I might neither offend their feelings by an open disrespect to their ceremonies, nor compromise myself by honouring that which I believed to be foolish superstition. I have seen some of our countrymen place themselves in a conspicuous position, that they might in this way show more clearly their opinion of the folly of whatever ceremony they might be witnessing. This does not accord with what I consider right. In passing through a foreign country merely to gratify our curiosity, we are bound to respect the prejudices of the people; and if we cannot look on their superstitious observances without lifting up our testimony, we had better stay at home.

After remaining a short time at this village I proceeded forward towards Castro . . . As the sun was approaching the horizon I began to look anxiously for the village of Castro . . . The path along which we were proceeding led us to the commencement of a ravine, and on turning a corner of a hill a ruined castle or fortress appeared, at the distance of a quarter of a mile. Here, therefore, I determined to remain for the night, or rather I had no alternative; and I thought it not unlikely that I might find some apartment less ruinous than the rest in which I should be able to shelter myself from the heavy dews of the night. The path led us down to the ravine, but we could see no path by which the mule could ascend to the castle; and, as I knew that another quarter of an hour would render every object indistinct, I directed the muleteer to remain where he was, and scrambled up the face of the hill to the foot of the wall, which I began hastily to perambulate in search of some ingress. On turning one of the projections I came suddenly on a priest, who was as much startled at my appearance as I was surprised to see him. I found that this ruin was actually Castro,[1] and having received some directions respecting the path which the mule ought to pursue, I soon rejoined him.

1. Castro is now being developed as a seaside resort, but the old village on the hill-top remains much the same as in Ramage's day.

I found that there was a syndic, to whom the priest offered to conduct me. The village had at one time been of considerable size; but a visit of the Turks about a century ago nearly destroyed it, and since that time it has remained in its present dilapidated state. The walls are completely in ruins, and few of the houses are in a habitable state. It now contains about one hundred inhabitants, and is never likely to recover. We passed along the foot of its walls till we reached its ruined gateway, where we met a middle-aged man, who was introduced to me as Don Tommaso, the syndic. He was without shoes and stockings, and his clothes were in as dilapidated a state as the city, whose supreme magistrate he was. He could find me no lodgings, but the priest came forward and offered to accommodate me with an apartment – he was the true Samaritan. I inquired for a grotto in the vicinity – Zinzenusa – about which much has been said. The priest assured me that he knew it; and as I was aware that torches or lamps must be employed in examining it, I thought it advisable to set about it immediately. It was now quite dark. This was of no consequence, as the grotto would be dark at any time; so the priest, having procured everything necessary, I accompanied him down a steep declivity to the sea, and having embarked in a small boat, we rowed along a rocky coast for upwards of a mile. We reached the entrance, but advancing a few yards I found that a gulf extended between me and the interior, and that I must grope along the face of a rock rendered slippery by the constant dropping of water. I was aware that this grotto had been supposed by some to be the Temple of Minerva, spoken of by Virgil, and which I believe to have been situated at the Capo di Leuca. It was said to be adorned with columns and sculptures. Its entrance at once convinced me that to suppose a temple in such a spot was absurd, and I was prepared to find a cave with some stalactites, such as constantly occur in limestone rocks; but the miserable lamp, which was all that I could procure. would have rendered it impossible to make a satisfactory examination, while the slippery nature of the rock, with the slight ledge to save me from a watery grave, made me give up the attempt . . .

XXI

When I awoke next morning at Castro, in the hospitable house of the priest, I found myself very much in the state of one who had the rash of scarlet fever upon him. I do not believe that you could have placed a pin point on any part of my body which had not been bitten, and yet my fatigues had enabled me to sleep soundly during the whole attack. I felt feverish and uncomfortable when I got out of bed, but I went down to the shore and plunged into the sea, which was highly refreshing . . .

Having satisfied my obliging host, I left Castro, and proceeded in the direction of Otranto . . . We soon reached the small village of Vaste, whose inhabitants were all astir. This is the ancient Bastæ, some of whose sepulchral monuments still remain, where vases and bronze ornaments have been found. They had also discovered an inscription, said to be in the Messapian dialect. I saw what seemed to be the remains of the ancient walls.

The road for the last two days has been through an open country, interspersed with some copses of a jagged oak, dwarfish in appearance, and rendered so, I suspect, from exposure to the blasts from the sea during winter. As I approached Otranto, for which I looked anxiously, the landscape was less pleasing, from the quantity of dykes which divide the fields. In its immediate vicinity orange-trees began to appear, and the odour of the flowers is always delightful. There are many springs amidst laurel and citron groves, and the water in the wells is so near the surface – a very rare circumstance in this peninsula – that you can take it up with your hand.

The city of Otranto lies low, and we were close to it before it was visible . . . the castle[1] is the most picturesque object in the city. Its walls are massive, and there are two large circular towers, which were added by Charles V. In the streets and on the parapets you see several enormous cannon-balls of granite, which had been fired into the city, AD 1480, by the Turks, when they took possession of Otranto, and filled all Christendom with terror and amazement. At that time there were twenty thousand inhabitants, of whom twelve thousand were massacred, and many were reduced to slavery.

1. Constructed by Ferdinand of Aragon between 1485 and 1498.

Alphonso, son of Ferdinand, caused two hundred and forty of the bodies to be transported to Naples, where he placed them in the vaults of the church of St Catherine, in Formiello . . . [Inscription.]

Otranto is a city of some importance, chiefly as the port from which travellers usually embark for the Ionian Islands. There is a packet-boat regularly every fortnight to Corfù, and on that account I found the hotel by far the most respectable since I left Naples. On entering, I was not a little pleased to find an officer of the 90th, as I had not seen the face of a countryman, or spoken a word of English, for upwards of a month. I was amused to find that he did not recognise me, and I was not surprised, as my dress had none of the usual neatness that we generally assume, and my appearance was altogether Italian . . . I found that he had had a narrow escape of being detained here for ten days, from his passport not being countersigned by the English authorities at Naples. He was on his way to join his regiment at Corfù, and on leaving the kingdom of Naples it requires such a signature . . .

I proceeded to examine what ancient remains there were of Hydruntum, which was on the site of Otranto. The modern city seems to be built within the precincts of the ancient fortress, while Hydruntum in former times extended up the hill about half a mile towards a place called La Spezieria Vecchia, where the inhabitants are foolish enough to believe the ancients kept their medicines. It is evidently a fountain cut in the rock, which has long been dried up. I visited the church of St Basilio, regarded as an ancient temple, but there is nothing visible to prove its right to a remote antiquity. Within the walls of the present city I could discover no ancient remains, except a few marble columns in the *soccorpo* of the cathedral, which are supposed to have belonged to a Temple of Minerva. Of Gothic architecture, it possesses several green marble pillars mixed with granite pillars, which are said to have been transferred from this Temple of Minerva, situated where there is a chapel to S. Nicolò, a little distance from Otranto; but they are spoiled by having *stucco* capitals adapted to them; its pavement is what is called Saracenic mosaic, composed of pieces of serpentine, porphyry, and cubes of gilt glass, which have been formed into rude representations of animals, among whom are seen monkeys sitting on branches of trees.[1]

1. The Turks are reported to have used the cathedral as a stable and it is remarkable that this most interesting mosaic pavement remains in such a good state of preservation.

In a chapel you are shown the bones of seven hundred of the natives of this town, who were massacred in 1480 by the Turks, and the superstitious regard them with equal veneration as they do the reliques of the ancient martyrs . . .

I saw nothing interesting till I reached the vicinity of Lecce, when I passed several respectable people, who were picking up something on the side of the road and dropping it into baskets. I inquired what they were doing, and found that they were collecting a particular kind of snail to make soup, which they consider a great delicacy. I had witnessed the operation of boiling them, but I have never yet mustered courage to taste what appeared to me an abominable dish. Yet this is mere prejudice, and if I could taste it before I knew of what it was made, I am told that I should not dislike it. I found Lecce a large town, containing about fifteen thousand inhabitants, fortified by walls, in rather a ruinous state, and ditches, being defended by a castle or citadel. It is a well-built town, having wide and regular streets, very uncommon in this part of the world, and many rather handsome buildings. It is evidently an active commercial town, and I found that it had manufactures of woollen, cotton, and silk goods, besides oil and wine. The hotel is respectable, though not particularly clean . . .

Lecce is believed to be the site of the ancient *Lupiæ* or Sybaris, and is well known to classical scholars as the spot where Augustus resided for some days after his return to Italy, on hearing of the murder of Julius Cæsar on the Ides of March, 44 BC . . . No ancient remains are now visible, nor, indeed, is there anything to interest a stranger,[1] except, perhaps, the church of Santa Croce, which is not a bad specimen of architectural design. The cathedral has a wooden roof, richly carved and gilt. In the public square is an antique column, said to have been brought from Brundisium, and on the summit is Saint Oronzio, the patron saint of Lecce. Verrio, a native of Lecce, has adorned many of the churches with his paintings; he was employed in England, where his staircases and ceilings are much admired. One of the gates of Lecce is called Porta di Rugge, and this was to me the most interesting point connected with Lecce, as it led the way to the ancient

1. Norman Douglas, in *Alone*, remarks that 'at Lecce, renowned for its baroque buildings', Ramage finds 'nothing to interest a stranger . . . True, the beauty of baroque had not been discovered in his day'.

Rhudiæ,[1] the birthplace of the celebrated poet Ennius ... [which Ramage then visited.]

I had thus accomplished all that I cared to see at Lecce, and ... though the day was far advanced I ... started at once for Manduria, which was about eighteen miles distant. The country was thickly covered with olive-trees. There is nothing picturesque in slightly undulating plains, and the heat of the day did not tend to raise my spirits, so that I was glad when the village of Manduria appeared in the distance. On my arrival it was too late to examine its ancient remains and after I had submitted my passport to the chief magistrate, I retired to rest in a tolerable *albergo*.

Next morning I issued forth with a guide to visit the well of Manduria[2] ... It is at a spot called Scegno, about half a mile from the town, and is described by Pliny (ii. 106, 4) ... It is situated in a large circular cavern, and is approached by a descent of thirty rough steps. Light is admitted partly from the entrance, and partly from an aperture in the rock, which is immediately above the well. The rocky stratum in which the well is found is a concretion of sea-sand and marine shells, and the porous nature of the stone allows the water to percolate freely. The water is not now drawn by the inhabitants from the ancient well, but from a small reservoir, which is kept always full by the constant oozing from the sides of the cavern, the water being collected into an earthen pipe, and thus conveyed into the reservoir. It flows thence into the well, which is said never to show any change of level. The well gets gradually filled up with small stones, and at present is not above a couple of feet deep. It had, however, been once cleaned in the memory of the present generation, and was found to be of no great depth, with a bottom of very hard composition. There must of course be some very peculiar way in which the water passes off, and how it is supplied is equally a mystery. It must ooze through the joints of the sides of the well, and it is curious that it should at all times, whatever be the quantity of rain that falls, only receive as much as it can throw off ... The water was pure, pleasant to the taste, in no respect mineral, though not particularly cool, as if it had come from some internal reservoir exposed to the heat of the external air.

1. *See* bibliography, and M. Benardini, *La Rudiæ Salentina*, Lecce, 1955. The site is situated 2 kms, to the south-west of Lecce at San Pietro in Lama.

2. There is a custodian here and the well can be visited.

The city of Manduria was of some importance in early times, and is remarkable as the scene of the death of Archidamus, King of Sparta, son of Agesilaus, who had been invited by the Tarantines to assist them against their neighbours, the Messapians and Salentines. The battle took place on the 3rd of August, 338 BC, on the same day with the more celebrated battle of Chæronea, It revolted to the Carthaginians in the second Punic war, being taken by assault by Fabius Maximus just before he recovered Tarentum, 209 BC. It then disappears from history, having been probably severely punished by the Romans.

The ancient city[1] was at a short distance from the present village, or probably town, as it ought to be called, containing about six thousand inhabitants. The walls can be traced nearly in their whole circuit. The stones of which they were built are soft, and easily decompose from exposure to the air. They have, therefore, mouldered away, and the highest part of the wall which I saw was not above seven feet. They are composed of large rectangular stones, in regular courses above each other, without mortar. What is curious is that it had a double wall, with a fosse on the outside, while there was a wide passage between the walls. As far as I could judge, the outer wall, with ditch, had a breadth of twenty-three feet, and the inner passage, with the inner wall, of about fifty feet. The modern city is well built, though its streets are unpaved. There are numerous churches, and an immense baronial residence of the Francavilla family, without garden or prospect. The chapel of S. Pietro Mandurino is at a short distance from the city, and beneath it is a small chapel, whose walls are covered with paintings of saints of the Greek Church. This part of Italy was the last which the Greek emperors of Constantinople possessed, and in this way we may account for these paintings, which are nearly destroyed by damp.

Having examined everything that a stranger cares to visit at Manduria, I proceeded forward six miles through a country partly covered with olive and almond trees and partly a barren waste, from the entire want of water in the summer season, till I reached Oria, the ancient Hyria, situated on a hill of moderate height overlooking the level plains of Iapygia, which I have been traversing for the last week. You look down on the Adriatic, and have a Pisgah view of the Bay of

1. Excavations have recently been conducted here and three concentric rings of walls brought to light, the earliest dating from the fifth century B C. A vast necropolis has also been excavated just outside the walls, see bibliography.

Tarentum, with the mountains of Basilicata in the distance. The imme-diate vicinity of the town, containing about six thousand inhabitants, is well cultivated, having numerous vineyards and orchards, separated from each other by hedges of aloes. The large castle rises majestically on the highest point of ground, and here, too, the cathedral is placed. These are picturesque objects, seen to the distance of thirty miles. This city was of great importance in early times, being mentioned by Herodotus (vii. 170) as the capital of the Messapians, founded by a colony of Cretans on their return from Sicily ... [After 'baiting' his mule, Ramage sets off on the eighteen-mile journey to Brindisi, and, after passing Latiano and Mesagne, he enters Brindisi a little before sunset.]

Brundisium is full of world-known recollections, and I was, there-fore, anxious to see what survived of its ancient splendour. I sallied forth in company with the English vice-consul, Signor Monticelli, who kindly engaged to point out whatever was worthy of notice within his native city. Time, however, has laid a heavy hand on the works of man, and little now survives to excite our admiration. Still little change can have taken place in the natural scenery around, and I pleased myself with tracing the approach of Cæsar to Brundisium and the flight of Pompey by sea. The present walls are of a later date than these two heroes, and, before the introduction of gunpowder, must have been impregnable, if stoutly defended; but they are now in a sadly dilapi-dated state. The fosse, which once proved its safety, is now filled with stagnant water, and sends forth, during the heats of summer and autumn, most pestilential effluvia. In former times there are two har-bours, an outer and an inner; but the entrance is now nearly blocked up by sand, so as to render the inner little better than a marsh, and last year the malaria produced by it was so malignant that six hundred of the inhabitants were carried off by fever – about one-tenth of the popula-tion. The magistrates made a representation to government on the subject, and a promise has been made that the outlet to the outer harbour shall be cleared, yet they have no hopes that any steps will be taken. I was particularly struck by the ghastly appearance of the inhabitants, and my host told me that he looked forward with great dismay to the approach of autumn. Something might, no doubt, be done by the inhabitants if they were not so much accustomed to see everything undertaken by government. It is the narrow channel that leads into the inner harbour that is choked up with sand, and it is this that renders the inner harbour completely useless. This has been ascribed to the works erected by Cæsar for the purpose of obstructing the entrance, and till the piles, which he is believed to have driven in, are removed, my host did not think that any real benefit would be derived ... I find that the inhabitants will do nothing for themselves, even though death stare them in the face. Thus they drink the putrid water of their city rather than be at the trouble and expense of conveying a pure stream from some little distance within their walls. They were beginning, however, to think on this subject, and I accompanied the chief magistrate to a spring at one of the gates, which had been neglected for many years, and which he had given directions to be cleared out. It was to me an interesting spot, as the celebrated Appian Way, from Rome, had entered the city by this gate; and there lay the huge blocks of stone, so massive and so strong, that they were, no doubt, the identical stones over which Horace and Mecænas had passed eighteen hundred years ago ...

In all directions the eye is caught by a lofty pillar of cipollino marble nearly fifty feet high, whose capital is adorned with figures of sea-gods, and in the centre of each side appear the faces of Jupiter, Neptune, Mars, and Minerva. An inscription states that it was erected by Lupo Protospata in the eleventh century: but this is, no doubt, a myth, as it must be of a much more ancient date. There was another pillar close to it, the base and pedestal of which still remain. It was thrown down by an earthquake in 1456, when the city also suffered severely; and in 1663 the fragments were conveyed to Lecce, to be erected there to the honour of St Oronzo, the patron saint of Lecce, who was believed to have saved the province from the plague. There it is still seen in the public square of Lecce. It is difficult to determine whether these columns were merely ornamental, or served the useful purpose of a *pharos* or lighthouse. There is, indeed, a marble vase on the top, and it has been suggested that this vase might be to contain fire or lights; but the difficulty of reaching the top, which must have been by an outside ladder, renders it unlikely that they were intended for such a purpose, and, besides, they are placed so near the edge of the water, that they could not be seen at any great distance from the sea.

In the distance rose the fine old castle at the north-west end of the port, having its foundations washed by the waters of the harbour, and on the land side being defended by a deep ditch. It was founded by Frederick II, and completed by Charles V.[1] For what base uses are such buildings often reserved! It is now a common prison, and resounds with the clanging irons of the malefactors.

There is a library here, the only one I have heard of since I left Naples, and I was of course anxious to visit it. It is very respectable in size, though containing chiefly theological works, as it was bequeathed by the late Archbishop of Brindisi; and attached to it is a small museum,[2] containing a tolerable collection of ancient vases and coins . . .

I spent part of the evening at the public coffee-house, where the respectable inhabitants meet for amusement, to eat ices, and play at billiards. I then proceeded to the house of Signor Monticelli, English vice-consul, where I had the honour of meeting all the principal inhabitants at supper. We spent a few hours very jovially, and some time after midnight the *sotto-intendente* conducted me to his hospitable house. I shall be to-morrow on my way northwards, but I have determined to run along the coast in an open boat for a hundred miles, as I know that there is nothing to be seen on shore that will recompense the fatigue caused by the jogging of a mule.

XXII

[RAMAGE left Brindisi in an open boat 'under the boiling mid-day sun'.]

On getting clear of the islands we found the wind to be against us, but, by taking a wide tack, the captain expected to reach Trani in forty-eight hours. On looking round the boat, I found that they had furnished themselves with oysters, which were small and ill-fed – not like the natives in which the Cockneys delight. In the luxurious times of the Romans we are told by Pliny (xxxii. 21, 3) that the oysters of Brundisium were conveyed to the lake Avernus, near the Lucrine lake, in Campania, to be fattened; and certainly those which I saw would require some such process to render them fit for the epicure.

1. The four cylindrical towers were added by Ferdinand I of Aragon (1481) and it was further enlarged by Charles V (1550). It is now the headquarters of the *Comando Militare Marittimo.*

2. The new *Museo Archeologico Provinciale 'Franc. Ribezzo'* was opened in 1958.

We directed our course far into the Adriatic. No words can express the hazy brilliancy which hung around the coast, making me at last understand Claude Lorraine, whose paintings I used to imagine were drawn from fancy and not from nature. He who has seen such a scene will never forget it. Towards sunset the land had nearly faded from our view. The sky was cloudless, and the wind did scarcely more than ruffle the surface of the waters. There was a softness in the air and a cooling freshness, which formed a pleasing contrast to the heat which had so lately tormented us. I watched the sun descend behind the mountains of the Basilicata, and soon all was wrapped in darkness. It was a glorious night as we glided lazily through the waters of the Adriatic, though I should have preferred a stiff breeze to hurry us forward. Nature, however, was worn out, and I stretched myself on the bench to sleep as I best could. At daybreak I found that we had altered our course during the night, and had again approached the shores of Italy, which appeared at the distance of four or five miles. The coast was low and studded with watch-towers, one of which the sailors called Torre d'Agnazzo, all, I believe, that remains of a place – Egnatia[1] ... I could have wished to have landed if I had not known that we should have been captured by the coast-guard, and a report would have been spread that a detachment of Greek troops, under the command of a Scotchman, had attempted to land on the coast ...

[After a night at sea Ramage] ... entered the harbour of Trani towards eleven of the clock. The port is in the form of a circle, and has good quays. The Ventians, who occupied Trani towards the end of the fifteenth century, constructed this harbour, but the entrance, I was told by my boatmen, has long been blocked up by sand, so that none but vessels of light burden can enter. On approaching the landing-place we were at once seized hold of by a custom-house officer, and hurried off to the police-office to have our passports overhauled. After we had waited about half an hour in a miserable room, I begged one of the subordinate officers to present the compliments of an English traveller to his superior, and to say that I should be much obliged to him if he could examine my passport and allow me to go, as I was anxious to get some repose after the fatigue of two nights in an open boat. Such a request was not unreasonable, and no gentleman would have refused

1. Excavations are being conducted at Egnazia, the Greek Gnathia, see bibliography.

it, but the answer sent was that I must wait. Another half hour passed, and you may be sure that my temper was not improved by the delay, and that I had made up my mind to teaze the fellow in every way possible. At last I was summoned, and ushered in to a little prim, consequential man – Il Signor Mirabile – who evidently thought that all must bow before him. He looked at my passport, and began, as I knew he would, to inquire where I was going. So much I was obliged to answer, and I told him he might insert Barletta as the next town I should visit. Then, looking at me sternly, he asked why I was allowing my moustache to grow. To understand the meaning of this question, I must tell you that an incipient moustache, as I found from my plague the lieutenant at Pizzo, is considered the secret sign of the *Carbonari*, a political society in the country. Here he opened the door for me to poke in to him, and I said, for the same reason that he allowed his black mop to grow on his head. If a thunderbolt had fallen at his foot he could not have been more astonished . . .

I proceeded to examine Trani, which I found to have a population of somewhere about sixteen thousand. Its walls and bastions – which have been ordered to be put in a state of defence, lest the Greeks should invade the country – are sadly dilapidated; and it has a sort of citadel, which would certainly not stand a long siege. Some of the houses are handsome, but the greater part of the town is ill-built. I was much struck with the appearance of the cathedral, which is situated close to the sea, and has a spire said to be two hundred and fifty feet in height. The interior is elegant, and less gloomy than is generally found in these buildings. Some of the windows are fine specimens of Gothic architecture. It has a theatre of respectable appearance, and a public garden along the sea-shore, where the higher class of citizens assemble in the evening to enjoy the coolness of the sea breeze. I inquired for ancient remains; I could hear of none, nor was it likely, as it is evidently a town of modern date. Still, there is no doubt that it is the site of the ancient town of Turenum, mentioned in the Tabula Peutingeriana; and Pratilli, in his account of the Via Appia, states that he found eleven milestones at Trani, some of them in good preservation . . .

[On leaving Trani, Ramage resorted to a mule to take him the nine miles on to Barletta where he only made a short stay. He then hired a cabriolet to continue to Canosa.]

My way lay across the plains of Cannæ, a spot which I could by no means pass without an examination of its appearance. As soon as my passport was procured, I mounted the cabriolet, and proceeded along an excellent road, till we reached a bridge which is thrown over the Ofanto, the ancient Aufidus, and here we turned up a by-road along the south bank of the river . . .

To the south of the river lay the wide plains of Apulia, as far as the eye could reach, already stripped of the grain, so early is the harvest in this part of Italy. They leave the greater portion of the stubble on the field, cutting off little more than the ear, and they afterwards set fire to the straw, which is thus burnt on the field, and serves for manure. The practice of burning the stubble upon the lands has been handed down from the earliest times, and is followed in many other parts of Italy. It begins here in the month of July, and it is surprising, I am told, in how short a time the fire runs over a whole field of corn. They never commence except when a brisk wind is blowing, and they set fire of course to windward . . .

Three miles from the bridge over the Aufidus we reached the memorable field of Cannæ, where the Romans were defeated by Hannibal, and here I alighted. I was fortunate enough to meet a gentleman who addressed me in French, and who turned out to be the proprietor of the ground. He had resided three years in France in the time of Napoleon, and was kind enough to act as my guide, giving the traditions of the place. The ruins of the ancient village, which was occupied by Hannibal before the battle, are distinctly visible on a small hill about four hundred yards from the southern bank of the river, and you can trace the foundations of what seems to have been a fortress. My guide told me that excavations had been made, and that Roman coins and small images of terracotta had been discovered. There is a tradition that Æmilius Paulus, one of the Roman generals, died near a spring, and of course the inhabitants have fixed on the very spot where that melancholy event took place, and, stooping down, I took a refreshing draught from the *Pozzo d'Emilio* – 'Well of Æmilius' – as they still call it. Immediately at the foot of this hill, in an angle formed by the curvature of the Aufidus, there is a piece of ground called *Pezzo di Sangue* – 'the field of blood' – and here they suppose the crisis of the battle took place.[1] This angle of ground of which I speak is united to

1. I was inclined to omit the following pages referring to Ramage's views on this battle, but Professor Arnold Toynbee has kindly allowed me to state that in his

the land on the north, yet has all the appearance of being traversed – as all low-lying lands on the side of rivers are – in various directions, according as the water excavates its course. It is, therefore, impossible to say how the river flowed in the year 216 BC, when the battle was fought, nor do I think that with the data before us we can decide authoritatively the point. The battle is said to have been fought on a *plain*, and this is the chief reason why that spot on the river is fixed on. Yet, though the character of the ground a mile down the river cannot be called a plain such as this is, yet neither is it hilly; there are merely slight eminences, sloping gently down, and they could have proved no obstacle to the movements of an army. The first question that arises in respect of the battle of Cannæ is, in what direction the Romans advanced towards the Carthaginians. Was it from the direction of Canusium, which lies about six miles from Cannæ on the same side of the river – that is, on the south side – or did they approach from the north, and reach the neighbourhood of Cannæ with the river Aufidus lying between them and Cannæ? The Romans and Carthaginians, according to Polybius (iii. 107), during the winter and early spring of 216 BC, lay, the Romans at Larinum, and the Carthaginians at Gerunium. This was between forty and fifty miles north of Cannæ, at a spot where the Apennines are beginning to slope somewhat down towards the plains of Apulia. The Romans were acting on the defensive, knowing that time was in their favour, and Hannibal was aware that every day he put off bringing matters to a point was lessening his chances of success. The harvest drew to an end in Apulia. I find that it is over now in a great measure, and this is towards the second week of June. Hannibal broke up his camp at Gerunium, and knowing that the Romans had collected at Cannæ large stores from the district of Canusium, which was particularly friendly, he pounced suddenly upon Cannæ, and secured the citadel of Cannæ, which was an important point, as it commanded the plains of Apulia. The city, or rather village of Cannæ, had been, we are told by Polybius, destroyed some time

---

opinion it might be 'a valuable contribution to the present debate, because it was written before the topography had been changed by the building of railways, modern roads, and river conservancy works'. This area has been extensively excavated in recent years and a museum has been opened beside the road near the site. For relevant publications see *La Guida d'Italia del Touring Club Italiano* – '*Puglia*', 1962, p. 467. There is now a well-arranged museum at Cannæ.

before. The Romans lying in Larinum did not immediately follow, as the generals sent several despatches to Rome to state what happened, and requested to know whether they were to pursue Hannibal to what they knew was the comparatively level ground of Apulia, which enabled him to bring his cavalry into full play. The armies in the field were under the command of the consuls of the former year, Cn. Servilius and M. Regulus, while the Consuls Æmilius Paulus and Terentius Varro remained at Rome to deliberate on the measures to be pursued, and to raise new levies. Servilius continued to act cautiously, and there is no reason to suppose that the army descended into the plains till the arrival of the consuls. I follow the account given by Polybius, though Livy appears to state that the consuls followed Hannibal as soon as he started for Cannæ.

Though Lucera is not mentioned in immediate connexion with these events, except as firmly attached to Roman interests, I should expect that the Roman army leaving Larinum would be encamped on these heights, the last slopes of the Apennines, before descending into the treeless flat of the Tavoliere, which they had to cross in pursuit of Hannibal.

What period of time it required to communicate with Rome and receive an answer we cannot say; but pretty nearly six weeks seem to have elapsed before the Roman troops – eighty thousand infantry and six thousand cavalry – came up with the Carthaginians. From the time the Romans began their march under the command of the consuls, they took two full days before they reached the vicinity of Hannibal, at Cannæ, and this is about the time the army might take in marching across the Tavoliere – fifteen miles to the neighbourhood of where Foggia now stands, and about the same number of miles to the vicinity of the lower part of the river Aufidus, towards the spot where the bridge spans the river, which I left on my right as I approached Cannæ.

Another point to be considered is, whether Hannibal had his troops occupying the ground round the citadel of Cannæ, which he had taken in the beginning of June, or whether he was on the opposite side of the river. Livy says that some of the fugitive Romans took refuge in the ruined city of Cannæ, and were obliged to surrender. If Hannibal's troops were in occupation of the citadel, it seems strange that the fugitives should have thought of taking refuge in the village in its immediate vicinity. This slight fact shows, in my opinion, that the battle must have been fought lower down the river than Cannæ, else the fugitives could not have come in contact with Cannæ at all, as their natural place of refuge was Canusium, six miles up the river. In none of the accounts is there any allusion made to Canusium till after the battle, nor of the army crossing the Aufidus, which they must have done if they advanced from the side of Canusium.

Besides this, any army of ninety thousand men and upwards would be sadly cramped in the narrow ground between Canusium and Cannæ, and were cut off in a great measure from its natural granary, the fertile plains of Apulia, and the towns along the coast of the Adriatic, which were still friendly to the Roman cause.

The natural and direct course for the Romans advancing from Larinum, or the neighbourhood of Lucera, would be what is now the great post-road which leads from Foggia to the bridge over the Aufidus, where I left the post-road. In those days there would be nothing more than a mere tract, or mule-path, such as we still find in every part of this country. There are no roads such as we understand, but mere paths, along which a mule may jog, but no wheel-carriage can pass along with safety. The Romans approached with caution, taking care to reconnoitre as they came near to Hannibal. They did not require to cross the river, but kept on the northern or left side. The ground on both sides of the river for a couple of miles up is comparatively level, and would be no great obstacle to an army. As you approach to the spot opposite Cannæ the ground rises about fifty feet above the river, but in some places slopes gently down. From the level and soft nature of the ground the river has a meandering course, having many curves, and, in some places during the winter, evidently overflows the level land on its sides. None of the curves are large, and the ground therefore enclosed is small. The largest, called *Pezzo del Sangue*, opposite to Cannæ, does not appear to my inexperienced eye at all capable of containing upwards of a hundred thousand men in order of battle, and yet this is the spot fixed upon as the site of the battle. I inquired of my intelligent guide, who had been a soldier in his younger days, whether he thought that a hundred thousand men could be deployed on the small plain before us, or whether sensible men would place an army in such a position; and he confessed that it was quite out of the question. I suppose the Roman army to advance from the north, and to encamp at first at some distance from Hannibal, fifty stadia, as Polybius says. The country is described by Polybius to be plain and open, very fit for cavalry; and this description I found to be such as exactly suits its present appearance. Hannibal is lying with his army at or near the citadel of Cannæ. The Roman consuls are Æmilius Paulus and Terentius Varro, who command the army alternatively. Varro is rash and headstrong; Æmilius cautious and wary. Æmilius wishes to wait, and, by his flank position, will be able to keep Hannibal in check from getting provisions from the plains of Apulia. This is the true Fabian policy; whereas Varro is anxious for immediate action, and on his day of command advances nearer to the Carthaginians – so near, that Hannibal sends a body of cavalry to attack them. The Carthaginians are repulsed, but Æmilius, though still earnest in refusing battle, saw that it was now impossible to retreat with safety, and therefore encamped next day with two-thirds of all his forces along the Aufidus. This is the first time that the river is mentioned in connexion with these transactions; and if the Roman army had been advancing from the side of Canusium, we can scarcely imagine that the river would not have been alluded to. It must have been passed to reach Canusium, and they must have marched along its right bank to reach the neighbourhood of Cannæ. Where the Romans struck the Aufidus would be about two miles down the north side, where I found the ground to rise somewhat above the river. There I place the larger camp of the Romans. The other third he ordered to pass the river, and (observe what Polybius, iii. 110, says) to *advance up* the stream, and then to entrench themselves about ten stadia, a little more than a mile, from his own camp, and about the same from Hannibal. If the Roman army had been advancing from Canusium, this body of men must have been going down the river, and not up the stream, as Polybius says.

Here, then, we have the position of the two armies lying in wait for each other, two-thirds of the Romans across the river on the north, and the main body of Hannibal at Cannæ. Hannibal harangues his troops, and says the gods had delivered the Romans into their hands by inducing them to fight on the level ground, where the Carthaginians had such an advantage. Hannibal then passes the Aufidus from Cannæ to the side where the larger camp of the Romans is placed, but it is not said how far he went down the river. The next day he allows for the refreshment of his army, and to prepare for the struggle. On the third day he offers battle, which Æmilius refuses to accept, and makes such dispositions as may secure his camp from insult. Hannibal then returns to his entrenchment, and sends a body of cavalry to fall upon the Romans of the lesser camp while fetching water from the Aufidus. Then comes the fatal 2nd of August, 216 BC, as Gellius (v. 17), Macrobius (*Sat.* i. 16) tell us, when the rash Varro had the command. He orders the soldiers of the larger camp to cross the river, and those of the lesser camp to join them. The ground is sufficiently level towards the great plains of Apulia to enable the largest of armies to deploy. No doubt the ground is not an even plain, like the *Pezzo del Sangue*, but it slopes away so gently from the river that it may be considered a plain. Hannibal then crosses the river nearer to Cannæ, which he had probably left unoccupied that he might have the advantage of all his forces. and arranges his troops in order of battle. There are so many curves in the river, that it would not be difficult for the right wing of the Roman army to rest on the river, and still have their faces somewhat to the south. This was the cause of the ruin of the Romans, as the wind brought clouds of dust from the plains of Apulia, and blinded them. I inquired of my guide if he had ever seen this phenomenon, and he said that it is not uncommon in autumn, after the stubble has been burnt, and the land exposed to the air, for clouds of dust to be driven along the plain. The Romans were defeated; and then comes the account of those who escaped. Varro fled on horseback; and if he crossed to the north side, and made a slight détour to pass Hannibal's entrenched camp, he would have no difficulty in passing the river higher up, and pursuing the same course which I did to Venusia, but it was not necessary to cross the river in order to get away from Hannibal. Though the ground rises to the south of Cannæ, it is by no means so hilly that seventy men on horseback could not pass it, and they would then get into another road in the direction of the small village Minervino, which I visited, and thereby reach Venusia without difficulty. According to Polybius, the ten thousand men left in the larger camp were many of them killed after the battle, and the rest taken prisoners. According to Livy, a portion of those in the smaller camp burst forth, and, fighting their way, joined their comrades in the larger camp. Thus united, they made their way to Canusium during the night, which they could easily do by a slight détour to avoid the entrenched camp of Hannibal on the north side. I am aware that this is a view of the precise locality of the battle which is now for the first time suggested, as it is usual to regard the Romans marching down the south or right side of the Aufidus from Canusium, and the battle is fixed at the isthmus of the small curve *Pezzo del Sangue*, made by the river opposite to Cannæ. I do not believe that such large armies could have been placed on such a confined piece of ground, and if I am wrong in the idea I have formed, I do not think that we have yet got at the truth. I had no time to look for the site of the entrenched camps; I have no doubt they may still be visible, like the camp of Hannibal on the hill above Capua, which I have seen and traced distinctly. All the banks on both sides of the river for six or seven miles ought to be examined, and I trust that some future traveller will make a point to do so. We may then hope to arrive at something like the truth.

I am aware that it will be said that there is no appearance of a stream falling into the Aufidus in the direction where I have placed the battle, and that there are such streams towards Canusium. To this I answer, that in August or even July, in whichever month the battle was fought, it is very unlikely that a drop of water would be found in these small mountain torrents, for they are nothing else. When I passed on my way to Venusia the next day all the beds of these streams were dry, and at this time of the year they must invariably be so. Neither Polybius nor Livy allude to any such stream, called Vergellus by Florus (ii. 6) and Valerius Maximus (ix. 2), on whose statements little dependence can be placed.

You may ask, why did not the Romans after their defeat, if the battle was fought lower down the Aufidus than Cannæ, fly to some of the towns along the coast rather than to Canusium? These small towns had already shown signs of wavering, and, after such a serious defeat, there could be no doubt that they would adhere to the conqueror, as, in fact, they were found to do. The Roman troops, therefore, were aware that no safety was to be found there, and they wisely fled inland to Canusium and Venusia, in which direction they were resting on a wooded country, where the Carthaginians could less easily follow them. I lingered on the plains of Cannæ till the sun had disappeared, and, taking farewell of my intelligent guide, who was under surveillance of the police for his liberal sentiments, I hastened forward over a very uneven road to Canosa, which was still six miles distant . . .

XXIII

THE *locanda* was good at Canosa, and, after a sound night's rest, I was on foot by daybreak to examine the ruins of the ancient Canusium. It must have been of large size, as the ruins extend in the plain upwards of a mile in all directions from the modern town, and the ancient walls may be traced for several miles. The remains of the amphitheatre are still visible, and show it to have been larger than that of Pompeii. A triumphal arch of brickwork, supposed to have been erected in honour of Trajan, though it seems more like a gateway, is nearly entire, and everywhere you see masses of brick, the remains of Roman edifices. At Sta. Chiara, the inhabitants fix the palace of the Lady Busa, mentioned by Livy (xxii. 52, 54; *Val. Max.* iv. 8) as receiving the fugitive Romans so kindly after the defeat at Cannæ. Numerous sepulchres are found cut in the soft rock; and towards the end of last century one was accidentally discovered full of beautiful vases, coins, and two brass lamps. There were, also, the skeletons of two figures clad in complete armour, which are still to be seen in the Royal Museum of Naples. I visited this tomb, which I found to be about twelve feet square, cut in the solid rock, with a bas-relief of a dog and boar on each side. It was discovered by the proprietor of the ground, while constructing wine vaults. The church of St Sabinus, the patron saint of the city, contains six very fine pillars of verde-antique, and is supposed to have been erected on the site of the Temple of Jupiter. There is a curious old pulpit, and an episcopal chair[1] sculptured in marble. In an adjoining court, under an octagonal cupola, is the tomb of Bohemond, son of Robert Guiscard, one of the firmest bulwarks of the Crusaders against the infidels . . . It is of white marble, with bronze doors, covered with sculptures and inscriptions in Latin verse; and within is a marble sarcophagus, in which the body is deposited. Whether he died here or at sea, on his way home from the first crusade, is a question which is undecided; but that he was buried here the inscription on these doors clearly states . . .

Horace (*Sat.* i. v. 89) complains of the bread of Canusium being full of sand . . . I find that the traveller has still the same complaint to make, owing to the soft nature of the rock from which their millstones are

1. Mounted on elephants.

made. Their maccaroni, my landlord told me, is sometimes so full of sandy particles that it can scarcely be eaten. It still makes good wine, if I may judge from what I tasted; as for its wool, from which a particular kind of cloth, prized for its durability, was formerly manufactured, they do not seem to pride themselves upon it. There are some remains of the aqueduct constructed by the munificence of Herodes Atticus to supply the city with water; it has long ceased to be of any use, and the inhabitants of Canosa again suffer from the same deficiency of water of which Horace complained. The modern city is built on the site of the ancient citadel, and contains upwards of five thousand inhabitants.

I had now seen all that was interesting in Canusium, and, ordering a mule, I started at once for Venusia, the birthplace of Horace, born 65 BC, which I found to be about thirty miles distant in the interior. My road lay for several miles along the south bank of the Aufidus . . .

I jogged on for twenty miles over a country chiefly pastoral . . . At the distance of a few miles Venusia appeared before us. It is surrounded on all sides by hills, which rise to a considerable height, particularly to the south-west. To the north-west rises Mount Vultur, a conical mountain like Vesuvius, and resembling it much in its form and appearance.

Venusia fell into the hands of the Romans 262 BC, when, we are told, it was a populous and important town . . . It was on the Appian Way, and it is mentioned more than once by Cicero as a customary halting-place between Rome and Brundisium. It appears, indeed, that the celebrated orator had a villa here, as one of his letters is dated 'De Venusino' (*ad Fam.* xiv. 20). Before I proceeded to examine the ruins of Venosa, I found it necessary to take some refreshment, and while I was at dinner my window looked out on the ruins of a Roman edifice of reticulated structure, and this I found to be what the inhabitants called the *Casa d'Orazio*, 'the House of Horace'. I fear that it had no right to any such name; but I did not examine minutely into the reasons of their belief, pleased with the idea that it was really the residence of Horace. The pigmy works of man might, indeed, pass away, but the grand features of nature still remain the same. There rose Mount Vultur as it was eighteen hundred years ago, and the country was still covered with the woods, the descendants of those trees which had shaded the poet. Observing two villages on the slopes of the hills to the west, I was told that they were called Acerenza and Forenza . . . Venosa stands on the ridge of a hill; the ground falls to the south and west, and the eye rests on a well-wooded country. The *saltus bantini* of Horace are still there, and an old abbey, Santa Maria di Banzi, the position of which was pointed out towards the sources of the river Bradanus, which I had crossed at Metapontum, still fixes the exact site of these woods. Of antiquities, Venosa[1] possesses not much. The church of La Trinità is adorned with some ancient pillars and sepulchral inscriptions. Its entrance is guarded by two stone lions; but the greatest curiosity it possesses is a single column, which, according to local superstition, has the power of binding those to lifelong friendship who walk hand in hand around it. The interior of the church is in sad neglect,[2] it contains the tombs of Robert Guiscard and of his first wife, Aberarda, the mother of Bohemond. The former, a plain marble sarcophagus, contains the bones of Guiscard, and of his brothers William Bras-de-fer, Drogo, who was murdered there on the feast of St Lawrence, in AD 1051, and Humphrey, who succeeded him.

Near this spot the Benedictines began in the thirteenth century a much larger church, which was never finished. The square stones of which it is built are said to have been taken from the ancient amphitheatre; but it is at present overgrown with vegetation.[3]

At the entrance you observe the mounds of the ancient fortress, and

1. Since I [Ramage] visited Venosa, the city has suffered severely from an earthquake in 1851, and in 1853 some ancient catacombs cut in the limestone rock, like the sepulchre I saw at Canosa, have been discovered. It has evidently been a Jewish necropolis, from the roughly painted or scratched inscriptions in Hebrew, Latin, or Greek. Twenty-four Hebrew inscriptions have been found, ornamented with the seven-branched candlestick and a pigeon with an olive-branch. The Latin and Greek inscriptions have been misspelt, but the Hebrew is much more correct. There are several corridors, the largest of which, in the centre, is about seven feet high and as many broad. There are cells of various sizes, ten on the right side and nine on the left, and, as far as it has been cleared, it is already nearly one hundred and forty yards long. The walls of these cells have numerous columbaria or niches of different sizes.

At what time the Jews occupied Venosa in such numbers is wholly unknown, but they were evidently in considerable force in Apulia and Calabria at a very early period. Some of the laws of the Emperor Honorius (AD 395–523) refer to them as being in this part of Italy. (*Cod. Theodos.* xii. 1, 158). 'We find that several classes of people are wavering in their allegiance because they are of the Jewish superstition.' [Note C.T.R.]

2. This church is now in good order.

3. These remains are now attractive to visit since the custodian has made a pleasant garden amidst the ruins.

on the opposite side the ruins of a strong castle of the Middle Ages, which was erected in the fifteenth century by Piero del Balzo, Prince of Altamura and Venosa. The walls of the dungeons under ground are still covered with inscriptions by prisoners who had been confined in them. Venosa has so often suffered in the wars with which Italy has been afflicted, that little now remains of Roman origin . . .

My muleteer met with an old friend here, and got at once into an animated conversation respecting some one, whom I could just discover that they united in ridiculing in no common way. The Italians of all classes make use of signs much more than words to express their feelings, and I could not help laughing at the way they showed their contempt for the person of whom they spoke. One of them waved his fingers up and down alongside of his temples, like the flapping of an ass's ears, while the other thrust out his tongue with a very expressive sound . . .

I met an intelligent inhabitant as I was strolling through Venusia, and had an interesting conversation with him on various points. Among other things, he inquired, laughing, if I had ever heard of the following mode of discovering whether a youth or maiden is still without knowledge of the other sex. He said that the custom was not unknown in southern Italy, and maintained that it was an excellent criterion. Measure the neck of a marriageable youth or maiden correctly with a ribbon; then double the length, and, bringing the two ends together, place the middle of it between the teeth. If we find that it is sufficiently long to be carried from the mouth over the head without difficulty, it is a sign that the person is still a virgin, but if not, we are to infer the contrary. This custom must have been known to the Romans, as Catullus (lxiv. 377) seems to refer to it . . . 'The nurse, when she sees Thetis on the day following her bridal night, will no longer be able to make the thread meet round her neck.'

. . . [Leaving Venosa, Ramage went on to Palazzo where the celebrated *Fons Bandusia* of Horace is said to have been. He put up at an inn where he was showed 'a passage, which was one of the entrances to the stable, having an outer and an inner door, and here they proposed to cage me'. Having dropped off asleep without taking off his clothes, he was suddenly awakened by a 'terrible uproar'. He started up in considerable fright and 'seizing my umbrella, prepared to show fight so far as I was able'.] When the door was opened, I issued forth in a scene truly ludicrous. The large chamber was lighted by a solitary lamp, which only served to make the darkness more visible. In the middle appeared as the most prominent figures the landlord, a muleteer, and the landlord's wife. The muleteer was belabouring the landlord for stealing the food of his mule, while the woman, a strong, masculine Amazon, the worthy representative of Meg Merrilies, was defending her husband, who was far inferior to her in strength and courage ... The muleteer was at last satisfied, and the hubbub ceased. I threw myself again on my couch – if so it could be called – and was soon soundly asleep. I awoke thoroughly chilled, finding a strong current of cold air passing through my cage. This was too dangerous, and I determined to pass the remainder of the night in the stable, where I should at least be free from the draught. This turned to be truly out of the frying-pan into the fire, for I found the stable in a state of stifling heat, and this caused the swarms of insects to receive renewed vigour. There I sat on a low stool for a couple of hours, like 'Patience on a monument', with all around me soundly asleep. I fear that I shall never be able to read with any degree of pleasure the beautiful ode to *Fons Bandusiæ*, as it will always call up my disagreeable associations with Palazzo ...

My landlord ... said that there were two fountains which claimed to represent the *Fons Bandusiæ*. He took me to them: the one is called *Fontana del Fico*, the fountain of the fig-tree, and the other *Fontana Grande*, which was nearly dry, little deserving of its name, as it was of diminutive size. The former has been lately repaired, and its white-washed, utilitarian appearance was a sad damper to all the poetical embellishments with which my fancy had invested it. Whatever trees had once surrounded it had disappeared; and though it may be much more useful in its present state, it would have little to recommend it to the fancy of the poet. If it had been in this state in the time of Horace, the world would never have been delighted by his address to Bandusia.

There is a dispute whether this celebrated fountain is not near the poet's Sabine farm, a little way from Tivoli, and where travellers are shown, in the valley of Licenza, a fountain called *Fonte Bello*, said to be the *Fons Bandusiæ* ...

[The next morning he went on to] ... Minervino,[1] the name of which had attracted my attention, and which I was told is the site of a temple of Minerva. I passed through a picturesque country, hill and dale

1. Minervino Murgie.

187

alternating, but with little appearance of cultivation. The inhabitants are clustered together, as in Calabria, in villages, and not scattered over the country as with us. When I reached the public square of Minervino, I addressed myself to a priest, who was seated at a door, and inquired respecting the antiquities of the place. He told me that the temple was now called the Grotto of St Michael, and that the saint had usurped the place of the Goddess of Wisdom . . . [Ramage found the grotto to be a natural cave with no pretensions to a temple. He returned to Venosa and then set off for Melfi (which he states is an Albanian Colony) and Mons Vultur via the 'miserable village of Barile'.]

On a hill I saw the village Rapolla, supposed to be the ancient Strapellum; my road, however, did not lead through it. The volcanic character of the country through which I had been passing is strongly marked, and the city Melfi I found to be built on a hill of lava. Passing through many vineyards, which seemed to flourish in great luxuriance, I entered the city Melfi, containing about nine-thousand inhabitants. Like most cities of Italy, its streets are narrow, to protect from the direct rays of the sun; it had at one time been defended by walls, but they are now in a dilapidated state. I was struck by the fine appearance of the cathedral and theatre, which had in early times been the hall, where the baronial councils of the Normans, who occupied this part of Italy, were held.

Whether it existed in Roman times is unknown; it became, however, the chief city of the Normans when they took possession of Apulia, and here they met, from time to time, to enact laws and transact public business. In 1059, Pope Nicholas II invested here Robert Guiscard as Duke of Apulia and Calabria. In 1089, Pope Urban II held here a general council of a hundred and thirteen bishops. The Popes Alexander II and Pasqual II also held councils in this city; while the Emperor Frederick II assembled a diet, and wished to make it the capital of his dominions. You thus see that it was a city in those times of great importance; but all this has passed away. Its public hall has become a theatre, and a portion of the castle is the residence of Prince Doria Pamphili, who has large possessions in the surrounding country.

Its cathedral is a remarkable building, erected in 1155 by Roger Guiscard, King of Sicily, having a richly carved ceiling. The episcopal palace is also a striking object. All this country is subject to earthquakes; on the 8th of September, 1694, it sustained great damage, and scarcely a year passes without some slight shock.[1] The vineyards through which I had passed I found to be celebrated for their produce, and I confess that I enjoyed a draught of what they call *moscato* with great zest.

This evening, as I jogged along, my fatigue was solaced by the long-drawn notes sent forth so sweetly by the nightingales . . . It was now necessary to make inquiries respecting Vultur, which towered a few miles from Melfi to a height of upwards of four thousand feet. It had an imposing appearance, being of a conical shape, and rising in a great measure perpendicular from the plain, though I found that it could be ascended by a winding path.

Next morning I started at daybreak with a mule, muleteer, and guide, who was recommended by my landlord as acquainted with the mountain. The approach to the foot of the mountain is through vineyards, and as we mounted the slopes on the north side, we saw the river Aufidus winding very beautifully through deep glens finely wooded. The scenery reminded me of what I had seen on the loftier pinnacles of the Apennines, which I had crossed in Calabria. My guide pointed to several large caverns, which had often been the refuge of brigands. At present they had been dispersed. For several hours we passed through the thick forest of Monticchio, and ever and anon, as I was humming the words of Horace (*Od.* iii. 4, 9) . . . flocks of wood-pigeons were roused from the woods, and passed over my head . . .

At last I reached a very striking and wild part of the mountain – a crater of a much more perfect form than that of Vesuvius. Its sides rose in nearly an unbroken line around, and were covered with old beeches and oaks. It had once been in active operation, but had ceased long before the most ancient historical records that we possess. There are several craters of different sizes, but this is by far the most perfect and striking to the eye. In the largest crater are two small lakes, from which at times issue sulphureous exhalations, like those which rise from Lacus Ampsanctus, which is at no great distance, and is no doubt connected with this ancient volcano.

I rested an hour at the monastery of S. Michele, and was kindly received by the Franciscans . . . I had now to determine whether I should climb the highest peak, called *Il Pizzuto di Melfi*. The view would have been magnificent from the pinnacle if the air had been

1. In 1851 it suffered severely from an earthquake with great destruction of buildings and loss of life.

clear, which I found at this season of the year was seldom the case, as
the heat raised a haze, which prevents the eye from reaching the distant
horizon. The mere boast of having put my foot on the highest point
of Mons Vultur had no temptation for me. It rises to a height of four
thousand three hundred and fifty-seven feet; but, gazing on its conical
peak, I bade adieu to the monks, and descended again towards Melfi,
very much in the same way I had mounted. There are said to be wild
boars in these forests. I saw none of them.

I hurried on to Melfi, and, getting my passport in order, started for
Ascoli, the ancient Asculum Appulum, about twelve miles distant.
I passed the Ponte Sta. Venere, rather a curious saint, an old bridge,
not in a good state of repair, spanning the river Aufidus, which runs
below over a rocky bottom, and continues to be a mere mountain
torrent ... The country seems to be favourable to the vine, as all
volcanic soils are, and I passed many vineyards. The wine is strong, and
requires, it is said, to be watered to make it palatable. If they were
accustomed to our port they would not think so. The Italians are a
sober race. I cannot say that I have seen a drunken man, or even one
much elated with wine, except the coast-guard at Trebisacce, and I am
ashamed to say that I caused my brother to sin by over-indulgence.
I was not sorry when I reached Asculum, a little before sunset, and found
it of respectable size, on a rising ground, where the Apennines are
beginning to descend into the plains of Apulia ... It was here that the
great battle between Pyrrhus and the Romans was fought 279 BC.
They believe it to have been fought in the plain beneath, where swords
and pieces of armour are said to have been found. The ancient city was
not on the site of the modern Ascoli, but a little way below it, amidst
vineyards, where I saw the foundations of ancient edifices, and here
sepulchral inscriptions and fragments of columns have been discovered.

XXIV

[For once Ramage was in no hurry to leave Ascoli for Foggia, and
he was apparently very tired because he says the 'fatigue' of holding
his umbrella 'was almost more than my strength was equal to'. On
arrival at Foggia he found a 'tolerable inn', and as soon as he had refreshed

himself, he went out to examine the town] which had every appearance of being in a flourishing condition. Most of the houses were small, but some were handsome, and had more air of comfort about them than I have generally met. The cathedral had a strange, patched appearance, which arose from its having been partly destroyed by an earthquake in 1731, and the upper part of it has been rebuilt in a different style. Foggia is the staple market for corn and wool, and the corn vaults – *fosse* – are extensive, extending under the streets and squares. It has a population of about twenty thousand. The inhabitants have lately erected a handsome theatre, which I visited in the evening, and saw it numerously attended. During the evening I took an opportunity of paying my respects to the governor of the province, Cavaliere St Angelo, who is a cousin of the Prince of Satriano, whose letters of introduction have been so useful, and was received with much kindness ... I told him that I wished to visit in his province Mons Garganus, known as the Spur of Italy, and he at once said that he would relieve me of all difficulties from the public authorities in his own province ...

Before I started next morning on my visit to Garganus, I rode out five miles to a spot called Arpi, where some slight remains of the walls of the ancient Arpi are still found. Many sepulchres have been discovered, with vases, cameos, and terracotta figures ...

Hastening back to Foggia, I proceeded through the same uninteresting flat country for twenty miles to Manfredonia, a city with a population of about six thousand inhabitants, on the shore at the foot of Mons Garganus, which rises to a height of five thousand one hundred and twenty feet. This city was founded about AD 1266, by Manfred, one of the early kings of the country, and is defended by walls, which seemed to be in a better state than those which I had seen on other parts of this coast. It is not unlike the 'lang toun of Kirkcaldy', the main thoroughfare being a long and wide street from one gate to the other. Its port is defended by a castle, and protected towards the north by a small breakwater, though there is depth of water only for light vessels. The inhabitants had a pale, unhealthy appearance, arising from the malaria of some marshes in its neighbourhood. The ancient city of Sipontum was situated a little more than a mile to the south of Manfredonia, to which I at once proceeded, and found an ancient church of no great size, called Sta. Maria di Siponto. It is situated close to a marsh formed by the overflowing of the river Candelaro, and the ancient town must at all times have been exposed to the unhealthy exhalations of the marsh called Pantano Salso. I examined the neighbourhood of the church in all directions for ancient remains; they had, however, all disappeared, nor is it surprising, as Sipontum was never a city of any importance. Having returned to Manfredonia, I resolved to hire a small boat to sail round the promontory, landing wherever I might feel inclined, though in this proceeding I expected to have difficulties started by the authorities.

Behold me again launched in a small sailing-boat on the waters of the Adriatic. The day was lovely; a gentle south-west wind wafted us forward, while above towered Monte St Angelo, as the promontory is now called, far different in height from that of Capo di Leuca, on which I had stood a few days before. The promontory juts eastward from Manfredonia for five-and-twenty miles, to the point near a small village called Viesti. The hill is in some parts nearly perpendicular, though generally it slopes gently upwards, affording several small harbours, in which small vessels can find shelter from the north wind. I landed at the village Mattinata . . . no doubt the site of the *Matinum littus* of Horace (*Carm.*, i. 28, 3), where the body of Archytas was thrown ashore . . . I asked whether they had any bees in the neighbourhood, and there was a grand chorus, '*molti, molti*'. They hive, as in other parts of Italy, in old trees, and when these trees are cut down immense quantities of honey are often found. The hills around I observed to be covered with flowers, and they said that the flavour of the honey is particularly odoriferous . . . There has been a great demand for wood during the last fifty years from the denudation of the mountains in the interior of the kingdom, and I understand that this demand has led to the cutting down of the trees on this peninsular promontory.[1]

I could hear nothing of the *querceta Gargani*, the oak-groves spoken of by Horace (*Carm.*, ii. 9, 7), but I heard enough of St Michael and his miracles at Monte St Angelo, which is now the name by which this promontory is known. The church of the Archangel St Michael claims to be of very ancient origin, going back to 492 AD for the period when the Archangel took up his residence on Garganus. It was sacked by the Saracens, 869 AD, again restored in greater magnificence by the gifts of the faithful, and it continued to enjoy great fame and riches, till it suffered, like many others, from the sacrilegious hands of the French.

1. This region is now well-wooded.

The priest, who seemed to be well acquainted with the legend of St Michael, talked of a stream which, as usual, claimed to heal all kinds of diseases, and this, no doubt, as in many other parts of Italy, is a mere continuation of a pagan superstition, as Strabo (vi. 284) mentions a small stream issuing from a hill in this neighbourhood called Drium, which healed all kinds of diseases in cattle. St Michael, however, has been kinder, as he has extended its healing powers to human beings . . .

[Ramage re-embarked for Viesti[1] a 'miserable village' standing on a 'kind of peninsula, and washed on three sides by the waters of the Adriatic'. His boatmen refused to go farther, and they put about returning to Manfredonia just before midnight. The next day he set off by mule for Lucera via Foggia. On arrival at Lucera he presented a letter of introduction from 'his friend, Miss White'[2] to Signor Nocelli. He went on to Volturara, Campobasso, and Boiano (here he spent a couple of hours examining the ancient remains on the low ground near the banks of the river Tifernus (Biferno). He remarks, 'it is curious that no specimen of Cyclopean architecture should be found in the southern parts of Italy which I have lately traversed. Is this because the cities of Magna Græcia were all of late foundation, and colonised at a comparatively modern period? The walls of Bovianum were the first polygonal blocks of a massive style which I had yet met'. Isernia was his next stop, then Venafro, the walled town of Alife, Caizzo, the church of S. Angelo in Formis, and finally, 'hastening on' to Naples where] . . . I need not tell you, I was glad to rest from my labours, having successfully carried out my original intentions. I have still much to see in this part of the country before I bid an eternal farewell to the Kingdom of Naples.

1. This is now quite a flourishing small fishing port.
2. Miss Whyte, with whom Sir Walter Scott stayed at La Cava and of whom he said, 'a lady not less esteemed for every good quality, than celebrated for the extraordinary exertions and benevolence on the occasion of the murder of the Hunt family at Paestum' (p. 203); and he expressed himself 'at all times much delighted with the admirable Miss Whyte': remarking that 'there was nothing cold about her but her house, which being in the mountains, is, in fact, by no means eligible at that season (February) of the year'.

APPENDIX
Letters from Ramage to his Mother 1825–28

My dear Mother,

I have no doubt you must be extremely anxious at not hearing from me sooner and I therefore hasten to inform you of my safe arrival after a tedious but fine passage of 40 days. The weather has been only too beautiful for we had a great many calms and light contrary winds. We have cast anchor but are not fairly fixed in our berth. There will be a quarantine of 12 days it seems and as letters go through a certain process of fumigation before they are sent off, I shall delay my journal until I get ashore. You will then receive a very long letter containing all the particulars of our voyage. I have been quite well all the time. I was sick at first but not very ill. We were 9 days getting out of the English Channel – 250 miles – I can of course give you no directions as yet as to writing me. This will be in my next. I hope you are quite well. I suppose the family have been with you and are away again. I hope Charles and Archy[1] are well. Remember me to all my friends. As there is a man waiting for this letter to take to the Post Office, I must conclude by subscribing myself

Your affectionate son,
C. T. Ramage.

Castellamare, 23 October 1825

I was agreeably interrupted tonight in a game of chess with Lady Lushington[2] by the arrival of letters. It was the very night I calculated I might possibly receive one and you may suppose I was happy in not being deceived – it gave me both sorrow and pleasure, but your recovery which I hope is complete by this time obliterated all matter of grief . . . You observe we are still in the country; in fact we are lingering as long as possible though the weather is at present very unfavourable and as unpleasant as I have ever experienced in Scotland. All our friends have left us sometime ago, so that we are completely by ourselves. We are going to Naples on Thursday if the weather will permit what it has no appearance of doing at present.

Naples, 27 October 1825

Here we are settled in Naples for the winter. We returned by sea in one of His Majesty's schooners but not a pleasant day. In the evening we dined at

1. His half-brothers, Charles and Archibald Black.
2. Wife of Sir Henry Lushington, 2nd Bart. (1775–1863). H.B.M. Consul at Naples, 1815–1832.

Field Marshall Lederer's,[1] we sate down at 6 – it was the first dinner I had been in an Italian house, it was curious enough to me. On the table when we entered there was nothing but fruit; in the centre between gold-branching candlesticks there were fancy flowers upon the middle – it had a very great effect – There were 25 in the party – everything was handed round to you and there were at least 30 dishes presented for none of which I would have given a roast leg of mutton and a dish of potatoes. Oysters came first which I know you would have liked but which I detest particularly when raw. Then came soup, and a number of dishes whose names and composition I knew not – about the middle they handed round spinach and butter which was odd enough to me and it concluded with fish – sweet meats came after, cheese then joint – of course wine during dinner of all sorts. I was very tired before it was concluded and I found afterwards I was not singular in this as Sir Henry[2] made the same observation – we retired to the small drawing room where we had coffee – it was seated round with dark tartan-like sofas – Scotch tartan – after this a suite of rooms was thrown open through which the party roved to amuse themselves, each as he chose – some at cards, some danced – music in the evening, and a number of German officers came to pay their respects to the General. The rooms were extremely elegant, but our suite in the Palazzo Bisignano is allowed to be the handsomest in Naples – when lighted up they are very beautiful. I forget whether in my last letter I mentioned that I had been at a ball given by Sir R. F. Acton[3] at Castellamare. It was marvellously attended by all the 'fashionables' here. You know the titled nobility are plentiful enough. They have a very mean appearance contrasted with an Englishman, so much so that the Italian is proud of being taken for one. It was kept up till 5 o'clock in the morning but I left at 2. My letters go with the English Ambassador's despatches to the Foreign Office, so they cannot be opened . . . As to my health, I never was better in my life . . . the climate seems to agree with me better than the northern one. At present the weather is very miserable – rain – wind, and lead one to believe one is in Scotland . . . We are beginning now to be settled in our house but there has been a great deal of confusion . . . Before leaving Castellamare I went with Sir Henry on board the 'Revenge' – 78 man of war. Admiral Sir H. Neale.[4] As I have never seen one before it was a curious sight. The Admiral is a very pleasant man and Capt. Sir Charles Burrard[5] is as much so.

1. Field-Marshall Ignaz Ludwig Paul, Freiherr von Lederer (1769–1849).
2. Lushington.
3. Sir Ferdinand Richard Edward Acton, 7th Bart. (1801–1833).
4. Admiral Sir Henry Burrard Neale (1765–1840). Commander-in-Chief Mediterranean, 1823–1826.
5. Capt. (later Admiral) Sir Charles Burrard, 2nd Bart. (1793–1870).

Naples, 9 March 1826

I received your letter sometime ago and am happy to hear you are well . . .
This winter has not been at all equal to my expectations and we have had a
great deal of cold wind and rain and a little snow which is rather remarkable
for Naples. For the last month however we have been recompensed by the
presence of most delightful weather – the soft balmy breezes that bring pleasure if not health in their wings – the clear blue sky and a warm but not too
powerful sun would far than counterbalance months of rain and snow.
Indeed now that I have become domesticated here I regard life but as a dream,
so quick does the time pass. I can no longer be surprised that pleasure should
be the chief good and principle pursuit of the Italians – everything invites
them to it – their outward senses are solicitated in a thousand ways to feast
on the gifts of nature and they would treat Nature with ingratitude if they
did not yield themselves to the enjoyment of what it presents them with.
The Carnaval lasted for a fortnight when all Naples was gayer if possible
than she usually is. Twice a week we had a *corso*, which is merely a suite of
carriages for perhaps two miles close upon another in which many appear in
masks – it was stupid enough as in a carriage no character can be kept up –
it is a custom to pelt your friends with sugar plums and the greater force
you employ in throwing them, the greater friendship do you show to the
individual – it is a foolish enough custom but it is curious to observe from
what follies man can derive pleasure. You may conceive what the *corso* must
have been when I tell you that it was calculated there were 100,000 people
present. One day a double row of carriages extended upwards of two miles
so that they could scarcely move forward. At night there used to be public
Masquerades which were stupid enough to those who did not know many
individuals. They were held at the public theatre and were crowded. I was
however disappointed in them. Private balls there were about every night.
We closed the Carnaval at Lady Drummonds'[1] – she gave an immense party
– about 300 present. The Princess of Parma,[2] who is in Naples on a visit,
honoured it with her presence. She is remarkably pretty as much as her
husband is plain-looking. She is young and just lately married – a daughter of
the King of Sardinia. After the Carnaval has come Lent which is intended
to be a penance for all light conduct during the former gaiety – no dancing
allowed – not even music. The 'fashionable', however, as the theatre is not
allowed to be open, take the opportunity to give card parties where all the

1. Wife of Sir William Drummond, (1770–1828). Envoy Extraordinary and Minister
Plenipotentiary at the Court of Naples, 1801–1803, 1806–1809.
2. Mr Harold Acton has suggested to me that she may be Maria Theresa, d. of Victor
Emmanuel I, Kg. of Sardinia (1759–1824). Maria Theresa was a sister-in-law of Ferdinand
II of the Two Sicilies.

world meet to talk scandal and while away the time as agreeably as possible. I was at General Lederer's the other night – cards and talking were the order of the night – it was quite a military party as all the General's officers were present. I am now beginning to talk Italian with considerable fluency and can converse in it without much difficulty. I have a master three times a week whom I have engaged for three months and by that time I expect to be then completely master of it as is necessary. I shall then commence French again with the same vigour . . . I shall hesitate whether to commence Spanish or German as there is such a number of them here. By the end of the second year I think I shall know both tolerably, then I know not to what I shall turn my attention. If Modern Greece recovers her independence and becomes a nation, I shall learn that language . . . It is not yet determined when we shall go to the country this summer as Sir Henry goes to England in all probability. Dr Lushington is brother to Sir Henry. Sir Henry is very liberal in his principles though he may be said to belong to no party. I bid fair however to be a Whig in my principles though I care little for politics . . . You may give Anderson[1] my compliments and say that I have not seen a tree since I arrived larger than the young trees in Montague plantation. Round Naples, though there is a considerable quantity of wood, it never arrives to any size as they cut it down every 7 years for charcoal – and if one proprietor was found wise enough to let it grow for his lifetime (which would be extraordinary) the next would certainly demolish it. Thus though Italy appears well-covered with green wood, it never comes to any size, and as for gentlemen's parks, where you would expect to find timber, there are no such things here . . . The eye is never refreshed by that grassy verdure which we have in Scotland. There is a small lake, Lago di Agnano, a few miles from Naples round which I often ride for the mere pleasure of the grassy circle which surrounds it. It is the centre of an extinct volcano – we have had a shock of an earthquake a few weeks ago – rather severe – it shook the houses considerably. There is a prophecy that Naples is to be destroyed this year as it escaped last.

P.S. March 14 1826. When you write me you may follow the following directions. Direct it to me, enclose that for Sir Henry Lushington, Bart. and enclose that again to Mr Hill,[2] His Britannic Majesty's Minister, Naples. You must enclose the whole again and direct it, George Canning, Esq., Secretary for Foreign Affairs, Foreign Office, London. In this way I shall get it free from expense. The 'Revenge' is in sight and Miss Louisa's[3] heart leaps for joy. I am just going to see her enter the bay.

1. Head Forester at Drumlanrig Castle.

2. William Noel-Hill, 3rd Lord Berwick. Envoy Extraordinary and Minister Plenipotentiary at the Court of Naples, 1824–1833.

3. Only d. of Sir Henry Lushington who m. Admiral Sir Charles Burrard in 1826.

Naples, 8 May 1826

I am happy to inform you that I am well and that everything is going on as I could wish. I am as busy as I could possibly be, and Italian, German and French fully occupy my time. I am alone at present as the family has gone to Castellamare with the young couple. They were married about a month ago when we had a very large party – Austrian Minister[1] and wife and Russian Minister.[2] Generals Lederer and Koller,[3] etc. They were married at 1 and we sate down to a magnificent breakfast at 2 – they have been in the country ever since. Sir Charles (Burrard) will make an excellent husband though he be not a very bright genius. That however is not at all necessary to procure happiness. Matt. Lushington,[4] the soldier, has arrived from Gibraltar and has been very extravagant but has promised to reform; he is very pleasant, his extreme youth makes his extravagances pardonable. We expect the Oxford gentleman in June. I am afraid he will have too high an idea of his own importance to be agreeable – these *college youths* are very apt to assume airs which do not become them. We have had horrible weather during the last week – snow on the hills and a cold bleak wind which reminds me of Scotland. It now rains and thunders tremendously – I have not yet changed my winter clothes. I hear Mr Pillans[5] is on his road thro' Italy and I expect to see him about the middle of June. He could not have chosen a more disagreeable time of the year as it will be so hot as to prevent him going out except in the morning and evening. The malaria too and tainted air is strongest at that time. Today I witnessed the liquefaction of the blood of St Januarius, which is one of the most unblushing pieces of knavery and priestcraft that can be met with anywhere throughout the world. It is the remains of that baleful superstition which has so long extended its withering grasp over the native energies of man and which has so often spread desolation over the moral world and crushed man's rising hopes by stemming the tide of civilisation – it is the same which in former times condemned Galileo to the stake and which now endeavours to draw again over us the veil of ignorance by condemning knowledge and science as the bane of society. Let us hope that there is a mandate gone forth which thunders the language that cannot be misunderstood 'That for *her* Time is no longer – that she has ruled the world during the ages allotted to her and that now she must yield her

1. Count Karl Ludwig Ficquelmont (1777-1857), Austrian Minister at Naples, 1821–1829.
2. Count Gustav Stackelberg.
3. Field-Marshall-Lieutenant Franz, Freiherr von Koller (1767–1826).
4. Matthew, 4th s. of Sir Henry Lushington, (1808–1839).
5. James Pillans, LL.D. (1778–1864). Scottish educational reformer and prominent in academic life in Edinburgh.

sway to the goddess of Reason'. In witnessing such a scene I felt my blood curdle in my veins at the cold calculating knavery of my fellow creatures and could with difficulty restrain my indignation at their unfeeling and disgraceful conduct. The higher classes of this country, who have received sufficient education to perceive the tissue of absurdities their religion teaches them, have discarded it altogether and they sometimes submit to perform outward observances for the sake of society: they show by their conduct that they consider everything sacred and holy as the mere ravings of a sickman's dream. At this ridiculous ceremony you saw none of this class – The audience consisted wholly of the lower orders and of strangers. The ceremony takes place in the Santa Chiara towards evening though you may find it difficult to discover the time from a Catholic who will tell you with the utmost gravity that it is impossible to say when the Saint will manifest his presence. In the morning there is a procession to bring the statute to the place where the miracle is performed. About four in the afternoon, you find the Church open to receive the public, with a strong body of soldiers before the door to prevent all disturbance; you find no difficulty in entering if you tell them you are a stranger. There are two acts, and in the first act there are two scenes – in the first place there is a procession of flags and priests of all the different orders in Naples. It is amusing to observe their various costumes – it is not surprising that man should devote himself to a monastic life for it is flattering to his pride – it implies a command over the suspicions and a self-denial which at once the most difficult and the most honourable victory which a man can obtain – as they pass in review before you there is a solemnity in their appearance and a melancholy sadness in their countenances which leads the mind to contemplation, and yet in some you can perceive a lurking superciliousness and symptoms of that spiritual pride which does not well correspond with their outward look. Then come a procession of the statues of 40 saints who pay their respects to St Januarius, are presented with a little incense, and are carried back to their respective churches. The statues are silvered over and are draped with great magnificence. At last comes the blood under a purple canopy which is supported by monks of the highest order. It is carried to the altar and the Archbishop of Naples in his robes takes it down from its place. Meanwhile the family of those lineally descended from St Januarius are placed to the right handside of the altar and are privileged to blackguard him in the most rude language. They commence long before the blood comes and bawl and scream in the most discordant tones, and as each saint makes his appearance they address him thus, 'And so you, Sir, are come to pay our saint a visit – get away with you – you are far inferior to him – he wishes not your company'. Their language is sometimes quite indecent. They are a parcel of old women, fit supporters for such an absurdity. At the moment it is liquefying, they utter the most piercing screams and threaten to discard him for ever if he does not listen to them instantly. The substance in the bottle is at first firm, and after the Archbishop begins to move, it begins to melt.

Naples, 10 October 1826

We were on the point of starting for the country when I wrote you last and we are now returned to Naples for the winter. We remained six weeks at Sorrento. I intended to have finished two months there, but I made an expedition to the island of Capri and the violence of the sun's rays gave me a *coup de soleil*. Though it was slight, yet it incapacitated me from doing much, and as we had no physician at Sorrento I determined to return to Naples. A few leeches applied behind my ears soon gave me relief and I have since gone down to Paestum without suffering anything.

It is about 50 miles distant and we were four days on the road. We might have done it in three, but as we went for pleasure we did not hurry ourselves. The temples are the most magnificent that can be found in the world, at least in Europe. There are three, supposed to have been built at different times. They lie so extremely low that you can see nothing of them till you arrive within a mile of them. At a little distance we were shown the spot where the poor Hunts[1] were murdered some years ago. The place is quite open and several houses are a very short distance. The first *coup d'oeil* of the Temples is magnificent. They rise in lonely solitariness upon the eye and seem to be mourning the desolation that surrounds them. I refer you however to the Encyclopedia for a description of them as they are too well-known to require illustration from me. The country is extremely barren and reminded me of the extensive heath of Scotland. There were numerous herds of buffaloes scattered over it. We spent the first night at Salerno and proceeded next day to Eboli which was journey of only 18 miles – visited Paestum next morning and returned to Salerno to sleep. My two companions were merchants here who were going to Salerno on business. I intended to have gone down with Charles Lushington,[2] but he is so dilatory in all his motions that I thought it best to take advantage of the present opportunity. I have only another expedition in contemplation this autumn which is to Benevento and its neighbourhood. The heats are over now and at this moment it is raining severely ... I am busily engaged with my German which I find laborious

1. Thomas Welch Hunt, of Wadenhoe. High Sheriff of Northamptonshire in 1823, m. 1824 Caroline, eldest d. of Rev. C. E. Isham, Rector of Polebrook, and *see* p. 5.
2. Rev. Charles, M.A., 3rd. s. of Sir Henry Lushington.

enough, but I have overcome the driest part. I am on the point of engaging a master for 3 months which will complete me in great measure.

We expect Naples to be very gay this winter and to have several English noblemen with us. Lord Normanby[1] and a party of amateur actors is expected down – Marquis of Huntly[2] is reported too. The Duke of Buccleuch[3] is also mentioned but you must know that. Of course there will be the usual rabble from every part of the United Kingdom which are regular visitors during the winter. It is said that we shall lose the Austrians in the spring, but I think this is extremely doubtful as the country is by no means in a satisfied state. In Sicily there have already been several disturbances and they are in great terror. Lord Cochrane[4] frightened them at Mespina and they would not allow him to land.

By the way, I passed through a forest of oaks belonging to the King near Paestum and think that they are in general far inferior even to Dalkeith Park.[5] Indeed the climate does not appear to agree with them. Hanning[6] may have heard of the roses that appear twice a year there. We saw them and they are a pinkish red colour and very delicate-looking. They were famous among the ancients. Alas, what farmers we have here. They carry everything on mule's backs – their plough is the most rude possible. Carts in this country are never seen. Butter is generally horrible except when it can be procured from the King's dairy.

Naples, November 30 1826

I have just been told this instant that a courier goes tonight with the news of the Marquis of Hasting's[7] death, and I shall endeavour to finish this letter before he goes. By my last letter, you must perceive that a letter has miscarried, that one in which I gave you an account of Mr and Mrs Pillans and which was written about the beginning of August . . .Mr and Mrs Pillans remained here about three weeks and I did everything in my power to show them the Seiano Cave.[8] I devoted myself entirely to them and though the weather was insupportable for its heat, yet we contrived to see everything in the neighbourhood of Naples . . . Mr Pillans was kind enough to say that he had

1. Constantine Henry, at this time Viscount Normanby, eldest s. of Earl of Mulgrave (1797–1863).
2. George Gordon, 8th Marquis of Huntly, later 5th Duke of Gordon (1770-1836).
3. Walter Francis, 5th Duke of Buccleuch (1806-1884).
4. Thomas, Lord Cochrane, Admiral RN, later 10th Earl of Dundonald (1775-1860).
5. Seat of the Duke of Buccleuch.
6. ? Employee at Drumlanrig Castle.
7. Francis Rawdon-Hastings, 1st Marquis of Hastings (1754–1826). Died at sea off Naples.
8. Grotto di Sejano: a tunnel c. 90 m long, constructed by the Emperor near Posillipo.

never found any young man so comfortable and so completely at home as I was. About the middle of October, Charles Lushington, Dykes, and myself with a servant started an expedition to Caserta, a palace belonging to the King and one of the most magnificent said to be in the world. The Gardens are laid out in the English fashion but their plots of grass are burnt up by the sun. The Staircase is magnificent beyond all conception from its pillars and beautiful marbles – the rest of the house does not correspond to the entrance. We next visited a very fine Aqueduct which is near it and then went to the Caudine Forks, a place famous in Roman story. We were on horseback and arrived about 7 o'clock at a small village called Airola about 27 miles from Naples. Here we were surrounded by the people and after a great deal of botheration we discerned a place where we could sleep. We got two rooms and then to forage for a dinner. We found a *trattoria* where they came in crowds to see us. We then went to bed and I think I slept, my companions were kept awake all night by their bedfellows! We started next morning before day-break and rode through a most beautiful country to Benevento; a town which is in the Neapolitan dominions but belongs to the Pope. It swarms with priests and we discovered long before we reached it that we must be near it from the shoals of them that we met. It is a walled town with narrow and dirty streets – the Triumphal Arch of Trajan is the one thing which is worth seeing. There is an ancient bridge also where the stones are of immense size. We arrived there very early in the day, but were rather fatigued, so we agreed to sleep in Benevento as we were sure of tolerable good beds, which we could not be if we proceeded, particularly as we scarcely knew where we would arrive at. Our object was to visit the Lago Ampsanctus, a boiling sulphurous lake which few have seen as it is quite out of the common road. Its situation we scarcely knew, but I made myself pretty well master of the topography of the place. Next morning we were off before day-break as we considered ourselves to be approaching the Lake, and as we might lose ourselves among the hills we thought it well to have a long day before us. You must know that the roads this day were so bad that we could scarcely proceed at a pace quicker than a walk. We arrived about 11 o'clock at a small village, Taurasi, which we were inclined to think must be near the Lake. Here we determined to rest our horses and take what breakfast we could get. The people here had once before seen an Englishman, but they seemed to consider us monsters as they crowded round us and filled the hut when we were eating some coarse bread and cheese which were the only things to eat. They were however very civil and here a man offered to guide us to the Lake about 5 miles distant he said. This was the best we could do, and as we believed he must have seen it, we started confidentially a little after twelve. After leaving this village the road became nearly impassable and we were obliged to lead our horses the greater part of the way. The country became gradually bleaker and bleaker and gave evident proofs that we were in a volcanic region – the further we went the less near we seemed to approach our destination till we at last discovered our guide had never even seen the Lake and only knew the direction in which it lay. We were far from feeling comfortable on this discovery as the day was far advanced and as we looked around us we saw no place where we should be able to obtain lodgings for the night . . . We travelled on and met with two cut-throat-looking chaps with whom we thought it best to enter into conversation, and we found they could conduct us to it. At last about half past five in the evening after we had travelled fifteen miles from Taurasi we came to the long-wished Lake. It certainly was worth the trouble. It is about 150 yards in circumference and is continually boiling up to a great height, and in some places it throws the water 6 feet high – the fumes of sulphur that proceed from it made it very dangerous, nay impossible to approach it and we were obliged to content ourselves with viewing it from a precipice 40 feet above it. The sun was now setting, and what was to be done a distance of 8 miles from any village? On consultation we determined to make our way to the nearest. The day soon closed and as the road was nearly impassable by day, you may conceive our difficulties by night. Dykes and his horse came down and he bruised his arm considerably; with the exception of this we arrived safe at Gesualdo about half past eight and found a tolerable inn. They gave us the best room in the house and made up three beds. Also here, the people had only once before seen an Englishman and the chief men of the village came to pay their respects – we asked the priest to dine. We went on next day to Avellino on our return to Naples through a most lovely country, and the next day arrived there highly pleased with our tour. Since then I have been in Naples. It is full of English at present – Marquis of Huntly and Marquis of Bath,[1] Prince Leopold,[2] Mr Lambton,[3] Lady Warwick,[4] Bishop of Ossory[5], and thousands of plebeians. We are now beginning to be very gay indeed. The young Lushingtons are on the point of leaving us. Lady Burrard[6] has been here a few days, but the ship is expected to sail every day and she will go again. Charles Lushington has decided to enter the army much against all inclinations. His father has applied for a commission and there seems little doubt but that he will receive it. In that case he will join his regiment in

1. Henry Frederick, 3rd Marquis of Bath (1797–1837).
2. Prince Leopold of Saxe-Coburg, later Leopold I, King of the Belgians (1790–1865).
3. ? Kinsman of John George Lambton, later Earl of Durham.
4. ? Henrietta, widow of 2nd Earl of Warwick.
5. Robert Fowler, Bishop of Ossory, Feins and Leighlin (1813–1842).
6. *Née* Louisa Lushington.

about 4 months. I have received Charles's letter and one from Mr Tait[1] by Mr Stewart, Lady Shaw Stewart's[2] son. I have shown some little attention to them as also Ramsay of Barnton[3] and Rocheid of Inverleith[4] and Buchanan of Ross.[5] Ramsay is a remarkably fine young man – Sir A. Campbell[6] comes here in March when I shall have the pleasure and honour of waiting on him ... Mr Tait thinks that I should direct my attention to the English Church and I am inclined to it myself, but all my interest in it is yet to be made. What depends on my own exertions I am not afraid to execute. Within 3 or 4 months I shall be tolerably master of German, but it is very difficult to find books here. I shall then commence Spanish. It is a laborious thing acquiring these languages and nothing but the prospect of the great advantages I may derive from them would induce me to persevere. Their acquisition only requires great industry, for talent or abilities is out of the question. Before you receive this, A New Year will have been ushered in and I wish you, dear Mother, many happy returns of such a day. I only wish I were among you to join your dinner party. I dine out that night with one of the principal merchants here, Mr Oates.

Naples, 28 March 1827

Time to me at present is beyond all measure precious and even the short time for this letter I cannot always find. All my Scotch friends have left me and gone to Rome. Holy Week, where there are great Festivals at Rome, is fast approaching and all the English in Italy flock to it. We have had some lovely weather here lately though the winter has been detestable. A number of English have died – a niece of the Marquis of Huntly, daughter of the Duke of Manchester[7] and several others. As this is a town to which invalids resort, it is to be expected that there should be numerous deaths. There were some gentlemen who were shooting in a marsh at some distance from Naples and they were all seized with the malaria fever as soon as they returned and one died in 3 days; the rest with difficulty escaped. They were warned of the danger but laughed at it. I had a letter from Rocheid the other day from Rome – he tells me that Sir A. Campbell is there and has some intention to come down to Naples. I don't know whether I had commenced

1. Craufurd Tait, m. 1796 Susan, d. of Sir Islay Campbell of Succoth, whose ninth and last child was Archibald Campbell Tait, Abp. of Canterbury. *See* Introduction.
2. ? Widow of Sir Michael Shaw-Stewart, 5th Baronet.
3. William Ramsay Ramsay of Barnton (1805–1850).
4. James Rocheid of Inverleith: suc. to estate of father in 1824.
5. ? Sir George Alexander William Leith-Buchanan, 2nd Bart. of Ross Priory, Dumbarton: died 1842.
6. Sir Archibald Campbell of Succoth, 2nd Bart. (1769–1846).
7. Emily, d. of William, 5th Duke of Manchester. She died unmarried in 1827.

Modern Greek when I wrote you last. I get on slowly with it but find it easy, infinitely more so than German. The latter I can speak tolerably well but it is the most difficult I have ever attempted. The truth however is I have only been studying it about 7 months and I can scarcely expect to master it fully in that time. Sir Henry has been very ill, but is recovered and has an intention of going to England, and will take Franklin[1] with him. The rest of the family is well. We have heard of the safe arrival of Charles in England after a dreadful tossing in the Mediterranean on his voyage to Marseilles. Matthew has also reached Gibraltar. I suppose he will be in Lisbon by this time. There seems every appearance of another war in Europe; people seem to have forgotten the miseries of the last and require to taste them again in order to be convinced of their unpalatability. I shall be very sorry if it breaks out. I am sorry too to see the Catholic claims rejected in Parliament. It appears to me a very impolitic plan. They speak of shutting up the San Carlo Theatre which will tend more to cause an insurrection than the imposition of a new Tax to support it. The Carnaval is finished, it has been more gay this year than for many of the preceding; you would suppose that the whole people required a strong dose of Hellebore to cure them of madness. There was a Masked *Corso* twice a week, that is a string of carriages that went backwards and forwards, occupying a space of about three miles, and crowded one upon another. These carriages contained masked individuals, some exhibiting the most ridiculous appearance. The *Corso* is along the finest street in Naples and at the windows of the Palace appeared all the fair of the Kingdom . . . It was closed this year by a Masked Ball given by the Neapolitan nobility to His Majesty – It was the most brilliant scene I ever witnessed in my life. Foreigners were invited by ticket and I received one. There were 4 rooms magnificently lighted up. There were about 800 people invited and the rooms were so crowded that you could scarcely move. There were a number of beautiful masks as it was a masked ball, all were at least obliged to wear dominoes. The King[2] and Queen[3] appeared in splendid Persian dress attended by the Royal Family in various fancy dresses. There were quadrilles got up for the occasion. There was one called Scotch quadrille but it denied the applicability of the name, as it had nothing Scotch except ugly checked silk in imitation of tartan. The dresses of the different characters glittered with diamonds. After the quadrilles were finished the King and Queen walked about the rooms and talked to those of the Company whom they knew. Afterwards a supper room was thrown open and there were refreshments of all sorts. It broke up about 5 in the morning but I left long before that hour. It was a truly brilliant

1. Franklin, 5th s. of Sir Henry Lushington. In later life he was a close friend of Edward Lear and was Lear's executor.
2. Francis I, King of the Two Sicilies (1777–1830).
3. Maria Isabella, Infanta of Spain, m. Francis I as his second wife in 1802.

scene. Mrs Lambton has been residing here this season and has given further amusement for the 'fashionables' – a number of comic plays in a little theatre which has been fitted up for the purpose. I have not seen any of them but they are much applauded. The fact is that pleasure here is the only thing people think of, anything serious is quite out of the question. I was at Count Ficquelmont's lately where he himself and his wife acted. She is one of the prettiest women in Naples . . . This life is a strange mixture of pleasure and pain and upon my word, I am sometimes at a loss to decide which of them predominate. You may indeed know little pain or trouble, but the very anxiety of looking forward to the future, which everyone must do, is sufficient to throw a melancholy over the soul. Besides I am a complete Scotchman and am very apt to anticipate disappointment which is much more distressing than ever when the event happens. At present my great anxiety is to know what to do on leaving Naples. Though my time is to finish in July 1828, I cannot leave before the end of August on account of the heat. It will be the summer of 1829 before I can be in Scotland as I must spend some considerable time visiting the different parts of the Continent. But I have to consult Mr Tait and Mr Pillans on my projects . . .

Naples, July 1st 1827

. . . You must have heard from Mr Tait of my determinations, and likewise his opinions regarding them. I know not whether I have acted in a manner which I shall afterwards approve, but it appears to me the most feasible plan to forward my view of life. It is a bold project, and my success depends on the cast of a die. There can be no doubt that I come forward backed by many advantages, but life is too much in the nature of a lottery to make me over-sanguine in my expectations of drawing a prize. I shall have much to struggle against, and I am afraid, I shall have much more than I am at present aware of. However, after a year's trial, we shall see the probability of success, and if it is a vain attempt, I must think again. My views are high, but if I fail in gaining all I am at, I may yet gain a part. I know not what urges me on for I care not for money, and distinction has but little real charm for me. I believe it is a conviction that if I had not some object in view which requires all the energies of my mind, I would be more miserable than could be conceived. If Fortune favours me, as she has done, I shall be quite satisfied. I have my time almost wholly at my disposal, and am able to employ it in a manner which will turn to account hereafter. I shall in this way be able to acquire with great ease Spanish. I have some thoughts of adding Arabic . . . Dr Quin[1]

1. Dr Frederick Forster Quin, one of the first exponents of Homœopathy.

has been made by Prince Leopold his private Physician and I have a certainty of his assistance. He is a very great favourite with the Prince and is on the high road to professional eminence. They have left Naples but the Prince means to return in the Autumn. One great bar to my rising in the world is a diffidence which I find enormous difficulty in overcoming. We go to Castellamare on 16 July and shall be there during the hot weather. At this I am both sorry and glad; sorry, because it will stop my lessons, and glad, that we leave the intolerable heat of Naples. Count Ficquelmont, the Austrian Minister, has been very kind in lending me German books, and wrote a note to me in answer to a German one which I had written him, expressing his surprise at the progress I had made in acquiring the language. Wilkie, a gawky compatriot, and his mother will be there. A pretty Mrs Anderson from St Germains is also living there. There is a great dearth of English ladies, so that I have kept my heart pretty whole, as I have an utter contempt for the whole batch of foreigners. I consider myself as beyond all measure fortunate in never having fairly entangled myself in a love affair, at least in having always got out of it honourably. Believe me, it is no easy task and can only be accomplished, I am confident in certain situations, when you are not thrown much into their company. I hope Archie will keep clear, though I fear his susceptibility will be too strong. He must take his chance, and however much I may regret any foolish match he may make, if it be at all respectable, I shall not feel called upon to say much against it. It will no doubt be unpardonably foolish in him but we must hope for the best. Charles, I think, is less likely to act foolishly in such a matter . . . I believe I mentioned to you that I would leave Naples in all probability about the beginning of next May and shall be in England at the end of the year. Whether my funds or time will permit of my visiting Scotland then, must be determined when I arrive there. I believe it will be most inadvisable to proceed direct to Oxford and sacrifice the pleasure of seeing you for my eventual good . . . Mr Tait's letter was very satisfactory and gives me every hope of success. It was very fortunate that Quin urged it to the end he did as I had no thoughts troubling my head about it till I was compelled by time. We had several consultations about it when I last spoke to Sir Henry and obtained his offer of all support in his power. I am sorry to tell you that Lady Burrard has had a miscarriage but is doing well. He is in England. Mat. Lushington, the soldier, has gone all wrong, he has been gambling and nearly ruined himself. He is giving great grief to his parents and deserves to be confined to a madhouse. It is the second time he has got into debt. By the bye, I had almost forgot to mention to you a very distinguished honour which was conferred some time ago, at least those who conferred it seemed to think so! After this introduction, you no doubt expect some Prince or royal personage but, alas, it was only a Scotch Baronet! Sir

Archibald and Lady Campbell.[1] To counteract the bad effect such an important event might have on my mind and yet to prevent it from turning my
brain with high-flown notions, I was treated, however, with marked neglect.
Everything was done for me, that this must be considered an *era* in my life.
In fine, I was by no means pleased with their behaviours, particularly the
lady's, and in any other personage would have thought it meant to insult me
grossly. In her, I believe it is ignorance. I took pretty good care that I should
not show any more than the common and indispensable civility of leaving
my card afterwards. They were only here for three weeks. The Balfours and
that family are as good specimens of Scotch pride as I would desire. It is the
first disagreeable thing I have met with here. I would wish myself away from
this heat; in the interior at a distance from the coast it is much worse, but it
should not surprise me if the Government by their measures should drive
people to despair, everything they do seems to lead to some desperate event.
The family is very small at present. There are only the three ladies, Franklin
and myself. The changes in England seem to give very general satisfaction
but I feel it will only be for a short time, as people seem foolish enough to
think Canning will bring back the golden age. My opinion however is that
he is better than some we have had and will no doubt try to do some good to
sustain the high opinion the country has formed of his talents; but that he will
succeed in lessening in any perceptible degree the burdens, which some
foolish ancestors have entailed on us can scarcely be expected in the present
state of the world. I should prefer Lansdowne[2] at the head of the Administration . . . Our accounts of Greece are most melancholy, and indeed everything
seems to point at their bitter extermination. The European powers seem
very slow in interfering. To gladden all our hearts, we had an opera last
night and in the absence of Sir Henry, I have a kind of charge of the ladies.
The Neapolitans cannot exist without music and they prefer suffocation to a
deprivation of their favourite amusement. It was the birthday of the King's
brother[3] and the theatre was brilliantly lighted up to add to the heat . . . I had
always expected that our fruit here would be delicious, but it is the contrary.
The heat seems to render everything tasteless. Peaches, apricots, apples,
nectarines are not eatable though it may proceed from the little attention
paid to their cultivation. Strawberries ever had little taste. Grapes are
certainly sometimes excellent but this is not the season. Fish is also in general
very bad. Something comparable to our salmon and large trout. Mackerel,
much the common fish, is one of the best, and John Dorry is sometimes good.

1. Lady Campbell was Elizabeth, d. of John Balfour of Balbirnie.
2. Henry, 3rd Marquis of Lansdowne and 4th Earl of Kerry (1780–1863). Home
Secretary, 1827–1828.
3. Leopold, Prince of Salerno, who m. his niece, Maria Clementina, Archduchess of
Austria.

There is a small fish called *calamarella* [*sic*] – very tasty but you must shut your eyes when you put it in your mouth else you will not prevail on yourself to taste it, it looks so nasty.

Naples, 30 October 1827

If you will forgive me for making a classical allusion, I must tell you that I believe poor Scotland has met with the same fate as Plato's island of Atlantis, and has been submerged by the billows of the deep. But to be serious, I am quite surprised at the silence of my friends in Scotland and can only suppose you have been busily employed with the Duke's company . . . We have just returned from the country after a residence of three months at Castellamare, a most delightful spot. It may perhaps interest you if I give you an account of our limited but very select society. At the head of it we place Countess Ficquelmont,[1] the Austrian Minister's wife, a most lovely woman and though she be not free from the frailties of her sex, she is much less spoilt by flattery than you might expect. She takes the lead, and is of course woman enough to have some caprices. She is a great friend of mine, and has been remarkably kind. She is at home 3 times a week, and I generally wait on her. Parties at present commence about half past nine and at half past twelve, though we are often willing to break them up sooner, but in this, we are obliged to submit to her caprice. Count Ficquelmont is a remarkably well-informed man, and far superior to the common herd of diplomatic characters we meet here. He is much older than she is, I would suppose 30 or 40 years. They have one child, a pretty little girl. I may add to them Sir Richard Acton, an English Baronet, whose father was Minister in Naples. The good people here are pleased to say very ill-natured things respecting the Countess and him, but I have no doubt it is all from scandal. He is very rich, not a large portion of wit but remarkably good-natured. He and I are good friends. The next among the 'fashionables' is Count Privelle,[2] Neapolitan High Admiral, but a French refugee. He is very old but has two pretty daughters and is therefore obliged to give parties for them. They are much better educated than any young ladies I have met here. They possess all that feminine timidity which pleases the English taste, and have but little foreign forwardness. The next I may name is a vulgar Englishman and his wife whom all despise but still frequent their house because he is able to give a good dinner and splendid parties. He is Mr Bisse,[3] but I should say 'Colonel',

1. Dorothea Tiesenhausen, d. of Count Frederick Tiesenhausen, A.D.C. to the Emperor Alexander I of Russia.
2. Comte de Préville.
3. Dr Chaloner Bisse of whom Lady Blessington remarked, 'his hospitality and urbanity have rendered him very, and deservedly, popular'.

for so he dubs himself, though no one knows exactly of what regiment. You must know that military men are held in great respect on the continent, and that many Englishmen wear His Majesty's uniform on occasions, who have no right to it except that they are British subjects. I myself may yet find it advisable to submit myself *Captain* Ramage, for nothing under Captain will pass! Well the said Colonel gives *good dinners*, and his wife, perhaps still more vulgar than her husband, makes *good tea*. She is said to have been a toast in Dublin many years ago for they are from 'Paddy's land' and have a good deal of brogue. He is one of the most insipid characters you can meet and yet he is nearly at the head of society here. So powerful is the *golden key* here: money will cover a multitude of sins. With all her vulgarity, I like Mrs Bisse, though our family find a great deal of faults in her. But to say the truth, they are hypocritical and should look at home, where they might find things quite as ridiculous. Next in the rank of 'fashionables', we may mention Mr and Mrs Anderson of St Germains, and I am sorry to add, two as great fools as Scotland ever produced. I know them only from meeting them at parties, but Anderson is weak-minded in my judgment to a degree that is lamentable – His wife *is* or *has* been, or it *is* said *has been* remarkably pretty, but her affectation is too much for me and completely disgusts me, so I never ask her husband to introduce me to her. I fear they both pay dearly for their Castellamare residence, but time will show. I may add Prince Butera,[1] a Hanoverian subject and married to a Sicilian Princess whom he neglects in a most shameful manner. He is a clever man and has succeeded by his address to raise himself from a Captain in the English service to be Prince in the Neapolitan dominions. You see I have added no Italians, but these do not remain any time and were only visitors. Among them were Signor Mele, a rejected suitor of Louisa Lushington. I am inclined to think he was a poetaster and sung sonnets in praise of his mistress's eyebrows. He is a well-informed young man and had been obliged to fly on account of his *constitutional* principles, which don't suit the climate There was a Signor Lo Greco and son, who had been a distinguished character under Murati,[2] and is, of course, in bad odour with the Government – Prince Colonna, a branch of the famous Roman family, so well-known in the history of the Middle Ages, honoured us with his presence – Duchess of St Angelo,[3] daughter of the late King's wife and a remarkably pretty little doll, was occasionally here. I forgot

1. It appears that Ramage was confused here because the Prince of Butera in 1827 was Giuseppe Lanza, 8th Prince of Trabia (1780–1855), who by his marriage to Stefania Branciforte (1788–1843) – the last of her line – inherited many titles including that of Prince of Butera. This title was created in 1563 by Philip II.

2. Joachim Murat (1767–1815), King of Naples. Assassinated at Pizzo.

3. Duchess of Santangelo, d., of Lucia Migliaccio, widow of the Prince of Partanna and morganatic wife of Ferdinand I, King of the Two Sicilies, who created her Duchess of Floridia.

to mention Monsieur Mollerus[1] and wife, two Dutch beings, as heavily built and as dull in intellect as that nation generally is. He is Chargé d'Affaires for the Netherlands.

Besides them, we have an invalid, Mr Wilkie and his mother, an excellent woman, but who is making a mere gawky of her son to keep him out of the temptations of the world. She has certainly succeeded to a great degree at the expense of his intellect, and at the risk of making a booby of him all his life. At the close of the season we had a Mr Burgess, a Scotchman, but an English clergyman who had made his way in the world. He was chaplain to the late Duke of St Albans and married his eldest daughter,[2] who died in childbed. He has been very kind to me in pointing out what he thinks I should do. He was a Cambridge man and thinks that university would be preferable to Oxford, but his knowledge is of ancient date, and I cannot depend on it as things may have much altered. My studies have been very desultory during our summer residence – English, French, Italian, German, and Modern Greek and Spanish have all claimed a part of my attention. Scott's *Napoleon* we got, and that occupied some time as well as the new works from the English press. I have commenced with my Greek master again. I am enjoying a translation of a German work which you must find out from Black immediately whether it has been ever translated into English. The work is *The Thirty Years' War* of Frederich Schiller. Some of his German friends may be able to tell him if he does not know. Enquire also whether the *Agathadamon*, a work of Wieland has been translated – also *The Revolt of the Netherlands from the Spanish Yoke* by Schiller, and also *Perigrinus Proteus* by Wieland or *Agathon* by the same author. You might also enquire what is the duty on books imported into England, as it will determine me as to the number I shall bring home with me. Whether prints, if bound up like a book, are charged for duty. My studies this winter will be on Spanish and Modern Greek. This instant I hear 'Miss Louisa' cry out and go and see if the steamboat is in sight which brings her father and lady Burrard and husband to Naples. We shall be quite gay again when Sir Henry returns ... The gaiety of Naples has not yet begun and we know not yet how it will get on this winter. At present there is a very bad prospect here. This petty Kingdom is showing some activity in arming herself ready to take part in any general disturbance in European politics. I am afraid nations are tiring of peace, and that we shall soon have war and all its horrors. There is no account yet of Turkey having yielded the confederated powers ... I am sorry to say Lady Lushington has been complaining all this summer

1. Jonkheer Nicolaas Willem, later Baron Mollerus (1787–1865), Chargé d'Affaires at Naples from 1806, but in 1827 became Consul General, and later was Dutch Ambassador at Constantinople.
2. Lady Catherine Elizabeth Beauclerk.

and is far from being well. Franklin is getting fat as a porpoise and as lazy as possible – he is a complete Neapolitan . . .

Naples, 28 April 1828

I do not leave the Kingdom of Naples as soon as I intended as I have still a number of interesting points to visit. I do not expect to be in Rome until 10 June from which place I shall write you at that time. We have had a slight eruption of Vesuvius as you may have seen in the newspapers; it is now finished and everything is again tranquil. It was a most magnificent spectacle on the summit of the mountain. I ascended twice and was very lucky in arriving at the time it was most active in discharging liquid fire and stones. It was truly terrific in the interior of the crater. The depth of the crater is about 400 feet and fire was discharging from an opening in the bottom with a noise far exceeding anything that can be conceived. The ashes and stones – red-hot – rose above our heads to the height of 1,000 feet and had the wind changed a few points, they would inevitably have come upon us. Before we ascended we saw several fall in the direction we must mount by, and this alarmed us a little and so frightened our guides that they refused to go up with us. I had Franklin with me but was obliged to return to leave him at the Hermitage. My two companions proceeded and I again met them at the top of the crater. At the moment we were there, we saw a part of the opposite side of the mountain give way and fall in from the inward working of the volcano. It was rather an alarming moment as we could not be sure that our side might not give way too. We continued about an hour till we saw its force gradually exhausted and the mountain become comparatively tranquil. We descended and arrived in Naples safely about 2 o'clock in the morning. I consider myself extremely lucky in seeing one of the most sublime phenomena of Nature. I had scarcely seen before this time any smoke from the mountain and could have no idea of the irresistible force of a volcano in action. On the 2nd of February I witnessed the effects of a still more tremendous power of Nature – an earthquake on the island of Ischia about 16 miles from Naples. It was by mere accident that we had not experienced its effects as well as seen them. I overslept myself (I never was a good riser in the morning) and delayed our party for an hour. We arrived at Ischia at 12 noon and found the island in the utmost consternation from the shock of an earthquake that had taken place an hour before we arrived. We were at first not inclined to believe it and proceeded to examine the spot – a little village (Casillichio) – where the shock had been strongest. Then indeed we saw only too evidently its dreadful force. There was not a house in the village that had not sustained more or less damage; above 40 were completely destroyed and had buried, it was impossible to say, how many inhabitants. The survivors were displaying images of the most frantic despair. Some had lost a mother – others children, and one poor man said he had lost a wife and mother and 3 children. The streets were deserted and the inhabitants were seen in the neighbourhood [unread] waiting with terror lest there should be a repetition of the shock. We passed hurriedly through the midst of desolation, fearful lest a breath of wind should overthrow some of the overhanging walls. It was our intention to have remained at Ischia, about $\frac{1}{4}$ mile from this village, during the night but the people were unwilling to receive us and as we were unable to be of any especial use to the poor wretches who had suffered, we determined to make our way back to Naples. On returning Dr Henderson[1] and myself drew up a representation of the misery of the sufferers – The English, who are ever ready to assist the distressed, came forward with the utmost promptness and in 2 weeks we had collected upwards of 200 sterling. On Saturday the shock was felt, and on Thursday I returned to Ischia with the Hendersons to discover in what manner the funds we expected to get could assist the sufferers. We got a list from a clergyman of the parish, a most respectable man, of those who suffered most, and with his assistance Sir Henry has distributed the sum we collected. We remained at the village 2 days and examined more minutely the damage that had been sustained.

I cannot possibly get to England before the beginning of October and must be at Cambridge[2] at that time, if I intend to commence my studies there . . .

Naples, February 7 1828

I am rather sorry at the prospect of leaving Naples as I have been, on the whole, happy, at least as much as the nature of human affairs will permit. It may be too that some little affair of the heart may make me regret it, but it is only very slight. I think it improbable I shall remain a bachelor. Lady Burrard and husband leave Naples about the time I do but they go by sea, and I by land. They are very pleasant people, and also very good which is better.

1. Author of *History of Ancient Wines* see Norman Douglas, *Alone*.
2. On p. 210 he writes about the prospect of going to Oxford. In fact, he went to neither.

Rome, 26 June 1828

I hasten to inform you of my safe arrival in the Imperial city of Rome last night after a long and fatiguing tour through the Kingdom of Naples. I did not mention my intentions to you last time I wrote to prevent you having that anxiety which would naturally have arisen when you imagined I was on a dangerous journey. It was impossible for me to write from those remote parts of the world. I left Naples on 28th of April and proceeded alone with a small rucksack, principally on foot, for 300 miles towards the extreme point of Italy. The heat had so increased by the time I arrived at Maida that I found it necessary to mount on horseback and proceed to Gerace, crossing the Apennines at Casalnuovo ... I coasted along the Ionian Sea with immense labour and visited the sites of all the cities of Magna Græcia. In every part of this desert coast I was received with the utmost kindness and hospitality as I should otherwise have never accomplished my tour from the miserable accommodation of public inns. I was furnished with letters by General Filangieri, Prince of Satriano,[1] to almost every place I visited. This was absolutely necessary. At 50 miles distant from Taranto, at Policoro, I was left without mule or horse from the rigorous precautions of the Neapolitan Police, and if mere accident had not brought me in contact with some muleteers proceeding along a sandy coast where not a house was to be seen and not a drop of water to wet the parched lips of a weary traveller, it would have gone hard with me. I arrived safe at Taranto about 4th of June and went on to the Capo di Leuca. I then proceeded northwards to Brindisi, embarking in a small coastal boat to Trani – visited Canosa, Venosa, both places of Horace, crossed the fertile plains of Apulia, ascended the lofty range of the Apeninnes by Campobasso, descended by Venafro, St Germano, Frosinone, and arrived in Rome yesterday evening from Ferentino, a little fatigued but in excellent health. It has been one of the most interesting tours imaginable and I have traversed upwards of 2,000 miles while in Italy ... I received great kindness from Sir Henry and he has offered to give me an additional reference to that of the Duke's[2] respecting a living in the Scotch church supposing I choose to enter it. I shall remain here until the 24th or 25th of July before going on to Florence. During these last months, I have only seen one Englishman, a Captain of the 90th Rifles, on his way to join his regiment in Zante. I breakfasted with him at Otranto and the sound of the English language was strange to my ears.

1. Carlo Filangieri, Prince of Satriano, Duke of Taormina (1784–1867) to whom Ramage dedicated his book.
2. Duke of Buccleuch.

Rome, 2nd August 1828

Before this can reach you, I shall in all probability have reached Florence. I have remained a few days longer in Rome than I intended, owing to a short excursion of 300 miles I made in the neighbourhood. I visited Palestrina and Tivoli, proceeded to the Sabine farm of Horace near Licenza, crossed the mountains – a most picturesque ride – to Coresi, the site of the ancient Cures, and got on through Sabina to Rieti on the confines of the Papal States. I discovered on my way many ancient remains, unknown to the world in general. At Rieti I met Sir W. Gell[1] who detained me two days in that neighbourhood and we made excursions into the Neapolitan territories without passports to visit the site of an ancient town. We expected to be arrested, but as we travelled in a carriage and four in style, we were not molested. On leaving Rieti, I went down to the Falls of Terni – the most magnificent object I ever witnessed – then visited Narni, Amelia, Giove, Orte, Città Castellana, and by that road returned to Rome. Malaria, or bad air, in Rome is all humbug as I never saw a finer or more healthy people. There is no doubt that the air is more heavy, and that our spirits are less buoyant in Rome than in Naples. Write to me next in Vienna. I shall be there in all probability towards the middle of September. Dr Nott, formerly Tutor to Princess Charlotte,[2] now Dean of Winchester, is very much inclined to join me on the tour which I mean to make to some ancient cities in Tuscany, and if not, I shall meet him in Florence.

Florence, 24 August 1828

I am got on this far to the north and am at present detained by the non-arrival of Dr Nott to whom I entrusted manuscript notes of considerable value. I left Rome at midnight on the 2–3 August with feelings not of the most pleasant kind, as I was aware we must pass over the *maremma*, said to be one of the most dangerous parts of Italy for malaria. There were two travellers besides myself and we all agreed that it would be better to run the risk of suffocation than of fever. We closed the windows of the diligence and made every effort to keep awake, as to sleep in these regions is to wake in the fangs of death. At daybreak I found myself worn out with the miserable pace of a Roman carriage and when we stopped to change horses 24 miles from Rome, I got some stuff to refresh me which they persuaded me was coffee. The country, through which we were passing, was almost dead flat, and had only the appearance of the regions of death. About 10 in the morning

1. Classical archaeologist and traveller (1777–1836), who was then living at Naples.
2. Charlotte Augusta, only d. of George IV and Caroline of Brunswick.

we arrived at Città Vecchia, where I ordered dinner or at least a substantial breakfast to be prepared immediately. I found here the magnificent harbour constructed by the Emperor Trajan. An hour after midday I mounted on horseback to pursue my course to Corneto. It was 15 miles distant and I arrived there at night completely knocked up. I fell into bed instantly, and at the moment of falling asleep, a rascally *cicerone*, to whom I had given orders should be ready the next morning, came in to annoy me in a manner that almost drove me mad. I got rid of him at last by ordering the people to turn him out and slept soundly till daybreak. I then went to visit some Etruscan tombs which were very curious. I then started in a *caritella*, a sort of carriage, for Toscanella, 18 miles distant, and after being well shaken and several times nearly overthrown by the badness of the roads, I arrived safe. In the morning I started on foot to explore some ancient tombs 8 miles away. I was much disappointed. I stumbled on the remains of some ancient city which seems unknown to ancient geographers. I passed on to Viterbo and then to the ruins of Ferentinum. At Monte Fiascone, I drank the celebrated wine, said to have been fatal to more than one Cardinal, and admired the beautiful Lake of Bolsena. There I left the public road and crossed the country to Orvieto where you find one of the finest Gothic cathedrals in the world. I found it necessary to take to horseback to cross a mountainous country to Todi, which is situated very picturesquely on the banks of the Tiber. I started a little after mid-night and got to Todi at about 10 o'clock. Next morning I crossed another lofty ridge of the Apennines and came down safe to Spoleto, having twice lost the road on the summit of the mountain – the view from the top was magnificent. From Spoleto, I went to Trevi, Bevagna and Assisi – on to Nocera, Gubbio, Urbino and San Marino – the celebrated Republic – here my purse became very light and I found it absolutely necessary to husband my resources and proceed alone through an almost impassable country. There were only two places I was anxious to visit, and being so near them I was determined a little fatigue should not frighten me. I was more alarmed respecting the weather, which had every chance of changing, and in that case I should be a complete prisoner as the rains that fall at this season render the torrents impassable. Between Urbino and San Marino, I was ducked twice and was obliged to descend from my horse to avoid the danger of being upset by the violence of the tempest. My poor guide here commended himself to all the Saints in Heaven, and begged me earnestly to turn, assuring me that some streams we had passed would be very much swollen. I determined to see them as I considered it beneath my dignity as a son of a Caledonian to allow a mere storm to stop me. I went on to San Leo and Sarsina; then to S. Piero in Bagna. From these I crossed a very high mountain to Bibbiena and found I had sufficient money to take my place in a carriage to Florence. I now await with impatience the arrival of Dr Nott. The instant he makes his appearance, I shall start for Bologna, and thence to Venice. The fatigues I have undergone during the last four months have knit my bones together and rendered me doubly strong. I had imagined I had got rid of my laziness in the morning as I never found any difficulty during my tour in rising at any hour I thought proper, but, alas, my old habits return, and I am as lazy as ever.

BIBLIOGRAPHY

For those wishing to know about the archæological sites visited by Ramage, the two most important works relating to Magna Grecia are:

T. J. Dunbabin, *The Western Greeks*, Oxford, 1948, which from a geographical, topographical, and archæological aspect has not yet been excelled, and J. Bérard: *La colonisation grècque de l'Italie méridionale et de la Sicile.* Paris, 2nd edition, 1957.

These books contain references to all reports and discoveries of any importance up to their date of publication. J. Bérard: *Bibliographie topographique des principales cités grècques de l'Italie méridionale et de la Sicile dans l'antiquité.* Paris, 1941, is an invaluable guide to publications up to 1941. U. Zanotti-Bianco and L. von Matt, *La Magna Grecia*, Stringa, Genoa, 1961, have here produced a very beautiful picture-book of landscapes and works of art with good captions and a concise and up-to-date text.

Reports of recent excavations and discoveries, with relevant bibliographies, have been given by Italian Superintendents of Antiquities for their respective regions in the following:

Atti del VII congresso internazionale di 'Archeologica Classica'. Rome, 1961. 'Greci e Italici in Magna Grecia.' *Atti del primo convegno di studi sulla Magna Grecia*, 1961. Naples, 1962, and 'Vie di Magna Grecia', *Atti del secondo convegno* etc., Naples, 1963,

and a useful list of recent publications, and relevant articles in periodicals, is given in A. G. Woodhead: *The Greeks in the West*. London, Thames and Hudson, 1962, pp. 166–168. M. Bernardini: *Panorama Archeologico dell'-Estremo Salento*. Trani, 1955, gives a full bibliography relating to that region.

Picture-books illustrating the monuments of Apulia are: Alfredo Petrucci: *Cattedrale di Puglia*. Carlo Bestetti, Rome, 1961. C. A. Willemsen and D. Odenthal: *Apulia*, London, Thames and Hudson, 1959, also Elizabeth and Raymond Chevallier: *Mezzogiorno*. Ides et Calendes, Neuchatel (no date).

In addition, the *Ministero della Pubblica Istruzione, direzione generale delle antichità* have published short guide-books to many museums, galleries and monuments of Italy. The volumes of *La Guida d'Italia del Touring Club Italiano* are the standard works of this kind; and the recent volume on *Puglia* (1962) includes an excellent bibliography and up-to-date archæological information. The *Enciclopedia dell'arte antica classica e orientale* of the Istituto della Enciclopia Italiana Fondata da Giovanni Trecani, Rome also contains many articles of interest.

Printed Books

ACTON, HAROLD: *The Bourbons of Naples.* London, Methuen, 1956
The Last Bourbons of Naples. London, Methuen, 1961
BATTY, MISS: *Italian Scenery from Drawings Made in Italy in 1817.* London, Rodwell and Martin, 1820.
BLESSINGTON, MARGUERITE, COUNTESS OF: *The Idler in Italy.* Paris, Baudry's European Library, 1839, 2 vols.
BOARDMAN, JOHN, *The Greeks Overseas.* Penguin Books,Harmondsworth 1964
BRIGGS,M. S.: *In the Heel of Italy.* London, Andrew Melrose, 1910
COXE, H.: *Picture of Italy*; being a Guide to the Antiquities and Curiosities of that Classical and interesting Country. London, Sherwood, Neely and Jones, 1815
CRAVEN, HON. RICHARD KEPPEL: *A Tour Through the Southern Provinces of the Kingdom of Naples.* London, Rodwell and Martin, 1821
DOUGLAS, NORMAN: *Old Calabria.* London, Secker and Warburg, 1956
Siren Land. London, Secker and Warburg, 1957
Alone. London, Evergreen Books, 1940
DUPATY, THE ABBÉ: *Travels Through Italy in a Series of Letters, 1785.* Dublin, 1789
ERNLE BRADFORD: *Ulysses Found.* London, Hodder and Stoughton, 1963
EUSTACE, REV. J. C.: *Classical Tour in Italy, 1812.* London, Ward Lock – 3 vols – (no date)
EVANS, REV. G. W. D.: *The Classic and Connoisseur in Italy and Sicily.* London, Longman, Rees, Orme, Brown, Green and Longman, 1835. 3 vols.
FINLEY, M. I.: *The World of Odysseus.* London, Chatto and Windus, 1956
FORSYTH, JOSEPH.: *Remarks on Antiquities, Arts and Letters during an Excursion in Italy in 1802 and 1808.* London, John Murray, 1816, 2nd edition
FREEMAN, KATHLEEN: *Greek City States.* London, Macdonald, 1950
GISSING, GEORGE: *By the Ionian Sea.* London, Chapman and Hall, 1901
GORDON, PRYSE LOCKHART: *Personal Memoirs or Reminiscences of Men and Manners at Home and Abroad during the Last Half Century with Occasional Sketches of the Author's Life.* London, H. Colburn and R. Bentley, 1830 – 2 vols.

BIBLIOGRAPHY

HAMILTON, SIR WILLIAM: *Observations on Mount Vesuvius in a Series of Letters Addressed to the Royal Society*. London, T. Cadell, 1774

HARE, AUGUSTUS J. C. and BADDELEY, ST. CLAIR: *Cities of Southern Italy*. London, W. Heinemann, 1911.

HOARE, SIR RICHARD COLT: *A Classical Tour Through Italy and Sicily*. London, J. Mawman, 1819 – 2 vols

HUTTON, EDWARD: *Naples and Campania Revisited*. London, Hollis and Carter, 1958

Edward Lear in Southern Italy. Journals of a Landscape Painter in Southern Calabria and the Kingdom of Naples. Introduction by Peter Quennell. London, William Kimber, 1964

LENORMANT, F.: *La Grande Grèce*. Cosenza, 1961 – reprint – 3 vols

LOCKHART, J. G.: *Life of Sir Walter Scott*. London and Boston, reprint of 1839 ed. (no date) 10 vols.

MASSON, GEORGINA: *Frederick II of Hohenstauffen*. London, Secker and Warburg, 1957

ORIOLI, G. I.: *Moving Along*. London, Chatto and Windus, 1934

PAGE, DENYS: *The Homeric Odyssey*. Oxford, 1955

History and the Homeric Iliad. Berkeley, Los Angeles, 1959

ROGERS, SAMUEL: *The Italian Journal, 1814–21*, ed. J. R. Hale. London, Faber and Faber, 1956

ROSS, JANET: *The Land of Manfred*. London, John Murray, 1889

SASS, HENRY: *A Journey to Rome and Naples performed in 1817*; giving an Account of the Present State of Society in Italy; and containing Observations on the Fine Arts. London, Longman, Hurst, Rees, Orme and Brown, 1818

SIMOND, L.: *A Tour in Italy and Sicily*. London, Longman, Rees, Orme, Brown and Green, 1828

SITWELL, OSBERT: *Discursions on Travel, Art and Life*. London, Grant Richards, 1925

SLAUGHTER, GERTRUDE: *Calabria, The First Italy*. University of Wisconsin, Madison, 1939

STRUTT, ARTHUR JOHN: *A Pedestrian Tour in Calabria and Sicily*. London, T. C. Newby, 1842

SWINBURNE, HENRY: *Travels in the Two Sicilies, 1777, 1778, 1779 and 1780*. London, Nichols for T. Cadell and P. Elmsly, 1790 – 2nd edition – 4 vols

VAUGHAN, HERBERT M.: *The Naples Riviera*. London, Methuen, 1907

WALL, BERNARD: *Italian Art, Life and Landscape*. London, W. Heinemann, 1956

WARNER, OLIVER: *Emma Hamilton and Sir William*. London, Chatto and Windus, 1960
A Portrait of Lord Nelson. London, The Reprint Society, 1959
WEST, MORRIS: *The Devil's Advocate*. London, W. Heinemann, 1959
WHELPTON, ERIC and BARBARA: *Calabria and The Æolian Islands*. London, R. Hale, 1957
WILLIS, N. P.: *Pencillings by the Way*. London, 1845
WILLIAMS, H. W.: *Travels in Italy, Greece, and the Ionian Islands*. In a series of Letters descriptive of Manners, Scenery, and the Fine Arts. Edinburgh, Archibald Constable, 1820 – 2 vols

Additional Bibliography

1. DAVID H. TRUMP: *Central and Southern Italy before Rome*.
   London. Thames and Hudson, 1966.
2. PETER GUNN: *The Companion Guide to Southern Italy*.
   London. Collins, 1969.
3. BRIAN FOTHERGILL: *Sir William Hamilton (Envoy Extraordinary)*
   London. Faber & Faber, 1969.
4. RALEIGH TREVELYAN: *The Shadow of Vesuvius. Pompeii A.D. 79*
   London. Michael Joseph, 1976.

and, for further reading on Naples and its surroundings in Ramage's time, there are my 2 books:
Sir William Gell in Italy – Letters to the Society of Dilettanti, 1831-35.
(in collaboration with the late Martin Fredericksen)
   London. Hamish Hamilton, 1976.
Lady Blessington at Naples, Introduction by Harold Acton.
   London. Hamish Hamilton, 1979.

INDEX

INDEX

INDEX